THE BLUE CASCADE

THE BLUE CASCADE

A MEMOIR OF LIFE AFTER WAR

MIKE SCOTTI

GRAND CENTRAL
PUBLISHING

NEW YORK   BOSTON

Grand Central Publishing
Hachette Book Group
237 Park Avenue
New York, NY 10017

www.HachetteBookGroup.com

Printed in the United States of America

First Edition: May 2012
10 9 8 7 6 5 4 3 2 1
RRD-C

Grand Central Publishing is a division of Hachette Book Group, Inc.
The Grand Central Publishing name and logo is a trademark of Hachette Book Group, Inc.

The Hachette Speakers Bureau provides a wide range of authors for speaking events. To find out more, go to www.hachettespeakersbureau.com or call (866) 376-6591.

The publisher is not responsible for websites (or their content) that are not owned by the publisher.

Library of Congress Cataloging-in-Publication Data

Scotti, Mike.
The blue cascade : a memoir of life after war / Mike Scotti. -- 1st ed.
p. cm.
ISBN 978-1-4555-0348-3
1. Scotti, Mike. 2. Iraq War, 2003---Personal narratives, American. 3. Iraq War, 2003---Veterans--United States--Biography. 4. United States. Marine Corps--Officers--Biography. I. Title.
DS79.766.S46A3 2012
956.7044'345092--dc23
[B]
2011047665

For Mom and Dad,
You are the sunshine.

Acknowledgments

I would like to thank my brilliant editor, Ben Greenberg, whose keen eye for structure, content, and all the other bits and pieces helped take the raw manuscript to a place that I hadn't imagined possible. For this, especially given the emotional intimacy that this work holds for me personally, I am eternally grateful. You know that life is good when you get to work with people as good as him.

I would also like to thank my agent, Erin Cox at Rob Weisbach Creative Management, for braving the 30 mph winds and driving sheets of cold rain on that Saturday afternoon in March 2010 as she set out to see *Severe Clear* on its opening weekend at the Angelika Theater in New York. I thank her for all her effort, for her gung-ho attitude, for her vision, for her seemingly endless knowledge of the publishing industry, and for her strength.

I wish to thank Rob Weisbach for his guidance, unwavering leadership, and friendship. Rob always has the right answers, and he makes his authors feel as if anything is possible. He is a true visionary, and he is also a hell of a lot of fun to work with.

I would also like to thank the additional members of the Grand Central Publishing team who made this book possible: Jamie Raab and Deb Futter for their kind consideration and leadership, and Erica Gelbard, Pippa White, and Erica Warren for

ACKNOWLEDGMENTS

their continued support. I would also like to thank artists Flag Tonuzi and Rob Santora for creating a cover that perfectly captures the theme of the book and is not only thoughtful and meaningful—but also beautiful.

I wish to thank Suzanne and Jason Moore and Lou and Gene Quigley for their friendship and for their support. I would also like to thank Jason Frei, Joe Choi, Vick Cruz, Evan Wahl, Tom Del Cioppo, Eric Sibert, Ryan Pounds, Ismael Gallardo, Kyle Nickey, Coby Moran, Martin Casado, Mike Borneo, Jeremy Davis, Jerry Roeder, and Jiemar Patacsil for their brotherhood and for their support of the book.

I wish to thank Kristian Fraga, Marc Perez, Camille Cappola Gidich, Sehban Zaidi, John Sikes, Andrew Torkelson, Benjamin Charbit, and the rest of the Sirk Productions team for their kindness, understanding, and hard work during my dark time after the war. Without each and every one of them, this book would've never been possible. I would also like to thank composer Cliff Martinez for his consideration and for the beautiful original score he composed for the film—which in turn became the soundtrack playing in the background as I wrote the book.

I would also like to thank those who have been a constant source of love and creative inspiration to me: my mom and dad, my brothers Dave and Dan, my dear Laura, Sam, Alex, Missy, Jim, Uncle Bernie, Aunt D, Ed, Brenda, Brian, Bill, Ben, Nanny, Joe Holecko, Jim Beal, Joe Russo, Tim Lynch, John Stefan, Chris Whitley, Cory Maukonen, Scot Jaworski, Tom Willis, Vic Lomuscio, Dave Lewis, Billy Clark, Michael Cuomo, K. Lorrel Manning, Anton Sattler, Lucas Detor, Elizabeth Hayes, Anie Borja, Bruce Tracy, Krystal and Daniel Lange, Norm Parton, Reshma Sapre, Lindsay and Doug Lehtinen, Polly and Nick Weidenkopf, Sheila Brunsell, Troy Steward, Genevieve Chase,

ACKNOWLEDGMENTS

Ariane Montoy, Tara Orazi, Dennis Yerves, Peggy Yerves, Karen and Glenn Guenther, Michelle Racicot, Corie and Scott Norris, Gerry Byrne, Joel Cheney, Tom Martin, Dave Hochman, Manuela Harding, Matt Downes, Meredith Boylan, Paul Rieckoff, Deshawn Marie, Matt Salanga, Margaret Park, Tim Haber, Lynn Yaali, Brian McNamara, Petrina Easton, Tom Clark, Jasmine Fuller Pedder, Tedd Black, Jeri Klein, Kathy and Ron Ballek, Gwen and David Gary, Kevin McGrath, Mike Abrams, Noreen Eustace, Jenny Holbert, Amalie Flynn, Sister Joanmarie McDonnell, the Stovicek family, Jennifer and Bill Dinger, Jane and Geoff Bailey, Patricia Bailey, Barry Kaplan, and Jackie and Jim Iversen.

Lastly, I would like to thank the Marines of

- Bravo Battery, First Battalion, Eleventh Marines
- Charlie Company, First Battalion, First Marines, and
- Weapons Company, First Battalion, Fourth Marines

for their continuing service, sacrifice, and dedication to duty, and for allowing me the honor of serving alongside such magnificent human beings. Semper Fidelis.

THE BLUE CASCADE

Part I

—————

DOWN

Chapter One

"ITEM 1. LITTLE GIRL'S brain lying on the side of the road," she read aloud from the checklist attached to the clipboard she held gently in her hands. The "on the side of the road" part came out much more slowly and softly than the first part. Like she was confused about what the words meant.

We had met only a few minutes before, and for a moment, we just stared at each other in awkward silence. The air was heavy as both of us tried to ignore the photograph that stood frozen on the large monitor on the desk in front of us. The photograph I had snapped of the little girl's brain lying in the dirt and gravel on the side of the road in central Iraq.

The brain had a large-caliber bullet hole through it.

And I wasn't sure what was going to happen when I told that story to a stranger. *A civilian.* What would happen when I cracked the seal on the high-pressure valve and all the things trapped inside came out screaming and running and attacking. Things that had been locked away since they'd happened.

She sat looking at me, with her back straight and her fingers perfectly arched on the keyboard, ready to start typing every word I said. *Maybe this whole thing was a big mistake*, I thought. *Well, you signed on for this.* So, reluctantly, I cleared my throat, glanced out the small window, and began...

3

Twenty-one months earlier, in June of 2003, I stepped off the bus that took us from the airport to Marine Corps Base Camp Pendleton, in California. Captain Jason Frei stood outside, just beyond the last step, smiling and waiting to greet each of us. He had lost his right hand just a few months before when a rocket-propelled grenade (RPG) struck his vehicle. He now had a hook where the hand once was.

His eyes were proud. I sensed no self-pity or regret about what had happened to him. I was sure that I wouldn't have taken such a thing so well.

"Welcome home, Marine," he said.

After an awkward pause, we shook with our left hands.

"Thank you, sir," I said.

The crowd of wives and parents and children cheered and clapped and whistled as we filed off the bus. They held signs that said WELCOME HOME, DADDY. It was to be a celebration. Because we'd made it home.

There was a picnic table piled high with cakes and cookies that had been baked with the same gentle touch that had gone into the carefully selected items we received in our care packages overseas. Treasures from a far-off land that we opened with dirty hands as gunfire barked in the distance.

All around me were families and wives. Happy reunions. But I wondered how many of the wives had been fucking the neighbor or some surfer out in town. How many of these happy unions would soon end because hubby got drunk and saw demons and dead Iraqi kids and Marines and then his wife was the enemy and he wanted out of *all of this*.

As I walked toward the armory, I watched as a young Marine

from another unit, like me just home from the war, was served with divorce papers. Right in the parking lot.

There were a few old vets among the crowd. They shook our hands and looked at us like we were their own sons. I could look into their eyes and know instantly that at some point, they had been under fire. There was desperation to their happiness. And there was something deeper behind their eyes. Decades-old wounds resurfacing. They wanted to be there to welcome home the new generation. Which was us.

Before we deployed, I'd known that I would be getting discharged from the Marine Corps and moving back to the East Coast after I came home. I'd moved out of my apartment before we left, to save money on rent while I was gone. So I headed to the self-storage facility I'd rented in San Clemente to get my truck, which was packed with everything I owned. *The paychecks will soon end*, I thought, so I checked into the cheapest fleabag motel I could find. It would become my home for the few weeks it would take for me to be processed out of the military. But it didn't take more than a few hours for that tractor beam to pull me into a bar where the slightly hot bartender had big beautiful breasts. I drank alone. Her cleavage line was just below that point that says, *I will let you stare at my tits while you get hammered and I serve the drinks. Just tip me well.*

She was a good bartender. I tipped her well.

Something was off from how I used to feel when I sat in a bar eyeing a beautiful woman. Some part of me had dislocated. My body and soul felt used, dirty, weak. I weighed 118 pounds but had left for the war at 137. I looked like a refugee. Hollow eyes glazed over. Gaunt old-man face at twenty-seven.

I had seen too much. And I'd needed to swallow all of the emotion while we were still fighting. Swallow it down and move it out of the way so I could do my job and focus on the enemy and the mission. But when you did that, it became forever a part of you. In combat, especially in an infantry battalion, there was no room for error, because when things went wrong, they went terribly wrong and the whole situation could quickly unravel and turn into a real-life nightmare.

I finished my beer. *And…oh. Thank you, yes, I would like another. And another after that.* I looked at my reflection in the mirror behind the bar. I saw the darkness in the eyes of a stranger, and a day in Baghdad just a few months before when the sky was overcast and full of the dust and smoke from the fires burning in the city.

I'd sat on the bloodstained seat in my vehicle. Billy, a staff sergeant in our artillery detachment, had been shot by a sniper while sitting there only a few hours before. I was too tired to wash his blood off, so I just sat there. A stack of twenty-six letters, all mine, lay next to me. I could smell the ink, the clean paper, the perfume. They were from another universe. From safety and sleep on soft clean sheets. Where there were no men who were trying to kill me.

The letters had been written to Mike Scotti, the Marine who left the States just a few months before. But I was no longer him. I was now a citizen of war.

I had still felt sick from whatever it was I'd caught in the cattle-slaughter field next to the Tigris River three days before. It was the flies. They landed on the dead bodies and on the piles of shit and then on our lips and on our food. My vomit was still all over my gear, and the remnants of my diarrhea were still crusted to my trousers. There were bruises on my arms where the docs had given me the IV as they looked worriedly at each other, wondering if that first handful of us who'd become sick were the

6

first wave of casualties in some biological attack. Someone had snapped a picture of me with the IV bag clipped to the radio in the back of our vehicle as I listened to the Artillery Conduct of Fire Net.

Earlier that day we had raided a downtown warehouse looking for weapons. It didn't matter that I was sick. Our unit, like the rest of the Marine Corps, was undermanned, so each of us needed to pull our weight. On the way back to our perimeter, we were ambushed. I was almost shot in the face. And I could *feel* the snap of the bullets slicing the air as they flew by my head. Needles jabbing. Heart pounding and visions of what one of those things would do to me if it hit me. An overwhelming instinct to duck behind cover or drop back down into the vehicle. To preserve myself. Then random things popped into my head as dozens more of the sharp full-metal-jacket bullets carved the air just above our heads. *I wonder what it felt like to be scalped alive by the Indians*, I thought.

Once we were back, happy to be in one piece, and in what we thought was the relative safety of our perimeter, I found out that Billy had taken a round in the arm. They had medevacked him to Germany. I never had a chance to say good-bye.

I then spent three hours helping the battalion mail clerks sort through the thousands of letters that had finally caught up with us. This much mail was supposed to make us happy, but then we'd find a letter in the pile for a Marine who had been killed. *We Love You* and *Come Home Soon* written on the outside of the envelopes. They drew hearts and XOXOs and stuck American flag stickers on the front. Addressed so neatly, so carefully, with so much love. Because whoever had written that letter wanted to make sure that those words would find their way into the young wanting hands of *their* Marine. As I held the letters to the dead, faces of ghosts looked back at me, and I could feel the cries of the mothers and wives and children eight thousand miles away. Middle-aged moms answered their doors as two Marines in dress blues were about to say the unthinkable.

And so all of these thoughts intruded upon my mind as I sat alone in the San Clemente, California, bar watching the slightly hot bartender with the big beautiful breasts. It was like all of us who were in the fight had been hit with an ugliness. We'd soaked and bathed in it for weeks, and now its stench was upon us and there was no way to escape it.

As we fought our way up that never-ending highway in Iraq, we chipped off pieces of our souls. And those pieces became a currency that we spent quickly in a manic shopping spree of automatic weapons fire and violence and death. But soon we ran low, so we ran up a tab and borrowed all that we could and then spent that too. Some ran up a higher balance than others, but in the end, each of us in our own way would have to eventually pay the price.

That night, my first night home, I thought to myself that I wanted to do nothing more than drink, fuck, sleep, and hide. Forever.

The next day, I was given a checklist to complete, each section to be signed by the appropriate officer in charge. Training for civilian job hunting, the Veterans Affairs office, medical, dental, gear supply, the armory, the chaplain, the administrative building, base vehicle services, the base library. I hoped to set the land speed record for the quickest checkout the Marine Corps had ever seen. It usually takes two or three weeks. I planned to get it all done in five days.

Before I could get the supply sergeant's signature on my ticket to freedom, I had to clean all of my war gear. Dried puke. Blood. Food and fly guts. Dirt and filth and death. I found a coin-operated Laundromat out in town that had two huge washers in the back, and spent $16 washing all of my U.S. Government standard issue. Sixteen bucks in exchange for my freedom seemed like a good deal. I watched as the bored locals pumped their hard-earned quarters into the machines. *This is a good business*, I thought. People will always need to do their laundry.

I ran into Billy on base. He was one of the best Marines I had ever served with. One of the few who could be relied upon to do just about anything, and to do it well. I trusted him with my life and I considered him a close friend. He was the Staff NCO for the artillery detachment that I'd been responsible for in Iraq. He looked the same way I did. Terrible. Except that he had a much better reason.

"Hey, sir, how's it going?" he asked.

"It's going great, Billy." I lied. "How's it going with you? How's your arm?"

"I'm alright, sir. I was just over at the battalion medical aid station getting a checkup." He had lost a lot of weight and seemed like the negative imprint of the Billy I'd known before. Everything reversed. The energy that had once seemed so light now felt dark.

He showed me the three ten-inch incisions, still raw but healing, that ran the length of his forearm. When the bullet had embedded itself in his flesh, there was massive swelling. The surgeons had to quickly slice him open in three places to drain the fluid, or he would have lost his arm.

"Check this out, sir."

He pulled out a medicine bottle from his pocket. He held it up to the bright California sky. Inside, silhouetted against the sun, I saw it. It was the 7.62mm AK-47 bullet that had lodged in his forearm.

It was good seeing Billy. But he had the same look in his eyes that those vets in the parking lot had. And I was slowly starting to come to terms with the fact that I did too.

Shortly after, I ran into Major Joe Russo. He stood five feet five inches tall, with salt-and-pepper hair and a friendly, cherubic face that reflected the deep goodness that was in his soul. He was tough as nails and had a commanding presence that, when mixed with his friendly demeanor, was very powerful. In three years and through two wars, I never once heard him yell. He never had to, because just by being himself, Joe Russo made you want to be a better Marine. He made you want to be a better man and to do the right thing and to accomplish the mission—or die trying.

A year and a half before this tour in Iraq, he'd been my artillery battery commander. I'd served as one of his three lieutenants who became attached to infantry companies in Afghanistan in late 2001. By the time we invaded Iraq, he'd become the artillery battalion's operations officer. Just his voice on the other end of the radio could have a calming effect that steadied the scared forward observers—spotters who direct artillery fire amid firefights up on the front line with the infantry. I knew it, because I'd been one of them.

I couldn't, *wouldn't*, ever do anything in combat that would let him down. He was by far the best leader that I had ever served under and was one of my favorite human beings on the planet. I would follow him through the gates of hell, and die for him without a moment's hesitation.

Major Russo didn't look like me or Billy or the vets in the parking lot.

"Scotti! Good to see you in one piece. How are you doing?" he bellowed in his loving and larger-than-life voice.

"Good, sir, just going through the checkout process," I responded, my eyes now avoiding his.

Hide it, I thought. *Don't let him know. Don't let him down.*

"You know we would love to have you stay in the Corps, Scotti. You are one hell of an officer, and Bravo Battery could use an executive officer like you."

I wanted to tell him that there was something wrong with me, but I was ashamed. He looked perfectly fine. He looked normal. I wondered how he could be normal while I felt like I was going to come unglued at any moment. I wanted to ask him if he too felt the sadness, but I was not brave enough. So instead we talked about simple things.

"Thanks a lot, sir, I really appreciate that. But I've got plans. A new mission. I'm going to go conquer the world of business."

"I have no doubt you'll do well. But damn Scotti...you look skinny as hell. You need to go eat something," he said with a joking tone.

"Roger that, sir. I think I might have jet lag or something. Haven't been that hungry since I got back."

"I've been eating everything in sight. I had a nice thick steak, mashed potatoes, and blooming onion last night. Ice cream. Everything. The works." His hands tapped his belly.

I needed to get away from him before he dug any further. I needed to run for the hills. Because something inside of me didn't want to see anyone. I wanted to disappear. To fly down to Costa Rica or to the Atacama Desert in Chile or to Antarctica. I was vacant. I was half insane and underweight and felt like complete hell most of the time.

I said good-bye to Major Russo after promising to grab a beer with him before I headed east, knowing that I would break that promise.

I knew my mom and dad were probably wondering where I was. They had no idea if I was patrolling Baghdad, or in Kuwait, or in California. I had not wanted fanfare on my return. No forced parties or obligations or chitchat. So I didn't tell anyone that I was coming home. But it was inevitable that word would get out through the Marine Moms network that I was back Stateside, and mine would've been upset if she found out that way. The last thing I wanted to do was hurt Mom and Dad. I'd put them through enough already. Two combat deployments in two years.

I held the dirty receiver of the pay phone at the 7-Eleven in my hands and dialed the number of my parents' home in Colts Neck, New Jersey. Another world that existed on the other end of the phone. And in the instant it took for me to pick up the receiver and begin to dial, that other world came alive in my mind.

———

My mother snapped a picture of me at three years old, lying in the green grass in the backyard of our house in New Jersey. In my hands, a plastic M16 rifle. On my head, an oversized, plastic, olive-drab army helmet. Behind me, a small stream. Beyond that, woods that seemed to stretch forever. I aimed the rifle directly into the lens of the camera and looked too serious for a three-year-old. That look, common in children born with a certain type of DNA that meant one day a real rifle would find its way into their hands.

From an early age, I always wanted to go to a war. That was a man's job: to kill the bad guys. To protect my mom and my dad and brothers and friends. Those were the sleepy days of the

12

Cold War, when maybe some boy named Ivan was doing the same thing on his parents' farm on the other side of the planet. Or the young son of some mujahedeen in the Korengal Valley in Afghanistan.

I am the youngest of three brothers. Dan, who is eight years older than I, has always had a knack for business and a natural eye for the beauty of detail and design. My brother Dave is ten years older than I and is a highly talented actor.

My brothers looked out for me and taught me the ways of the world. Like how to win at the neighborhood game of kick the can, and when I was older, where their old *Playboys* were hidden in the basement. Our tree-lined neighborhood was full of adventure and good friends, and every fall the geese in V formation flew south for winter as we dug for worms and rode bikes. A happy childhood filled with love and compassion from my family.

My father's mind and work ethic led him from being the son of a butcher in the poor part of the town of Red Bank to the Ivy League. He won full academic scholarships to Harvard and the University of Pennsylvania Medical School. He became a doctor with a career spanning nearly five decades. He was beloved by his thousands of patients because he truly cared for them and really listened to them and spent enough time with each of them to figure out what was really wrong. Early on, he taught me the value of compassion and hard work and humor and discipline.

My mom was raised in a tough Italian neighborhood in North Jersey. Her father died when she was four, leaving her mother to provide for three young children by working fifteen-hour days in a birth-control-pill packaging plant. Mom entered nursing school at eighteen. Within a year, she found herself as one of only two young caretakers in a room with two hundred mentally disturbed patients in the psychiatric ward at the Philadelphia

General Hospital. She passed the compassion and sense of perspective she learned in those tough days in the wards on to her three sons. She taught us to always do our best and never compromise our values. She taught us integrity. She was a beautiful lioness who would have fought to the death for her boys.

My parents met in that psych ward. A young medical student and a twenty-year-old nurse.

When I was eight, one of the networks aired a TV movie called *The Day After*. It was about nuclear holocaust, and it scared the crap out of me. *Could the Russians really blow us all up like that?* I tried to convince my parents to put a nuclear shelter in the basement.

I became fascinated with war. Battle. Weapons. Combat. When we took our weekly trip to the bookstore, my dad would buy me one book. I always picked a war book. My collection grew. Many were stories of combat with photographs from Vietnam, Korea, and both of the World Wars. I would read the stories and look into the faces of the tired, haggard infantrymen. *Could I do that? Would I be a real man? A warrior?*

On Saturday afternoons my father would take me to the Army Navy store in Red Bank, which was owned by a former Marine. The store smelled of old GI canvas and leather holsters and the cheap cigars that the owner always smoked. On the wall inside the store was a picture of a bulldog, the mascot for the Marines, with the letters U.S.M.C. written below. I would stare at the picture. I understood what it meant: it meant that you didn't need to be big if you had a warrior's heart.

Ten years later, I would have that bulldog and U.S.M.C. tattooed on my right arm.

The phone rang a few times, then I heard my mother's voice for the first time since we'd said good-bye before I shipped off to Iraq six months before.

"Hi, Mom," I said when she picked up the phone.

I wasn't sure what else to say.

"Michael! Michael! Where are you? Are you OK?" she asked excitedly. My mom was the only one who called me Michael. Sometimes my dad and my brothers called me Michael T as a nickname because of my middle initial, but that was it.

"Yeah, Mom, I'm OK. I'm back in the States. In California. Safe and sound."

"Angelo, go pick up the other phone! He's home. Oh, he's home!" she yelled to my father.

I could see him as he hurried up the stairs—ignoring the pain in his one bad hip—and into their bedroom to pick up the other phone.

"Welcome home, Marine," they both shouted, almost in unison.

"We are so proud of you. Good job," my father added.

They'd watched the war on TV. The cruise missiles exploding. The statues coming down. My mother hadn't left the house for weeks. Her eyes locked on the screen as she constantly scanned the news channels. Hoping for a glimpse of her youngest son.

Some thoughtful high school buddies had brought her flowers on Mother's Day, assuring her that everything would be OK. Now my parents' hearts would no longer stop beating every time the doorbell rang.

I could feel the joy coming through the receiver, and for a second, I felt good.

They wanted to know all of the details. When did I get home? Was I home for good? Where exactly was I? I answered all of their questions, and assured them that I was OK and in one piece.

A high school friend was getting married in California that weekend, and I felt I had to go to the wedding. I was too embarrassed to admit I felt exhausted or that maybe there was something wrong with me and maybe I just didn't want to go. Marines don't feel exhausted, and there is never anything wrong with them. Ever. Because that is weakness. And weakness is vulnerability. And vulnerability means that the enemy can infiltrate the perimeter and kill your brothers and toss hand grenades into the helicopters.

So I went.

I boarded the flight from Orange County, California, to Oakland. The plane was brand-new, a huge 767. Everyone moved with a sense of purpose. Nowhere could I sense that we were at war. The colors of their clothes were bright, and they read their *Wall Street Journals* and *Vogue* magazines. The cleanness of the plane and the brightness of the light and the ladies on the covers of the magazines—everything was so vivid. My eyes were not yet used to it. They were used to seeing things like pale desert sand or rifles that were gun-metal gray or the drab washed-out colors of unfriendly Iraqi cities.

I sat next to a man who had a white beard and darkness in his eyes. It was strange how I could just tell. I guessed at his age.

"Korea?" I asked.

"Yup." We shook hands, and I told him about Iraq and Afghanistan, and he told me about the Korean War and how *the cold itself became another enemy.* And when he started talking about his buddies, the look on his face told me that the conversation had gone too far. So I went back to reading my book, and he went back to his newspaper.

At the reception, I sat in my dress blues, at a table by a window with seven or so other people. I listened to their conversation. About how much you could make in the real estate market. And how funny *My Big Fat Greek Wedding* was. And about whether mortgage interest rates were going up or down. About a dentist's office. And about the differences in cell phone coverage for Sprint versus Verizon. Oh, and can you believe they're making *The Lord of the Rings* into a movie? And did you hear what happened on *Survivor?*

I looked around. There was the chamber music quartet and the Reidel crystal glasses and the beautiful bridesmaids with hints of their nipples poking through their dresses. And there were the people at my table stuffing their faces with bread and lobster and Chardonnay. And then there were the guys from Weapons Company whom I'd just left back in Iraq. Guys who were probably on patrol and maybe fighting for their lives at that moment on some side street in Al Hillah. Shortly after I had left to return to the States, they'd taken fifteen casualties. One of them was a young Marine who'd been in my vehicle in the war and who'd been pictured on the front page of the *Los Angeles Times* holding his baby girl and kissing his wife good-bye the day we had left for Iraq. He took a fragment in the neck.

They were there and I was here at this wedding. Sitting at a table with normal everyday American people listening to them talk about normal everyday things. *But didn't they know that we were in the middle of a war?*

I hated them.

I wanted to turn the table over and bash their fucking heads in. I wanted to take a belt-fed weapon and machine-gun the chamber music quartet to death. A hand grenade into the kitchen. Drop a few 155mm white-phosphorus artillery rounds on the place. Burn the fucking building to the ground. Set up grazing fire in the courtyard to gun down all the guests as they ran out.

I was not even the same species as these people anymore. Someone who had not seen combat could never even remotely understand what I had just been through. Nor did they want to. Why would they? I was a creature from some other planet.

"*Lord of the Rings*? Wow. That's great," I said.

Back in town outside of Camp Pendleton that Monday, I went to pick up the twenty-five rolls of film that I had shot in Iraq. When I gave him the stubs from the envelopes, the guy behind the counter, realizing which order I was, looked spooked.

"Just back from Iraq?" he asked.

"Yeah."

"Some interesting shots you got."

"Yeah, I guess they are."

"Take care of yourself, man."

"Thanks, I will."

His concern seemed genuine. Because he had *seen* some of what I had seen. He had a taste of what it was like over there.

There were two other employees in the shop working the large photo-processing machines. One was clearly trying not to look at me, focusing on his work. The other was a pretty Southern California blonde girl in her early twenties. The kind of California girl who usually hates Marines, especially this close to base. By the look she gave me, I could tell that she had seen the pictures. And she would probably never talk to a Marine again.

It was time for the post-traumatic stress disorder (PTSD) seminar back on base. It was a true child of bureaucracy. So dry, academic, and ineffective. Certain to fail miserably at achieving its objective. The uninspired speaker added to the uselessness of the whole thing. You could tell that not one of the Marines in that room *gave one fuck* about what the lady from the Veterans Administration (VA) had to say. We just wanted to get our checklist signed so we could get the hell out of the military.

She went through the list of causes and symptoms of PTSD. The causes can include violent physical or sexual assault or abuse, natural disasters such as earthquakes, kidnapping, intrusive medical procedures, car or train accidents, plane crashes, and war. Symptoms can include difficulty falling or staying asleep; irritability or outbursts of anger; difficulty concentrating; feeling jumpy or easily startled; intrusive, upsetting memories of the event; acting or feeling as though the event is happening again (flashbacks); intense physical reactions to reminders of the event (pounding heart, rapid breathing, nausea, muscle tension, sweating); depression and hopelessness; feeling alienated and alone; feelings of mistrust and betrayal; substance abuse; guilt, shame, or self-blame; and suicidal thoughts and feelings.[1]

"But how about if I was kidnapped and raped and beaten in a war and then the plane crashed and was then hit by an avalanche?" asked some smart-ass as the room immediately erupted in laughter.

The lady from the VA said that any of us who thought they might be suffering from PTSD could walk up to the front of the room and take a brochure. We all watched silently as one guy, out of the fifty or so of us, walked up and took one. *Damn, that was brave.* Statistically, at least ten of us should have.

---

[1] See, for example, "Symptoms of Post-traumatic Stress Disorder (PTSD)," http://www.oregon.gov/ODVA/docs/PDFs/Criminal_Justice_Portal /Symptoms_of_PTSD.pdf?ga=t.

That's it? No mandatory screening? No conversation with a shrink? No questionnaire? They expect guys in their early and midtwenties to delay their exit from the Marine Corps and to immediately admit that they may be feeling symptoms of post-traumatic stress? Do they have any idea at all who we are?

Well. Fuck it. Sign my checklist. One step closer to freedom.

The Navy surgeon at the medical clinic said that one of my blood tests came back a little off. He said that the results from my liver function test were not where they were supposed to be, but that they were still within allowable parameters, so he could approve my release.

A little off? I didn't care if I needed a goddamn liver transplant; I was getting off that base and out of the Corps by the end of the week. And nothing was going to stop me. I wondered, though, what had caused it. Was it the beers I had the night before the blood test? The military-issue Meals Ready-to-Eat (MREs), with their preservative-driven seven-year shelf life, that I had consumed for months? Or the smoke we breathed in from the market that was on fire in Baghdad, when I had said, "I'll see you all in the VA hospital in ten years from whatever the fuck we breathe in from this fire"? Or the Iraqi cigarettes we bought from the locals that bubbled and popped when you lit them? Or that one pack of smokes we took off the dead Republican Guard captain on Route 7? Or a low dose of chemical weapons when the engineers blew up those giant weapons caches just south of Baghdad, like what many think happened to the guys who had Gulf War syndrome? Or the air in the room at the UN building that had biohazard stickers all over the door?

It didn't matter. The surgeon's signature was the last I had needed for the final checkout. I was as good as free. I had been a Marine for all of my adult life. Four years in the enlisted infantry reserves in college, in which I'd made it to the rank of corporal, and four years as an officer, a lieutenant, after graduation. A few hours later, sunroof open, windows rolled down, I drove through the Las Pulgas gate for the last time. Ready to start my new life. I was done. Free. Away.

———

I was headed to a small, old mining town in the Colorado Rockies for a few months. I had driven through it three years before on my way to artillery school in Oklahoma, with a nineteen-year-old waitress I had met out in town. She was itching to go somewhere, and she was beautiful, so I took a shot and invited her along for the ride out. She drove out with me, then flew back to California once the school started. Along the way, while exploring the Rockies, we found the town of Ouray, Colorado. It looked like it hadn't changed much since the 1800s. It sat quietly in a canyon, surrounded by the majestic, immovable mountains.

"This is the perfect place to write a book," I'd told her.

Now, three years later, I found myself headed to that same town with those mountains. I needed to go somewhere to decompress. A buffer between civilian life and the war.

On the seat next to me was a bag filled with Mini-DV cassettes containing footage that I'd shot in the war. I'd wanted to try to write a book after I made it home, and I'd taken the footage to help me remember. I also had a written journal I'd kept, and the twenty-five rolls of film that had been developed by the blonde who probably didn't like Marines. I planned on spending the summer in Ouray writing, then heading east to New York City to find a job in finance while I applied to graduate business schools that fall. That was the plan, anyway.

The twenty-three-mile stretch of Highway 550 from Silverton, Colorado, to Ouray was nicknamed the Million Dollar Highway. The scenery was truly and purely beautiful as the Rockies rose above twelve thousand feet on either side of the road. At some points, there were several-thousand-foot drop-offs just inches from the edge of the highway. And there was the light. The energy. The air. A fitting approach to my mountain sanctuary.

I would stay at the Western Hotel. Built in 1891, it was one of the largest and oldest wooden structures still in use as a business establishment on the western slope of Colorado. It had been a place for the miners to stay when they weren't up in the hills, deep in the mine shafts, breaking their backs and praying for a miracle. The rooms had character. Some of them still had their original hand-painted wallpaper. The rooms had no phones or TVs or minibars. And the fourteen standard rooms in each wing of the sixteen-room hotel shared a bathroom, one that still had the original claw-foot tub.

Rosemarie, the owner, was a beautiful Dutch woman in her late thirties or early forties who looked like Meryl Streep. She had moved to the United States to work as a nanny and had fallen in love with an American man she met while going to college. She had also fallen in love with the Western Hotel and had now given herself to the place. Unique and beautiful, the hotel was also, because of its age, a demanding master. Rosemarie fought a constant battle against decay while trying to run a business that made most of its money during the summertime. Pipes bursting in the winter. Electrical problems in the summer. The mortgage year-round.

"Do you give discounts for long-term stays?" I asked her as I checked in at the worn but beautifully hand-carved front desk.

"How long?" she asked.

Forever, I thought.

"The entire summer," I said.

She smiled, and said, "Let me think about it and get back to you later. I'm sorry. I'm a bit preoccupied today."

"Is everything OK? Is there anything I can do to help?" I asked, because she seemed flustered.

"My bartender and one of the kitchen staff both quit yesterday, and we are about to head into the busiest month of the entire year."

"If you are looking for a bartender, I would be happy to fill in. I went to bartending school while I was a senior in high school and worked while I was in college. And I just got out of the Marines, so I'm hardworking...and honest. I won't steal or skim from you."

She thought for a second and then smiled. And I saw an opportunity, so I decided to run with it.

"Alabama Slammer: amaretto, sloe gin, Southern Comfort, OJ. Red Devil or Red Death...same drink...a combination of an Alabama Slammer and a Kamikaze...which is equal parts vodka, triple sec, and lime juice."

"You're hired." She smiled more broadly. "And maybe we can work something out as far as the room rent goes."

We agreed that I would stay for free in one of the rooms, as long as I tended bar five nights a week. I could work in the evening, write all night, and sleep until early afternoon. It was the perfect place to decompress. And there also happened to be five college girls who would be working there for the summer. Three from Holland and two from Wisconsin. Between tending bar and chasing after the college girls, I wrote about six pages those first two weeks.

On the Fourth of July, I stepped out from behind the bar for a minute and watched, from the balcony above the front entrance to the hotel, as the fireworks exploded in the sky above the town. I could *feel* them as much as I could hear them. Just like in the war. And for a moment, I stood a bit straighter and was proud for having served my country. But then the cheers and the hollers from the crowds along the street below quickly faded from my ears until all I could hear were the explosions. And my mind and body suddenly became set and tense and ready for anything. Then the silent series of snapshots layered upon one another: dead dogs on the side of the road with tongues hanging out of their mouths, a dead child with black eyes, Marines dying in helicopter crashes, Marines dying in gun battles, Marines being killed accidentally by other Marines, destroying people's homes with artillery, killing other human beings violently, being terrified, being glad that you were killing other human beings violently, being exhausted, looking into the devastated eyes of the people whose homes you had just destroyed with artillery, sweating in the 110 degree heat for too long, being hunted, babies crying, things exploding, wishing you were anywhere else on the planet than where you were, bullets snapping by you, being horrified about making a mistake, thinking that at any moment you will be dead, thinking that you would not want to be anywhere else on the planet because this was your war and you were glad you didn't miss it, land mines, snipers, and the terror in your buddy's voice over the radio as he lies trapped underneath his vehicle begging for someone to get him some air support because they were taking fire from all directions and were sure that they were all about to die.

And you don't even realize that it's happening to you. You just breathe it in, every day, while you are trying to do your job. Like the poor son of a bitch who works for thirty years installing asbestos insulation, then spends his last three slowly drowning in his own blood.

I stayed at the Western Hotel, insulated and well hidden from the rest of the world, for eight beautiful weeks. But then one day, the light changed. And as I looked up at the late summer sun, I knew that it would soon end. The girls would go back to school. The weather would turn, and the hotel would close for the season. My mountain sanctuary was an iceberg that I'd been clinging to for dear life. But now it was melting. And when it was gone, I would find myself alone and adrift in a cold, dark sea.

Chapter Two

I FOUND A SMALL studio apartment on MacDougal Street in New York City's Greenwich Village. The weather was beginning to grow noticeably colder as the summer finally slipped fully into fall. It was now a little over four months since I'd returned home from the war.

A high school buddy of my brother Dave offered me an entry-level job at his commodities brokerage firm on the New York Mercantile Exchange. He was a crude-oil-derivatives trader, and he'd heard through my brother that I was looking for a job. I sensed that he would have given me one even if they hadn't really needed another clerk. And for that, I was thankful.

As soon as I accepted the job, I was happy—relieved, for a moment, to be moving forward with my postwar, postmilitary, post-killing-people-for-a-living battle plan. Clinging to its structure was comforting. It gave me the illusion of direction. Of stability. Of peace.

The plan was to go to graduate school to get an MBA. Then to Wall Street to make as much money as quickly as possible so that I could retire young and travel indefinitely. I was willing to jump through the hoops and buy into the corporate life for a decade or so in order to set myself up for a life of leisure. The best way I could think of to do that was to work in high finance. I'd majored in finance in college, so I already had some understanding of what I'd need to know. But what stuck out most to me were memories of the $10- and $15-million homes along the Navesink River in New Jersey. In high school, we would speed along the curves of the winding road that hugged the wooded hills above the river and point out the houses to each other: "That's Bon Jovi's house. That one belongs to Geraldo Rivera." Most of the rest, we'd heard, belonged to those who worked one place: Wall Street. Where men waged financial warfare upon one another—traders with their bonds, and bankers and private equity financiers with their hostile takeovers.

But I didn't want money to flash around and buy big houses. I wanted money so that there would be at least some time in my life when I didn't belong to someone else. A time when I wouldn't fear the boss or be accountable for anything or have to be in the office at a certain hour. And I didn't want to wait until I was an old man to get there.

The building next door to my apartment building was being renovated. There was a large, metal, mostly empty trash Dumpster on the side of the street in front of it, just next to a small café that had a few tables on the sidewalk. I hadn't noticed the Dumpster. But one day as I walked by, a construction worker threw a piece of concrete into it. It sounded like an explosion and I immediately dove to the ground.

A few seconds later, after realizing what had happened, I picked myself up off the sidewalk and tried to regain some sort of composure. A couple, obviously on vacation from somewhere, stood on the sidewalk and stared at me, looking both confused and horrified. Then I noticed that everyone in the café had seen me dive to the ground with a look of terror on my face.

My hands shook as the adrenaline pumped. I felt like I was going to puke. Then I felt like I was going to cry. What the fuck was wrong with me? I walked back to my apartment. As I lay down on my bed and closed my eyes, I was back on the battlefield once again.

There it was. Waiting for us as we drove slowly on that stretch of highway just north of An Nasiriyah in Iraq. *What are my eyes seeing right now?* Mangled corpses everywhere. Heads and faces split in two. Arms, legs, feet, and hands lying on the sides of the road. Charred piles of flesh slumped over melted steering wheels. Boots with feet still in them, the snapped bones sticking out. There was not much blood. Just meat, ripped and ragged. The faces contorted in agony, mouths open. A pungent acidic smell. The air tastes of metal. Burning flesh, clothes, ordnance, tires. And the faces. It was the faces of the dead that stayed with you.

I took the position of clerk for the oil-trading firm, hoping that a job in finance after my military service would increase my chances for acceptance into graduate school. It was my third day at work. I was a runner, helping the oil traders keep track of their current transactions as they quickly and violently bought and sold millions of dollars' worth of contracts, each one representing one thousand barrels of light, sweet crude. The day before, I watched a trader take home a $40,000 profit. *This is insane*, I'd thought. That's what a young Marine private first class or lance corporal makes in base pay in two years. *Two years* of getting shot at or driving over endless roads that could explode at any second. Or worrying about stepping on a land mine or carrying a pack for twenty miles or sweating his ass off in the 130 degree heat.

Rumors would pulse through the trading floor about oil pipelines being blown up in Iraq by enemy insurgents. The price of the crude would spike just a few seconds later as the traders bought furiously. And for the first time, I very seriously considered the truth behind the news: that at least part of the reason we cared about what happened in the Middle East and fought wars there was because we were utterly addicted to crude oil. It might as well have been tar heroin. The entire country—junkies. And then I realized that this had probably always been glaringly obvious for ages to everyone except me—and I was the one who had been fighting the goddamn war. Maybe I was naive, but I had never really given the Iraq oil angle serious thought. I'd thought we were fighting the terrorists. At least, that's what I'd been doing.

I was earning $30,000 per year and just wanted to do my job so I could get a good letter of recommendation for grad school, but many of the traders on the floor were multimillionaires. And many were arrogant and had bad attitudes and thought they were tough guys.

One day I was about to enter the oil-trading pit to get my trader's latest set of tickets, small pieces of paper torn from a pad upon which he scribbled each of his trades. As I stepped up to the entrance of the tiered platform, a trader from another firm pushed me back, with both hands on my chest, and yelled "Move!" in a condescending, "Fuck you, pal" sort of way. He wasn't just trying to slide by. He was clearly being an asshole. Because he thought he could be. Because he had been before and had gotten away with it.

Rage. Redder than the blood of a freshly slaughtered animal. I grabbed him by his stupid fucking colored trading vest and threw him into the railing. *This piece of shit.* I thought about punching him in the face. But I was sober and didn't want to go to jail. I clenched my teeth. My heart pounded. It seemed strange to feel this way surrounded by computer screens and coffee cups and fat people watching TVs tuned to CNN. I should've had a radio handset in my hand, a rifle at the ready in an assault sling on my shoulder, and a Kevlar helmet on my head. The thirty or so people in the vicinity couldn't believe what had just happened. Clerks like me were, as they say in finance, the whale shit on the bottom of the ocean. Traders were gods. Well, not today, asshole. Not today.

The trader immediately ran and got the chairman of the trading floor and pointed me out. I figured that I was about to get fired. And I didn't really give a shit. But the chairman was cool. He asked me what had happened, and I told him, as the guy who had pushed me stood in front of us. He asked if I was the new clerk who had just come back from Iraq. I said that I was. He smiled and explained to me that I couldn't go around fighting people. The whole time he was speaking, he had a wide grin on his face. Turned out that the trader I'd shoved was an asshole among assholes, and everybody hated him.

While the chairman spoke to me, I noticed that the guy I pushed had an eagle, globe, and anchor sticker on his trading badge. That was the symbol for the United States Marine Corps. I couldn't believe it. I walked over, shook his hand, and said, "Sorry, sir, I didn't know that you were a Marine. From one to another, Semper Fi. You understand how sometimes we can get a little nuts." If he was a Marine, he should totally understand.

The chairman laughed. The trader was not and never had been a Marine.

I was confused. It was incomprehensible to me that someone would wear that emblem unless they, their spouse, parent, or child had earned the right. I asked him if he had a son or someone who was a Marine; he had no answer. He turned his back to me and headed toward the crude-oil trading pit.

———

One morning on my way to work, something on the sidewalk outside my apartment building caught my eye. Among the trash and broken bottles and mysterious stains that seemed to accumulate each night was a freshly wrapped copy of the *New York Times*. And on its cover was a picture of suicide-bomber devastation in Iraq.

Not giving in to the thought of stealing my neighbor's newspaper, I bought a copy from the always-smiling man who worked at the kiosk down the street. I studied the photograph closely as I rode to work on the crowded subway train.

No one else seemed to notice the photograph of the soldier with the bright blond hair and big blue eyes. Eyes that were filled with terror. Next to her lay what was left of a man. Pieces of him. Fingers and a foot scattered in the road. Women who appeared to be his relatives stood next to one of the bigger pieces, screaming.

The soldier wore the patch of the Military Police on her shoulder. She looked like she was about to be sick from what her eyes were seeing. In her hands, a rifle. She held a death grip on that rifle.

I knew that look. Disbelief. Horror. She was now a vet. A veteran. A veteran of a foreign war.

At work, I walked around the trading floor, showing the picture to people, saying, "Look, look into her eyes. Do you see? Do you see that mangled corpse in the background?" I tried to show them, but no one gave a shit. They wanted to talk about baseball.

One of the traders, a heavyset guy in his midfifties with a white beard and serious face, had sewn a large POW/MIA patch onto the back of his trading jacket.

"Were you in 'Nam?" I asked him.

"Yep." He eyed me suspiciously, looking wary, wondering what I wanted.

"I was a Marine. On the front lines in Afghanistan and then Iraq."

He relaxed a bit and extended his hand. We shook and there was the trust between men who have been under fire, even if it was in wars that were thirty years apart. We talked of our units and battles fought.

"I'll tell you one thing that you better get used to. Nobody back home cares about what's going on over there." He had a thick Brooklyn accent. He paused.

"Nobody cares." A distant look in his eyes. "The quicker you realize that, the quicker you can move on with your life. And whatever happened over there... well, you've got to just *let it go*, son. You've just got to *let it go*."

He looked over my shoulder and out onto the trading floor, then disappeared into the crowd. And after he left me standing alone there next to one of the phone banks, holding the picture from the war in Iraq, I began to think about *what I'd done* over there. And more important, *why I'd done it*.

In Afghanistan in 2001, just after 9/11, I'd been an artillery forward observer attached to an infantry company. In Iraq in 2003, in much heavier fighting, I was an artillery liaison officer attached to an infantry battalion. But because of the way my battalion commander in Iraq maneuvered and fought—up front with his troops—I acted as a forward observer in Iraq, as well.

The job of the infantry is to do the killing—to locate and destroy the enemy forces. As a forward observer, I was responsible for directing the artillery shells down onto the enemy through a call for fire; as a liaison officer, for approving and transmitting calls for fire from other forward observers. I would do this by making a radio call for artillery support to the firing batteries, which were generally set up several miles behind us and grouped into three sections of six guns each. The main goal was to kill the enemy without killing our own people.

In battle, my eyeballs would see what was happening. My brain would process this information. On my map, my hands would mark a spot where I wanted there to be death. My right hand would key the Transmit button on the radio handset that was clipped onto my helmet strap. My mouth would speak the letters and numbers that matched the location on the map. Forty-five seconds later, the death would rain down.

The artillery pieces are giant cannons with a range of over twenty miles; they shoot hundred-pound shells that explode and splinter into thousands of shards of shrapnel in all directions. Each of the shards is the size of a heavy jagged-edged crowbar. Each is a maniac's sword hacking and spinning and slicing through the air at the speed of sound and easily able to take off a limb or cut a man in half. The shell bursts with such force that every living thing within a fifty-yard radius of the point of impact is either killed or severely wounded. And that's just one shell. We would regularly shoot eighteen, thirty, or fifty-four of them at the same time into the same general area. If the first barrage wasn't where I'd wanted it to be, I would make another radio call to adjust the coordinates so that the next salvo would be on target. Artillery is an *area-fire* weapon; it's like a chainsaw used to perform surgery.

Normally the shells would explode on impact with the ground. Sometimes I would instruct the firing batteries to set the fuses on the shells so that they would explode in the sky above the target. I would do this when I saw that the enemy was trying to hide in trenches. Other times, we would set the fuses to delay, so that the shells would crash through roofs and explode inside. I would do this when the enemy was trying to hide inside schools, houses, or other buildings.

I tried not to think about who else might be in the buildings.

In some situations, such as when the enemy was in a tree line or in vehicles, I would request a type of cluster-bomb artillery that was especially lethal. Each of these shells shits out eighty-eight smaller bomblets with shaped charges designed to rip through the armored vehicles. They are also devastating against personnel. It is a very effective killing tool, but we tried not to use it too much because a small percentage of the thousands of bomblets always fail to detonate. And to little kids, they look like toys. They like to pick them up and play with them.

———

Whenever I started to reflect on why we went over to fight, as I did that day on the trading floor after talking with the Vietnam vet, my thoughts always went back to Christmas 2002, just before we deployed to Iraq.

It was when I'd flown from Camp Pendleton back to the East Coast to spend the holidays with my family, as an active-duty Marine home on leave. I was staying at my brother Dan's apartment in New York City for a few days before taking the train to Boston to visit friends from college on New Year's Eve.

Most of the First Marine Division was home on holiday leave that December. Normally, it was a joyous time of rest and holiday cheer. But all twenty thousand of us in the division were on edge that year because the president and the other politicians had been rattling their swords and banging their drums and beating their chests for months. They used words like material breach and weapons of mass destruction. The UN Security Council was growing impatient with Saddam Hussein because he wasn't coming clean about the large stockpiles of weapons of mass destruction that he was supposedly sitting on.

When the phone rang in my brother's apartment and I heard the voice of one of my superior officers on the other end, I already knew what he was about to tell me. I'd been waiting for this call since I left Camp Pendleton. For security reasons, the Marine Corps always used landlines, never cell phones, to make those calls.

"Lieutenant Scotti, it's Major Coleman."

"Hey, sir, how's it going?"

"Did you have a good Christmas, Scotti?"

"I did, sir. How about you?"

"It was great. But the division just got the word that we're deploying to Kuwait shortly after leave ends."

He paused.

"I can't tell you the exact date because this is an unsecure line. The division commander decided to let everyone finish their leave past New Year's, but you need to have your shit wired tight and be ready to move quickly as soon as you get back."

Baghdad, I thought. *Eight million people.*

Would they fight us in the cities? The worst kind of fighting—especially when you're the attacker. Would they burrow down deep among the houses and the buildings and wait for us to arrive? That's what I would do. Hug up against us and hit us from rooftops and windows and alleyways. Attack at close range. Too close for us to use our bombs and artillery—because that would be suicide. Shoot RPGs onto the tops of our vehicles and rake us with machine-gun fire from above. An urban canyon of death. And after they had smashed us, they would melt quickly away, like ghosts, and hide in some distant part of the city.

In places like Grozny, Chechnya, and Hue, Vietnam, and Stalingrad, Russia, some units had taken 80 percent casualties.

"Roger that, sir. Should I let the guys know?"

"Negative. The Gunny is taking care of that."

"Roger that, sir."

"Happy New Year, Scotti."

"Happy New Year, sir."

I walked out onto the balcony of my brother's apartment on the twenty-third floor and thought about what had just happened. It was just after ten p.m. I looked out over Madison Square Park. A homeless man with a white beard was stretched across a bench, bedded down under his stained and tattered blankets, trying to stay warm for the night. I looked into the offices of Credit Suisse, to the south just across Twenty-Fifth Street. Inside, a few bankers sitting polished and well dressed in their cubicles, crouched in front of their computer screens, hard at work late into the night. They looked so sure of themselves, as though they knew a secret that the rest of the world was trying to uncover.

That New Year's Eve in Boston, I didn't tell my friends about the call I'd received from Major Coleman the night before. I didn't tell them I was about to head off to a war. *Loose lips sink ships*, I thought. And I didn't want to be the downer for the night, the guy with the bad news.

As midnight passed, I stood slumped against the bar in some crowded pub near Faneuil Hall. I watched all of the carefree people looking happy with their silly hats as they did shots of purple whatever-it-was and yelled things to each other and spilled their beers on one another. Then I looked at the empty champagne glasses that stood in front of me and wondered if I would be alive this time next year.

A few days later, I took the train from Boston's South Station to New York's Penn Station. There I would change to the New Jersey local train and head to my parents' house for a few quiet days before I said good-bye.

As the train rolled down the Connecticut coastline, I sat in my seat and prepared a predeployment checklist. Thirteen of us would make up an artillery detachment that would soon become part of an infantry battalion. And because of my rank, I was the one who was going to lead us. The infantry does most of the fighting in war. The rest of the Marine Corps is designed— as part of an interlocking system—to support the infantry. The logistics units bring ammunition and food and fuel when the infantry needs it. The air wing drop bombs on people when the infantry asks them to. The administrative sections try to make sure that a Marine's pay doesn't get screwed up, though it always seems to be.

Our detachment of forward observer teams would embed with the three rifle companies. One team of three men attached to each, plus four of us with the weapons company.

I'd been responsible for training these Marines during the last thirteen months, so that we'd be ready for whatever the hell it was that was waiting for us over there. We'd spent endless weeks and months together in the Mojave Desert in California. Training and being miserable and wishing we were out in the bars in San Diego pretending not to be Marines and trying to get laid. Weeks in the desert counting the hours until the goddamn training exercise was over. Eating MREs and smelling each other's farts and talking about what we would do when we got out of the Marine Corps. I loved each and every one of them. Most of the enlisted guys were just nineteen or twenty years old. I was twenty-six. And now I was the one in charge of bringing them home alive.

I flipped through a copy of our unit's Combat Standard Operating Procedures. I had brought it with me on leave to study. I needed to know these procedures cold. Make them part of my DNA, so that when I was tired and hungry and scared in combat, I would do the right thing.

> **Remains:** Collect as many parts as possible of dismembered bodies and wrap them in a poncho.

> **Nuclear, Biological or Chemically (NBC) Contaminated Dead:** While maintaining MOPP Level 4, place contaminated remains in a body bag and contact battalion-level NBC team or graves registration detail. Isolate remains from non-contaminated dead.

> **Selective Unmasking:** When the unit has been attacked with an NBC agent or suspected NBC agent and testing kits have run out or are not available: select the most junior ranking, mission non-critical Marine. Relieve him of his weapon, and order Marine to remove gas-mask and breathe normally for at least one minute. Observe closely for signs of NBC exposure described in Section 4.12.2A.

We would have to write our last wills and testaments. And be sure that our next-of-kin contact information was up to date. And give our wives or mothers power of attorney. There would be jokes about our moms hitting the "Marine Corps Lottery"—the $250,000 payout from the Serviceman's Group Life Insurance policy. And we'd have to confirm the identity of—and then sign for—each piece of equipment that had a serial number on it: rifles, pistols, night vision goggles, laser range finders, laser designators for the laser-guided bombs that we might call for, vehicles, radios, advanced cryptographic communications equipment, binoculars, gas masks, morphine doses for our individual first-aid kits, and special spring-loaded autoinjecting syringes with needles the size of coat hangers that we would stab ourselves with if we got hit with chemical agents.

On the train, I looked up from my notebook and combat manual for a moment as we approached New York City. The dull light of the weak winter sun came through the train's windows as rows of houses shot by. The car of the train was nearly overflowing: A frazzled mother traveling with her two young children tried to keep them from annoying other riders as they climbed all over the seats. A quiet couple in their fifties from somewhere in the heartland searched wide-eyed for the glimpses of the Manhattan skyline that appeared every few seconds in the spaces between the houses. A group of teenagers, laughing and ripe with youth. Proud grandparents, dressed in their best, probably off to see their grandchildren.

This is why, I thought. These are the ones whom it is my job to protect—everyday people doing everyday things.

As the train entered the tunnel that would end at Penn Station, I thought of the reports in the media about what a terrorist could do to the subway system. The Marine Corps had taught us a lot about nuclear, biological, and chemical warfare. About nerve gases like sarin and VX—how your nervous system becomes unglued and your cells and body systems can no longer communicate. You start to convulse, froth at the mouth, suffocate. Terror in your eyes, shit and piss in your pants. Lungs like fish gills just before the last gasp on the dock by the side of the lake. And about the blister agents, like mustard gas, which the unfortunate guys in World War I got hit with. It clings to anything that is wet or sweat covered. Your lungs, eyes, armpits, and genitals burn and break out in large pustules. Screaming in agony, you go blind and drown in your own lung fluid. And we learned about the biological agents, like smallpox or weaponized versions of the plague, Ebola, anthrax. About what a suitcase nuke set off in Times Square could do—instantly vaporize a third of Manhattan, including my brother Dan and my cousin Missy as they sit in their offices.

The personal risk that I was about to take was well worth it. If giving my life would prevent any of these things happening to even *one* innocent American person, I would do it.

Three days after New Year's Eve, I spent my last day of leave back at my parents' house. When I told them about the conversation I had with Major Coleman, they looked at each other briefly, communicating silently in a way that only two people who have been married to each other for thirty-seven years could. They had made it through my deployment to Afghanistan just after 9/11. They were now the seasoned parents of a Marine who sometimes had to go into harm's way for his country. I didn't tell them about my thoughts on fighting an urban war. I couldn't see the point of doing that to them.

The time came for my father to take me to the airport. I was to head back to Camp Pendleton, then Kuwait, and if the president decided to pull the trigger, Iraq. In the downstairs hallway of our home, just in front of our family portrait from 1984, my mother put her hand on my face and smiled gently. As I looked into her eyes, I smiled, each of us wondering if we would ever see those eyes again.

"Let me look at you. My baby boy," she said.

———

A few weeks after the day at work when I'd shoved the trader, I was standing at my console on the outer edge of the crude-oil options trading pit. As I entered a trade into the computer system, one of the other clerks tapped me on the shoulder. "Scotti...there's a guy over there who says he was a Marine in Iraq. Do you know him?" The guy had worked on the trading floor but had left before I started working there. He had come back for a visit.

The first thing I noticed was his screaming high-and-tight haircut. These are the haircuts they give new Marines—"boots," fresh out of boot camp. The sides are almost completely shaved to the crown of the head, the top buzzed short. They're ugly. They're great haircuts for drill instructors, because they scare recruits. But over the years I'd become wary of other Marines who'd been in for a while but still got them. Their owners always seemed to be just a little *too* motivated.

This guy had a smug look on his face. He was overweight, obviously not a fresh young recruit. I knew something was up and I already didn't like him.

"Hey, man, I heard you were in Iraq," I said.

"Yeah I was. And it was terrible. Dead bodies everywhere. Rockets blowing up all around us. Really crazy stuff." The smugness now dripping from him. He wanted me to shake his hand and scream, "Hey, everybody, this guy is a hero! Do you hear me? He is a *hero!*"

"Really? Wow, man. What unit were you with?"

"I was with the First Marine Division."

No kidding, asshole, I thought. *We were all with the fucking First Marine Division. All twenty thousand of us. What* unit *were you with?* He was being vague for a reason. And I was going to find out what that was.

"No, I mean, what regimental combat team? What battalion? What company? What was your MOS [military occupation specialty], dude?"

I could almost hear his asshole clench up. He realized that he wasn't talking to a civilian who would automatically gush over his bullshit just because he went to Iraq and had what he thought was the right haircut. His smugness disappeared. The other clerks who were standing with us looked at him. I continued.

"I was the arty LNO [artillery liaison officer] with Weapons Company One Four, dude. All the way up Route 7. An Nas [An Nasiriyah], Ash Shatrah, Al Kut, Baghdad. And I was an arty FO [artillery forward observer] in Afghanistan with Charlie One One in 2001. And a corporal in the infantry in the reserves out of Miami before that."

"I was a communications Marine out of the reserves in Brooklyn."

"Good to go. So what did you do in Iraq? Where did you go?"

"Well, mostly we set up antenna farms. I was actually in Kuwait most of the time. But we did cross over the border into Iraq for a little bit."

"So you guys were part of a comm battalion setting up ant farms out in the desert? How close did the rockets come to you guys? Did you lose anybody?" By this point I believed that he was a Reserve Marine, but I knew that he had never been in combat. I could see in his eyes that he was lying. And he knew that I knew.

"Oh, the rockets? Yeah...they landed a couple of miles from us."

"No kidding? That's really close." I decided not to embarrass him in front of the others. Yes, he was a Marine. And it wasn't his fault that he got stuck out in the middle of the desert putting up radio antennas. He had no control over that. But he sure as hell didn't have to go around acting like he had won the Congressional Medal of Honor. Plus, I'm pretty sure the clerks standing around us couldn't have cared less either way, because the war was something that was completely irrelevant to their lives. They cared more about their fantasy football leagues than they did about anything even remotely related to the war.

A bit later that day, I picked up a copy of a newspaper that someone had tossed aside. There was a story—not more than a paragraph long—about twelve Marines who were killed in action. All in one day. Fallujah. As I read the headline, I felt it in my throat. My stomach. My eyes. A quivering sadness as I began to unravel.

I wondered how it had happened and whether they were all buddies from the same unit. I hoped they had gone quickly and without pain. And not alone.

I left work early that day and walked north. Past Ground Zero. Past people with cold faces talking on their cell phones. Past the coffee shops and the churches and the jackhammers that sound like machine guns. And into a bar with only one small window.

"I'll have a Coors Light," I said to the bored bartender. That first cold crisp sip. The tonic. The battlefield memories now flashing across my mind like strobes...

Two Cobra attack helicopters banking slowly to the left, a pair of sharks swimming through the air, sniffing, searching for prey, their crews hoping they would get to let their rockets fly. Our guardian angels, our eyes, our fists, circling in the sky just ahead of us, spotting the enemy dug in along the streets, waiting to ambush us as we turned the corner. The sharks swooping down. The *whunk whunk whunk* of their heavy machine guns splattering men all over the walls and trees and roadside. Pink mist, we used to call it.

The entire First Marine Regiment attacked the Baghdad slums. Three infantry battalions, five thousand men. Fatigue from days and weeks fighting our way up Route 7. Catching forty-five minutes of sleep whenever we could. Circadian rhythms all shot to hell. Then Saddam City: narrow streets with civilians, families, and children all in the mix. Confusion. Dry mouth. Rooftop machine-gun nests. Radios crackling, interference building up. Radios not working. Cursing. Bullets flying at you from nowhere, from everywhere. Fear. Trying not to think about your buddies who had been wounded, or worse. Some units pushing farther into the slums, some units hitting resistance and falling behind, so the front line is everywhere. Friendly units ahead of you this way, enemy that way, don't know who's over there. Block to block. Building to building. Automatic weapons fire sounding like it was three blocks northwest. Or was it five? The sounds echoing off the buildings so it is almost impossible to be certain where things are coming from. More fire: a different firefight, five or six blocks northeast. What sounds like eight or nine blocks that way—due east—an explosion, then smoke. *What the hell was that?* A Bravo Company Marine shot, bleeding heavily. Urgent. Kyle Nickey next to me yelling on his radio. He's just twenty years old, yelling for the medevac birds to get the wounded Marine to surgery fast, or he will die. I'm making sure that the arc of the artillery rounds doesn't hit the helicopters, or our rifle companies, or our sister battalion. The artillery is parked across the river in the fields outside the city, shooting from miles away. Double-check the coordinates. Triple-check the coordinates. Read them aloud. Say each number and think it. Check the map. Check it again. Ask the operations officer who's where at this exact moment, as companies and platoons and squads and fire teams are constantly moving. Three minutes ago was an eternity. Everything fluid. Approve the barrage over the radio. Now I'm responsible for it. One number off in a six-digit coordinate means disaster. Fifty seconds later we hear the shells crashing. It feels good to be shooting back. "The Bravo Company Marine didn't make it." Now silence in our vehicle. We don't look at one another. Just the crackling of the radios. Two handsets are clipped to my helmet strap, one in each ear—left ear to talk to the forward observer teams with the rifle companies, right ear for the howitzers. Don't shoot at the mosques. No artillery fire to the west of that canal—that's our adjacent battalion's zone. No matter what, no fire west of that canal. Pass the word over the radio. Alpha Company. Bravo Company. Charlie Company. Make sure each understands. Get their position reports. Radio checks. Situation reports. *Why don't these civilians get the fuck out of here? Can't they see there's a war on?* Maybe they had nowhere to go. I wonder when we will get to sleep.

Then disaster.

Corporal Daniel Lange screaming over the radio from a few blocks away. One of the Marines in my detachment. Wife and newborn child. The fear in his voice beyond fear. Primal terror known only by men caught in an artillery barrage.

We have hit our brothers with our own fire.

No time to think—just make it stop. I key the handset. "Check firing, cannoncockers! Check firing! Check firing!"

Time in slow motion. *Please, God, let them not have fired the next salvo yet.* Check firing—fifty-four howitzers and the four hundred Marines manning them are frozen in an instant. Nobody does anything, because we now must unfuck this situation. What had just happened? Utter confusion as smoke rises from the impact area just a few blocks away. I knew it wasn't my guns shooting. I was sure of it. I hadn't told them to shoot. My boss hadn't given anyone permission to shoot into our zone. But we were so tired that we had to sit there going over the last three minutes in our heads, looking for mistakes. On the radio, right ear, I asked the artillery unit which battery had fired. *Please, God, don't let it be my guns. Please.*

They tell me, "Wait one," as they talk to the other firing batteries. It was a sister artillery unit in support of a sister infantry battalion. The call had come from them, and the cannons supporting them had shot into our zone. Relief—joy almost—that it wasn't my guns. My soul was clean. Then anger.

Who the fuck *just shot into our zone?* I grit my teeth. Anger boils. Who is the man responsible for this? I want to squeeze and crush his throat like an empty soda can. Because of his incompetence, an Alpha Company Marine—just a teenager—lies bleeding and kicking in the mud.

Shrapnel had ripped through his lower back and exited through his abdomen. He was classified as Urgent/Surgical. Corporal Nickey notified the medevac birds that were inbound to pick up the remains of the Bravo Company Marine that they will now be given another casualty. Captain Evan Wahl, the always calm and cool battalion air officer who sat next to me, pointed out that the death of the one Marine probably saved the life of the other, because the birds were already on their way.

My hands shook as I thought about the fact that if I had hesitated to call check firing, even by ten seconds or so, there most likely would've been another barrage on Alpha Company. My brain had chosen to say "Check firing, cannoncockers!" instead of "Check firing, Cobra!" *Cannoncockers* meant all of the Marine artillery in Iraq at the moment. There wasn't time to figure out which one of the nine batteries in the artillery regiment had fired, so I'd decided to shut them *all* down.

The Marine who'd been hit was near the edge of Alpha Company's position. The first barrage had been slightly off. Whoever the Marine was who was shooting at them would have made a correction, just as he had been trained to do. The second barrage would've landed on top of Alpha Company, and because they were patrolling, exposed and not dug in, it would have been devastating.

A few minutes later, an unfamiliar voice popped onto the Artillery Conduct of Fire Net. He was from another battalion, in another regiment. From the sound of his voice, he was the one who'd either made the call for or approved the barrage. He had thought he had approval to shoot into our zone but didn't, or someone had given him approval but shouldn't have, or our guys were in the wrong place, or the rounds were fired improperly and had fallen short of their intended target, or who the fuck knows what actually happened.

"Palerider, we just wanted an update on that wounded Marine, over," he said.

Regret and confusion in his voice. My rage against him turned to sadness as I thought about what he must be thinking—and would be thinking for the rest of his life.

———

I sat in the bar that had only one window. I sipped my beer and thought about the newspaper paragraph about the twelve Marines who'd died. And about the guys I knew who were gone and the ones who were still over there fighting. And about the terrible mistakes that people make on the battlefield. Mistakes that kill brothers. And about all the rest of those things that seem to crawl up from the dark depths at times when the cover has been knocked off and the trapdoor that leads down there is left wide open.

My eyes scanned the news channel on the TV high on the wall behind the bar, *looking for you*. But you were not there. A few weeks ago I saw your face on the TV, the story almost a throwaway between Donald Trump's hiring of Bill on *The Apprentice* and a stock market report. You were a truck driver in the Army. Ambushed. Dragged away. A POW, with the brim of your boonie hat flipped up in that grainy video. They stuck the camera in your face. You looked away. God knows what was going through your mind, but it looked like you knew what they were going to do to you. Those motherfuckers. But why wasn't our country holding its breath? Thinking and hoping and praying that the boys searching for you would find you alive. Why didn't the entire nation know your name—PFC Matt Maupin from Batavia, Ohio—captured by the enemy. I asked around, but no one I knew had ever even heard of you.

The band in the bar started to play to the three or four people who had wandered in at random. "We are now going to play a song called 'I Love My Country,'" the band leader said into the microphone, his guitar slung low around his hips.

No, you don't love shit, motherfucker. If you loved your country you'd pick up a rifle and go fight. You'd be over there right now instead of back here in this goddamn empty bar running your fat fucking mouth and playing with your shitty fucking band. I thought briefly about walking up onstage and punching him in the face. I didn't.

48

The place began to fill up with the after-work crowd. But I had been there alone for hours, so I was several drinks ahead of them. Well placed on my barstool with my back to them, lost in thought.

I remembered my Uncle Sammy. My father's uncle, an old-timer. A giant when I was a little kid. A gentle man who always had kind words. He had served in the Navy in the Pacific during World War II. Toward the end of the war, the kamikaze pilots would crash their planes into the ships, the explosions tearing through the decks, killing hundreds or thousands of our boys in an instant. And sometimes when the torpedoes sank the ships, sailors would drift for hours in groups in the ocean before the sharks got to them.

Uncle Sammy had given me some of his medals and the holster that had held his .45 caliber service pistol. His initials, JSC, were carved into the leather. At weddings and birthday parties, he would drink whiskey and end up with his head down on the table. As little kids, we would giggle and laugh and point. "Nanny, why is Uncle Sammy sleeping again?"

"Oh, he's just tired. He'll be alright."

He was long dead now, but I would always wonder if he, too, had seen the horror firsthand. Had he ever had to fight for his life? Were some of his buddies the ones who'd been hit by the kamikazes or the ones in the water with the sharks afterward?

During World War II, people grew their own food in victory gardens so there would be enough for the troops. Bands of kids scoured neighborhoods looking for anything made of copper. They would drop off the copper items at local collection points so they could be used in ammunition and for wiring for military vehicles and aircraft. Women went without their beloved silk stockings so there would be enough silk to make parachutes for the airborne infantry. People reached into their own wallets to buy war bonds, the government's way of financing the war. The civilians fought the war in their own way and through their own sacrifice, right alongside the soldiers.

But then came Korea. They called it the forgotten war. But it was not forgotten by the families of the Marines who froze to death at the Chosin Reservoir. Or by the soldiers who lived through it but lost their fingers and their feet and the tips of their noses. Or by their wives, who had to sleep next to the shells of what had once been their husbands for the next fifty years...each night hearing the nightmares and the names of buddies lost.

And during the Vietnam War, the draft had been in effect, so everyone was well aware of the war. They were well aware of the men who went to fight it. Because a few even spat on them in airports when they came home. It made me sick to think that people would do that.

The ground offensive in the Gulf War was over in four days. Not long enough to strain the public support. Not long enough to really make people have an opinion one way or the other. That war was filled with bombing runs that obliterated a hundred thousand Iraqi troops waiting in the trench lines in the desert.

And in Iraq and Afghanistan, there was nothing to bring it front and center to those who weren't fighting or who didn't have family members or close friends over there. Photos of the flag-draped coffins as they were unloaded at Dover Air Force Base were banned. There were almost no news stories about medals for bravery and those who earned them. Each report of those killed in action seemed just an afterthought. Back home, in the Northeast at least, it was business as usual. This was surprising to me, especially because I lived and worked in downtown Manhattan, just a few blocks from Ground Zero, where I thought people should've been most aware of the significance of our fighting and dying for our country. And yet as I saw on the trading floor, it just wasn't that important to most people.

But I thought that once the troops found the stores of nerve gas or whatever it was that Saddam had been hiding, it would all be worth it. Because although the people who surrounded me in that bar probably didn't think much about the war, they were still being protected by people in uniform. And they didn't deserve to die some horrible death on their way to work tomorrow morning because some guy squeezed an Afrin bottle full of liquid VX nerve agent on the E train at eight fifteen a.m.

Donald Rumsfeld came on the TV behind the bar. The sound was off because the band was playing, but I remembered a quote from him: "You go to war with the Army you have, not the Army you want." A man like him says something like that because he wasn't the one getting his ass shot off. We didn't have enough body armor when we invaded Iraq. We had flak vests, which were meant to stop or slow down small pieces of shrapnel, but bullets would slice right through them. Some were lucky enough to have reinforced porcelain plates that could stop an AK-47 round. They were made to be slipped inside our flak vests, one in the front and one in the back. They would protect almost all of the vital organs in the torso from gunfire. Our heads, limbs, the arteries that fed them, and the sides of our torsos were still exposed, but the plates offered a whole new level of protection. They were lifesavers.

But we didn't have enough for everyone.

So we gave the plates to the most junior Marines. But how long before we went to war in Iraq did we know that there was a chance we would invade? At least a year. And how hard is it to take the number of people that would fight and multiply that by two? How hard is it to call the suppliers a year before and tell them to retool and ramp up production? Maybe Rumsfeld should've been the one to look the next twenty-year-old Marine in line in the eyes and tell him that there weren't any more strike plates.

I watched as he mugged for the camera, his smugness telling of his arrogance and his holier-than-thou attitude.

I asked the bartender for a pen. On a slightly damp bar napkin, I wrote: "Donald Rumsfeld—I hope you die of cancer and are then ass-raped by a thousand demons in motherfucking hell, you smug son of a bitch." I folded the note and put it in my pocket.

Now I down the beers hard and fast. The band plays. The people talk, but I am only in the background. Then the fog starts to come. And I go. I go into the spirit world, where everything that is not OK is OK. Where the Route 7 corpses live.

Alcohol. Lack of understanding. Distance. The dead. Open mouths. Veteran.

Chapter Three

MY MOM CALLED ME early one night just after I got home from work. I could tell something had scared her from the way she said hello when I answered the call. There was a slight touch of panic in her voice.

"You got a package in the mail today from the Marine Corps. Do you want me to open it or send it to you?"

It was a gut punch. Not a letter. A package. Like when my brothers Dave and Dan applied to colleges when I was eight or nine. They would try to guess the response based on the size of what showed up in the mail. A package meant you were in, but a letter-size envelope was grim. "After careful consideration of the unprecedented number of applications this year, we are sorry to inform you..."

The package contains my original official orders, I thought. Involuntary recall. *They're sending me back to the war.* I'd heard that they were pulling lieutenants and sergeants and captains out of the Individual Ready Reserve (IRR) to use as combat-casualty replacements. Using us to plug the holes in the units where Marines of our rank had fallen in combat and also to fill spaces in the activated reserve units that just didn't have enough bodies to go around. The IRR was an in-between place for Marines who had finished their four-year active-duty commitment. For four additional years, the Marine Corps could call you back to go fight. It was in the fine print of the contracts that we all signed without reading. It was our purgatory.

"You can open it now, Mom," I said, trying hard not to sound alarmed. I couldn't believe she was going to have to endure another one of my deployments. Another year of her wondering and waiting and praying that two Marines in dress blues wouldn't show up on her doorstep.

"Can you help me out with this, honey?" I heard her ask my dad.

I thought of how I would have to show up at some regional IRR formation with all of the other shaggy-haired and pissed-off Marine sergeants and lieutenants and captains. Midlevel leaders who had done their time and gotten out and thought they were finished with it all. But then we got this goddamn package. We would be reprocessed back into the Marine Corps, and we would get haircuts, and then we would be sent back into the heat and dust and fear and violence and death.

I heard the crinkling of the package as my dad was trying to cut through the tape around the sides with a pair of scissors. *This will be my third tour. I wonder if this is the one that'll get me.*

"There's a plastic red folder and a small blue box," my mom said.

My father opened the small navy blue, gold-embroidered government-issue box.

"It's a medal! It's a medal!" I heard my dad yelling in the background. "Mikey got a medal!" he yelled to my brother Dave, who just happened to be visiting our family's house.

"Look, Angelo, there's a letter," my mother said.

It was the citation that accompanies a personal decoration. As she began to read it, I thought about the medals I had seen awarded while on active duty. The rest of the unit gathered, standing in perfect military formation, at attention in perfectly aligned rows. The Marine who was about to receive the decoration marched to the front of the formation. An officer read the citation, or official account of how and why the Marine had earned the medal. Then the commanding officer pinned the medal to the Marine's uniform. The Marine saluted the commanding officer, and the commanding officer returned the salute. Then he usually shook the Marine's hand and said something like, "Nice work, Marine. You make the Corps proud," as he slapped the Marine on the side of the shoulder.

I listened through the phone:

> During the battalion's movement to contact north, Lieutenant Scotti coordinated eight fire-for-effect missions in the support of engaged rifle companies. In every case, despite incoming fire, his coordination between forward observers and firing batteries was meticulous, which ensured that devastating artillery fires were delivered safely and accurately. The artillery fire coordinated by First Lieutenant Scotti was credited with destroying enemy strong-point positions and neutralizing enemy forward observers. His initiative, perseverance and total dedication to duty reflected great credit upon himself and were in keeping with the highest traditions of the Marine Corps and the United States Naval Service.

I could sense the tears in my mom's eyes. The citation was for a Navy and Marine Corps Achievement Medal with Combat V. It was the lowest-ranking of all personal decorations, which made me smirk for a second. *Leave it to me to win the lowest-ranking of all of the fucking medals*, I thought. And I had to laugh because, true to form, they'd gotten the number of missions wrong on the certificate. As I remembered and would later confirm when I read the Summary of Action (written by my superior officers) that accompanied the medal and gave a more detailed account, our battalion fired sixteen fire-for-effect missions, not eight. But that was a small detail that didn't matter. I was proud of what we'd done over there, and I was happy to accept the medal.

To my mind, all the citation *really* said was that a Marine had fought the way he was supposed to fight in combat, regardless of the circumstances. It said that a Marine had done his job. It didn't say anything about governments, politics, oil, the United Nations, the CIA, or intelligence that pointed to weapons of mass destruction.

But there was something that was starting to bother me. By this point, I'd expected to see photos of Marines or other soldiers with smiles on their faces because *they* were the lucky ones who'd found six thousand canisters of sarin or VX gas in the Iraqi Baath Party warehouse in eastern Baghdad. I'd expected the president or some general to hold a press conference full of phrases like, "...the massive cache of nerve-gas-tipped artillery shells...bunker in the desert..." But nothing like that had happened. So I couldn't help but wonder why we hadn't found the WMDs we all went over there to look for.

When I hung up the phone, I thought about the last time I'd heard that same worry in my mother's voice. It had been just a little under two years before, in July 2002, when I called home from Camp Pendleton.

In the morning on that day in 2002, I'd been ordered to report to the office of the artillery battalion commander. I'd wondered what he wanted. Or what I'd done. When I entered the battalion commander's office, I noticed a picture hanging on the wall. It was a cityscape of tan and gray buildings, red tracer rounds from machine-gun fire streaking across the foreground. The picture had been taken at a slightly crooked angle, as if it had been snapped in a hurry. I smiled briefly when I saw it, then remembered that this might not be a happy meeting. The smile went away.

I was more curious than worried about what the colonel wanted with me. The contract for my active-duty time in the Marine Corps was soon to expire. I was getting out and thus was unafraid of some career-ending conversation. If I had planned to stay in for twenty years, climbing through the officer ranks and retiring, I probably would've been shitting in my pants.

I stood at attention. Feet at a perfect 45 degree angle. Arms straight and extended down the length of my torso and upper thighs. Thumbs in perfect alignment with my trouser seams.

"Good afternoon, sir. Lieutenant Scotti reporting as ordered."

It felt good to know that I would be getting out soon. I would never have to kiss a higher-ranking officer's ass to further my own career. Or be stuck in a situation where someone above me had made a decision that looked good politically, but that also screwed over everybody in the unit below the rank of captain. I saw this happen sometimes in other units—when majors and colonels are scrambling for the ever smaller number of spots at the top of the pyramid. All I cared about was that the Marines under my command were well trained and that I'd provided them with every tool possible to help them stay alive in combat. Nothing else mattered.

"Scotti, take a seat."

"Yes, sir."

The colonel had noticed me looking at the picture. He pulled it off the wall and handed it to me.

"I took that photograph in 1984, in Beirut, when I was a young lieutenant like you. It was a hell of a fight."

"Sir, this is an awesome picture."

It was. And that fight was probably one of the proudest moments of his life. *Because he was there.*

"Scotti, you've spent a lot of time training with One Four. I just got off the phone with Lieutenant Colonel [John] Mayer. He has asked for you, by name, to be his artillery liaison officer for this fight. That's an honor, Scotti. And as you know, it's one hell of an important job. Especially with what lies ahead of us."

"Yes, sir."

"I know that your contract is up in February [of 2003]. Then the Marine Corps loses you. Now, there's a pretty good chance that Division is going to stop-loss everyone before then, which means that no one is getting out for a long time. But we haven't heard anything about that yet. So until then, General Mattis has asked for volunteers. He is asking certain Marines to voluntarily extend their active-duty time until major combat operations have ceased or until Division deems it's alright to release you. You did an outstanding job in Afghanistan, and we want you in the fight for the next round. You don't have to give me an answer now, but let me know by the end of the day."

"Roger that, sir."

I rose from the chair and stood at attention. I said, "Good afternoon, sir," did an about-face, and exited his office. Colonel Mayer was an exceptional leader, and I would have been proud to fight and die next to him. And the infantry battalion that he commanded, One Four, otherwise known as First Battalion, Fourth Marine Regiment, was one of the best in the division.

By the time I'd reached the parking lot outside, I'd already decided that I was going to say yes. There was no way in hell that I would abandon my guys, my unit, my Marine Corps, or my country. And if there was going to be a war in Iraq, I sure as hell wasn't going to miss it.

When I got back to our office in the barracks, I typed the colonel an e-mail. Then I called my mom and told her what I had done.

———

As I was coming home from work on the trading floor one day, I walked down the hall on the ground floor of my apartment building. Someone had set a paper and glue mousetrap on the floor by the side door that led to the alley where they kept the garbage cans. There was a small young mouse stuck to the paper. He was struggling to get away, his legs stuck to the glue. He was making a shrieking noise. Someone had come by and seen him. And they'd tried to crush him. A leg snapped and pointing the wrong way and some blood behind his ears. And now he had spit most of his insides up and they were in front of him. The way his insides had been spit up reminded me of something I had seen before. I clenched my jaw. He shrieked and struggled. I tried to pull him off of the paper. I couldn't do it without tearing his legs off. I thought about putting him out of his misery. But I couldn't do that either. I walked away and up the stairs to my apartment. I left the mouse back in the hallway.

I opened my apartment door and dropped the keys onto the counter. I searched through the box filled with stuff from the war that I kept in the cabinet underneath the counter. I found the large ziplock bag filled with footage I'd shot in the war. I took out my camera and scrolled through one of the tapes. It was the one from Route 6 in Iraq, just south of Baghdad. I *needed* to see that one scene, the one I'd just been reminded of. I didn't know why I needed to see it. I just did.

The dead Iraqis were on the side of the road. One had been hit with machine-gun fire. He had died in the fetal position, and his insides had come up through his mouth. The fluid had made the ground wet around his face and open mouth. The wetness had been sprayed in a way that it looked like he was probably still alive when it had come up. You couldn't tell if it was vomit or blood or the juices from his organs. It had already been soaked into the dirt. It looked like he had tried to cry out but no words would come. There were no words. Only the wetness.

And once I started watching the tapes, I didn't want to stop. The images and the memories that came with them hit me hard.

A young Iraqi boy with brown hair. Maybe six or seven years old. Lying dead in the road with one shoe missing. A look of final pain—or was it disbelief—frozen on his ash-charred face. Thrown from a powder-blue sedan with the roof pulled back like the lid on a can of sardines. Burning trucks and hulks of troop-carrying vehicles. Wounded Iraqi soldiers still crawling. Slowly. Arms outstretched in the fields along the road. Surrounded by their dead buddies.

The damned.

The wounded enemy who were left behind because their wounds had been too grave and they were beyond saving.

A cow dead and bloated in the sun with its legs stiff and extended. Attacked by thousands of flies. Its asshole blown wide open and its intestines spurted across the road. A mother standing in front of her home and next to her a young son who played in the dirt. Just a few feet away—a dead dog. The eyes of the mother not looking at us as we drove by. Vacant and hollow and not believing.

The M1 Abrams tanks firing their main guns. The shells splitting the enemy vehicles in half and blowing and peeling the walls back so that what was left looked like a flower. Men crawling through the mud and the gunners on the tanks hitting them with the coaxial machine guns. Thermal sights so powerful that the gunners in the tanks could see the facial expressions and contortions of pain as the bullets they had just fired ripped to pieces the bodies of the men who looked like green and white ghosts on the screen.

And a man who had been killed in the road. Right in the middle of the road so that you had to drive over him. All that was left of him was the hamburger meat that had been driven over by hundreds of tracked and wheeled vehicles. There was the main spot of what was left of him. Then the smear as each vehicle scraped more of the meat a bit further up the road in red and purple and green streaks. And the dead who had been blown out of their clothes with genitals exposed and backs arched and arms twisted. And I was done looking at them. I was done turning my neck to see what new horror could be possible. Because the number was infinite but my mind was not and so I was finished looking at them and hoped that they were done looking at me.

Yet still, I continued to dig through the box of war memories I kept in my apartment. I came across a letter I'd received the day before the war started and we crossed the border from Kuwait into Iraq. It was from a very good buddy of mine, Rob Secher, or Cubby, as all of the lieutenants used to lovingly call him. He was a year senior to me, so when I'd shown up in the artillery battery as a green young second lieutenant with no idea what the hell I was doing, he had been kind and showed me the ropes. He didn't have to do that. He could have let me learn the hard way, but kindness was a big part of who he was. He quickly became a combination of friend and a role model—someone whom I wanted to emulate.

Rob had spent four years on active duty as an enlisted man, had gone to college, then returned to active duty as an officer. He had blue eyes and strawberry blond hair. His manner was quiet and happy, and he was always smiling. But just underneath the quietness was one hell of a tough Marine. His Marines loved him, and after working with him for a week, I could see why. Cubby always did the right thing. There was no lying or false bravado in him. Just a pure, reserved confidence. He became one of my favorite Marines of all time, and over the years, one of my best friends. One of the handful of people that you meet in life whom you will always—no matter what—be buddies with. One of the ones whom you would die for in a heartbeat.

He and I were among the seven lieutenants who served together under our old commanding officer, Major Joe Russo, the officer I'd run into that day before checking out at Camp Pendleton. During the time Major Russo commanded our artillery battery, he had created something truly special. A unit whose Marines loved their leader and whose leader loved his Marines. Because of the example he set, the energy was good and the Marines did what they needed to do without being told because they were doing it for their leader. It didn't matter what the mission was or how much time you had left on your contract or whether or not there was a war brewing in the Middle East. For the time that you were a part of that unit, it was your home and your family, and serving in it would be the greatest thing you would ever do. And when it was over, you would miss it and search for the same meaning in other places, and you could come close, but you could never match it. And because of Major Russo's leadership, the bonds between the brothers who served together under him became especially strong.

After his three years at Camp Pendleton, Cubby rotated to a job as an instructor and staff member at Officer Candidates School (OCS). He was helping to build brand-new lieutenants. It was a tough job with long hours, and at times, I'm sure it was thankless, but it was an honorable one and one that was essential to the existence of the Marine Corps. But because the timing of his normal Marine Corps career path caused him to rotate out of the deploying units in the Fleet Marine Force, he missed the beginning of the war in Iraq.

The letter was addressed to Trashcan—my nickname and sometimes radio call sign in the Marines. I'd been given it by another of the Russo lieutenants, a buddy of mine named Chris Whitley, whom we called Whit. Whit was as tough as woodpecker lips and seemed to have almost superhuman strength. In November 2001, at three a.m., just a few minutes before we boarded the helicopters to become the first Marines into Afghanistan, Whit took one look at me and started laughing. "With all of that gear and ammo you have on, you look like a trashcan with arms and legs." Everybody in the room, including me, started laughing hysterically. At only five feet four inches tall, I *did* look like a trashcan, especially because I was worried about running out of ammo and carried both a rifle and a pistol, two hand grenades, 210 rounds of ammunition for the rifle and 30 for the pistol loaded into magazines, a bayonet, smoke grenades, an infrared laser pointer, signal flares, my giant Kevlar helmet, body armor, binoculars, night vision goggles, canteens and extra water, a compass, food, cold-weather clothing, a canvas map case, gas mask, wet-weather poncho, sleeping mat, and a whole bunch of other crap. We weighed ourselves on a scale with our gear to get an accurate weight so we didn't overload the helicopters that were taking off from the decks of the ships in the black night. Otherwise, the birds would plunge into the even blacker sea and quickly flip upside down, because the engines make the aircraft top-heavy, and we would be tangled in our gear and drown as the fuselage sank to the bottom of the Arabian Sea. After I stepped off the scale, I realized that my gear actually weighed more than I did.

March 18, 2003

TRASHCAN,

By the time you get this you will be a battle hardened vet, and if you're reading this, then you aren't dead yet!

I didn't get to bang Josh's sister in law. She, like all other women, dumped me inside of a month. It's alright though because I ended up meeting this other girl a few weeks back when I was out one night with Whit. This girl seems good to go. I'll let you know what happens.

So things are good on this end. We work long hours out here at OCS, but Whit and I both enjoy it. We'll be in Georgetown this weekend, getting shitfaced in your honor. We miss you guys.

On a serious note, I hope you will all be OK. It sucks to think that all our best friends are about to go into combat.

Give our best to Jim, Holecko, Maj Russo, Jaworski, and everyone else we know.

When you get back, we're all getting together in Jersey for some drinky drinky.

Semper Fi,

Cubby

As I read the letter, I remembered how it felt to be part of something meaningful, a unit of Marines who became brothers and close friends. It was a time when I got to know and see, every day, people for whom I would gladly have given my own life.

I sat alone in my apartment for hours studying for the Graduate Management Admission Test (GMAT). That was the test you needed to take to get into business school.

My small desk from IKEA wobbled a bit every time I sat down to work at it. Each time, I'd remember I needed to find that Allen wrench that came with the desk and use it to tighten the parts. But then I would open the study guide and forget all about the desk.

x is a positive integer and x raised to any odd integer is greater than zero; is $w - z$ greater than 11 times the quantity $9^{x-2} - 3^x$?

$z < 37$ and $w = 14^x$

$x = 9$

Choose the best answer:

a. Statement (1) ALONE is sufficient, but statement (2) alone is not sufficient.
b. Statement (2) ALONE is sufficient, but statement (1) alone is not sufficient.
c. BOTH statements TOGETHER are sufficient, but NEITHER statement ALONE is sufficient.
d. EACH statement ALONE is sufficient.
e. Statement (1) and (2) TOGETHER are NOT sufficient to answer the question asked, and additional data are needed.

What did this have to do with anything? How did it test the ability to run a business? Or the ability to accomplish a goal or a mission? Or to build a great organization? Or to lead and foster and develop employees? I would study for hours each day after work, trying to decipher the code of the test and shaking my head about the ridiculousness of it all. How meaningless this was compared to the consequences we'd face if we made the wrong decisions in combat.

———————

In the early spring of 2004, just under a year since I'd stepped off the bus at Camp Pendleton, I flew back to the West Coast to visit some business schools in California. I'd been given the advice that I should make sure to visit each of the schools, because an application wouldn't be taken seriously if the applicant hadn't made the effort to visit the school.

The University of California–Berkeley was one of the schools that would open doors at the investment banks. I signed up for a tour of the campus with a group of other hopeful applicants. We would then have a Q&A session with someone from the office of admissions.

After the tour, the group of us sat well dressed and nervous in our suits and blouses. We were uncomfortable because the woman we were about to meet was one of the people who would look at our applications and decide whether or not we got in. I got the sense that any one of the people in the room would have gladly murdered any of the other people in the room if it would've increased their chances. I hated myself for being in that room with them and those hard gray folding chairs and the hard gray people who were sitting in them. With my Brooks Brothers suit and my black shoes and my fake leather résumé holder that I bought at Staples. Everyone else in the tour group seemed to get it. They seemed to know something that I didn't.

When the woman entered the room, all movement stopped. Hands were folded and everyone did their best to give off their very best business-like energy. Their body language and their straight backs and the overly eager looks on their faces said *Yes, I belong here at Berkeley pursuing my MBA and yes, I will ask a very intelligent question to make an impression and yes, I will smile.*

Who the fuck are these people? I thought. *What did they stand for, and had they ever had a genuine thought in their entire lives?*

The woman was in her late thirties. She had straight dark brown hair cut to her chin and wore a business suit and earrings that dangled from her ears. From the look on her face, she knew that she had something over us. And it was clear that she enjoyed it.

When my turn came, I asked, "How does the admissions committee view military service, with its leadership development and decision-making experience?"

The woman smirked and shifted a bit in her seat. It was clear that she did not like me and that my presence annoyed her.

"The admissions committee does not usually consider military service as relevant work experience with regard to admission to Haas School of Business," she said sharply. Her tone and her eyes told me that I was the enemy. That I was one of *them*. Part of something that she hated. That she despised.

I fantasized about machine-gunning everyone to death in that fucking room. Especially her. People like her didn't deserve to enjoy the freedoms of our country. People like her didn't deserve to be American citizens. People like her deserved to have the shit beat out of them. And it was not because people like her were anti-war because anyone who's ever fought one knows that they are the most terrible of all things. So politics and idealism had nothing to do with it. It was because people like her hated the troops who fought the wars just as much as the people who started them. And for the first time, I had just a small taste—just a whiff really—of what it might've been like to have come home from Vietnam and been spit on by people like this lady with the dangly earrings.

I guess Berkeley is off the list, I thought.

———

On Easter weekend, I headed out to visit my family in New Jersey. It was rare for all of us to be in one place at one time, and my mother wanted to celebrate by going out for a nice dinner. We met at the restaurant, and I sat quietly at the table, sipping wine and not really listening to the conversation. I was angry that day. I was angry most days.

My mom could sense it as soon as I sat down. A bomb. Set and ready. I could tell it made her sad, because all she wanted was for her sons to be happy. I felt bad because she was the last person in the world whom I ever wanted to hurt. But the anger was strong and flowing inside of me.

"I'm thinking about writing a letter to Berkeley about how fucked up it is that they don't consider military service as relevant," I said out loud to make the conversation a bit more interesting. The wine was starting to take hold, and the rage was going to be right behind it. Various members of my family said that it was probably a bad idea, because I hadn't been accepted anywhere yet and I might be put on some sort of blacklist.

My brother Dave's girlfriend was sitting directly across from me at the table. She had two young boys from a previous marriage. One was in the Boy Scouts.

"My oldest son's Boy Scout troop is making care packages for the troops next week. Is there anything in particular that they should include?" she asked me.

The rage arrived. And this innocent mother of two, who was dating my brother and just trying to help support the troops, was going to catch the worst of it. For no other reason than because she was the one who happened to ask me a question.

"How about this?" I said loudly. "Send them some fucking body armor or some vehicles that don't have doors that are made out of fucking canvas. Have your kids send them cartons of smokes and logs of Copenhagen dip. Also, send them porn. *Lots* of porn. The nastier, the better. And if your kids want a really cool project for their Boy Scout troop, have the scoutmasters, once they're done feeling up the little boys, help the kids fill up Scope bottles with booze and send them to the troops. Because that's what the troops really fucking want. So they can sit back after a long day on patrol and sneak a few sips and forget where the fuck they are."

The table went silent. Everyone looking down, the only noise the sound of forks awkwardly hitting plates. The people at the other tables gasped a bit and looked—but looked away when I looked back saying *Fuck you, don't even look at me* with my eyes. *Fuck you* with your stupid haircuts and your condos and your tacky gold watches. Your home equity line of credit and your Cadillac SUVs and your whiny goddamn kids.

I gulped down the rest of my glass of wine, threw my cloth napkin on my plate, stood up, and walked away. I walked through the front door of the restaurant and out into the parking lot. I drove away, headed back to the city, ashamed of what I'd done.

———

In June of 2004, with much hype, the film *Fahrenheit 9/11* was released. I had never been a politically opinionated person. I never considered myself left-wing or right-wing. I was just a Marine who'd wanted to do his job. I knew the film was going to be very left-wing, so I'd prepared myself for some of the bias.

But when the lights came on in the theater, I sat in silence. Stunned. I sat and watched the people grab their things and file slowly toward the center aisle, stepping on the empty candy wrappers and soda cups. I did not move. My brain would not process the connections. The footage. The statements from the film.

The clip of the interview with Richard Clarke, President Bush's counterterrorism chief with Charles Gibson, host of *Good Morning America*:

"The president, in a very intimidating way, left us, me and my staff, with the clear indication that he wanted us to come back with the word that there was an Iraqi hand behind 9/11 because they had been planning to do something about Iraq from before the time they came into office." They didn't want to hear anything about any country other than Iraq. "It was, 'Iraq, Saddam. Find out, get back to me.'

"Well, Don Rumsfeld said when we talked about bombing the Al Qaeda infrastructure in Afghanistan—he said, 'There are no good targets in Afghanistan; let's bomb Iraq.' And we said, 'But Iraq had nothing to do with this,' and that didn't seem to make much difference."

Michael Moore had commented, "All [the troops] ask for in return is that we never send them into harm's way unless it's absolutely necessary."

All of it was swirling in my head. Talk of a prepackaged plan to attack Iraq. The business connections. The oil connections. The president not springing to action when he heard of the second plane. The Halliburton drivers being paid five to ten times more than the military guys who were protecting them in the same convoy. The eyes of the vets in the clinic who were clearly suffering from PTSD. The greed. The baby screaming and looking confused as they drilled a hole in his skull. The mother talking about her dead son in front of the White House, talking about the fact that there was no connection to Al Qaeda in Iraq and about the ignorance of the American people. Thinking how before the death of her son, that mother was just like my mother— proud and patriotic. But now that her son was gone, the costs of war were very real and heavy upon her. So she looked more closely than the others. Others who still had their sons and did not have to pay the price. And when she looked, she saw. Iraq. Based on lies. *Lies.*

I felt betrayed. Betrayed belief in our government. Betrayed trust. Honor. Duty. Things that had been hardwired into me since I was a young boy.

Things that men willingly die for.

Eyes wet, mouth dry, heart pounding. I walked on the sticky theater floor through the popcorn and the spilled soda and out into the aisle. Into the lobby with the worn red carpet and then pushed hard to open the swinging door, which struck loudly against the outside wall of the theater. The sun bright in the blue sky. Into my truck but eyes still wet and mouth dry. Then a tear. Then the rage. A fist into the dashboard. And then another. And I hit and I hit and then my fist was bleeding. The rage. The hurt and the sad and anger and not wanting to believe that any of what they said was true but knowing that at least some of it probably was.

The first glimpse of Meredith I had in a decade was while I was trying to flag down the overwhelmed bartender at our ten-year high school reunion. I went because I wanted to drink with the friends I'd known before things had become so complicated and confusing and ugly. And I wanted to thank the ones who'd been so thoughtful when I was deployed. Like the guys who brought my mom flowers and those who'd sent letters and care packages with the cookies and candy that we devoured once the mail finally caught up with us.

Meredith looked much as she had in high school, with her long dark brown hair and slender body and intelligent blue eyes that just drew you in. She was the supersmart, reserved girl who'd been in all of the honors classes. Never at any of the parties in high school, but always there in the back of your adolescent mind. She still had the underlying sensuality just below the surface that you always thought you could sense but were never sure.

She had become an assistant district attorney in Manhattan and lived on the East Side in Tudor City. After reconnecting at the reunion, we'd made plans to see each other again, this time where we both lived—in the city.

Meredith and I saw each other several times in the weeks after the reunion. The meetings went from lunches or coffee to dinner and drinks. And over time, we grew close, and she became one of the few people whom I trusted enough to open up to—even if only partially.

Meredith was a good woman. Her energy was different than that of most people I knew. She was naturally kind. Unjudging. And this put me at ease. I was ashamed of the way I was behaving, but I did not feel ashamed around her. With her it was OK if I was not OK, and no matter what I said or did, there was no shame for me. I had never felt that before. Around other people, I hid it, because there was a stigma in our society about coming home from war *fucked up*, so I wanted to seem OK. But I never hid it from her.

In a way, she filled a void. Some veterans, who had months or years left on their active-duty contracts after returning home from the war, were still back at work on base every morning with all of their buddies. Those who'd gone through all of it with them. But for vets like me, who went from the battlefield to the civilian world in a large, anonymous city, it was especially tough. When your whole world, your whole support system, suddenly vanishes after you're discharged, you're left fighting on your own. And as every Marine knows, you never want to be alone on the battlefield. I wished some of my buddies from the war lived in New York City, but they didn't, so Meredith helped to replace a part of that support network that had been taken away.

Meredith wanted more than anything else to be a mother. And maybe a wife. But definitely a mother. I could sense that she would be good at both. Things grew more serious between us, and we eventually started spending some nights at each other's apartments, but there was always a distance between us. I trusted her deeply and cared for her, but I made sure there was always that distance. I wanted it that way; the distance was my fault. Because something had broken inside of me. There was the rage and the sadness from the war, but there was also something else. Collateral damage from the bomb that went off inside of me. An inability to truly love someone who would've made a perfect significant other.

"One of my tapes from the war broke last night," I said to her across the table in the back of the quiet and dimly lit Italian restaurant. "The camera made a weird noise. The tape played for a second, but then the image froze and the tape jammed and there were just these weird lines going across the screen."

"Oh that's terrible. I'm sorry. What are you going to do? I know how much those tapes mean to you."

"I talked to some guy the other day—a student from NYU Film School—who said that I needed to get them put on a more stable format. Like DVD. He's an intern from some production company that he says does pretty good work, so I'm going to meet with them next week. I have to make sure the rest of the tapes don't break."

Then the conversation drifted to other things.

"Let's go get a drink," I said, and the night shifted from a quiet dinner with a bit of red wine to drinking beers at the corner table—my table—at The Back Fence, a bar in the Village at the corner of Bleecker and MacDougal Streets, just a few blocks away from my apartment. They said that Bob Dylan used to play there and they hadn't redone the place in forty years. They would give you small wooden bowls filled with peanuts, and you would crack the shells and eat the peanuts and throw the shells on the floor.

That table—in the corner where the benches that were attached to the walls met—was my favorite spot. I loved the safety of that one spot, especially in winter with your coats piled high around you, where generations of people had drunk almost on top of each other straight through the night.

The angry waiter in his fifties, with his round-rimmed glasses and long thinning hair, had been there for twenty-five years and would slam the beers down hard on the table. But if you just talked to him like a human being and maybe cracked a joke sometimes, you could get through to him, and he would smile, and then he wouldn't be so angry for a bit.

Meredith and I sat quietly in the corner of the bar. And the singer played his old beat-up acoustic guitar and sang his songs and poured his heart into them, and you could see that the words had meaning when he had written them. For those few minutes, everything was perfect, and I felt like my old self again. But after an hour or so at the table, things began to grow foggy and the light seemed to slip away. And when the light slipped away, either the rage or the sadness would take its place.

"I am thinking about volunteering to go back to Iraq with the Twenty-fifth Marines—the reserve unit out of Long Island."

"Really? When did you start thinking about that? You said before that two combat tours was enough. That you had done your part. And you were pretty adamant about it. You said that the third tour would be the one that would get you."

"Yeah I know I said that, but one of the majors from that unit called me the other day, and...I don't know, I guess I'm now thinking about it, anyway."

"What's going on Mike? Is everything OK?"

As soon as she said the word *OK*, I knew I was finished. It was to be the sadness tonight and not the rage. You never really knew which it would be until it happened. The tears started to drip from my eyes. There were no sobs—just quiet tears from eyes that just weren't that young anymore because they had seen too much.

I trusted Meredith, but I still couldn't look at her directly, because then she would see.

"They're short of officers, and they need an 81mm mortar platoon commander—and that job is somewhat similar to artillery. Plus, I was in the infantry when I was an enlisted Marine and spent all of my time in Iraq and Afghanistan attached to the infantry, so it would be a good fit."

I was hunched over the table clutching my beer with both hands, and the tears ran down my nose and dripped onto my arm. She could see the tears.

She rubbed my back gently. When I finally looked over at her, I could sense that she knew the real reason I was thinking about going back. She smiled softly and said nothing. Her blue eyes were kind, and I could see that there was no judgment in them.

A few days later, I met with the guys from the production company at their offices to see about doing the tape transfers. The intern I'd met had told them what was on the tapes. I sat for a bit in their offices with two of the owners, who were cousins, both in their early thirties. Marc Perez was quiet and had a friendly face and demeanor. He wore glasses and was starting to lose a bit of the hair on his head. Kristian Fraga, the other owner and founder, had a dark beard and dark curly hair and had an intense look in his eye. Like he saw everything in the world through the prism of filmmaking.

We spent a few minutes discussing the fragility of the mini-digital-videocassette format and the fact that one of the tapes had broken. He said that, because I was a veteran, he and Marc would be happy to do whatever they could to recover what was on the tape, free of charge. He was also very interested in seeing what was on the other tapes, and asked if it would be OK if we spent some time scrolling through a few of them.

Together, the three of us watched a few minutes of one of the battle scenes. At points, I would fast-forward to other parts of the tape, not wanting to dig too deep. But even so, they both seemed to be intrigued by the footage. It was easier than I'd thought it would be to show them the tapes. Because when we watched them together, it became a sort of shared experience. I would glance over and watch them watching the tapes, and it felt good to know that civilians were learning about what we experienced over there.

Kristian said it wouldn't be a problem to transfer the footage to DVD and asked that I leave the tapes with them for a week or so. Four or five days later, I got a call from him.

"You have some really incredible stuff, Mike," he said. "Marc and I would like to talk to you about an idea that we had regarding your footage."

The three of us met again, and Kristian said that they were interested in possibly using my footage for a documentary about Iraq. I told him I'd have to think about it for a few days. It was an interesting offer, but I didn't really know these guys, and didn't want them using my footage and editing it together in a way that made the Marine Corps look bad. We met again, and after a few hours of discussion, Kristian convinced me that the film, if they could raise the money and actually move ahead with the project, would be politically neutral. There was something about Kristian that told me I should trust him. So we shook hands and agreed that they would use my footage for their documentary.

Chapter Four

OVER THE LOUDSPEAKER, a woman's muffled voice said something I couldn't understand. The only other person in the subway car on the downtown E train was a homeless man who smelled like human feces. There was a trail of his urine running in streams across the floor of the car from the empty McDonald's soda cup that rolled gently back and forth beneath his seat as the train moved south. It was eleven forty-five p.m., and we were about to arrive at the last stop: the World Trade Center.

I'd been offered a job as a clerk on an international overnight trading desk at a financial company called Refco. A guy named Frank had interviewed me. He was in his late forties, with a friendly and calm, almost suave, demeanor. When you talked with him, you got the sense that he was a fairly straightforward guy. "This is a second-tier job at a second-tier company," he had said during the interview. His honesty was refreshing. The job paid $5,000 more per year than my job on the floor of the NYMEX, and I was hoping that the diversity of experience would help my business school applications, which were set to go out in a few months. But the downside was that my shift started at midnight and lasted until eight a.m.

And so I headed, alone, slowly up the wet and dirty subway steps to street level in front of the old Trinity Church across from Ground Zero. On the other side of the street was the large fence they had constructed along the perimeter of the hole that was now where the Twin Towers used to stand. Floodlights on stanchions shined down brightly into the hole. A large panel on the top of the fence listed the names of those who had died. It was just a few days after September 11, 2004, and the flowers brought by families and friends of the dead were still hanging on the fence. The bouquets were now wilted, with their stems carefully placed in the links so that the flowers would point outward toward the street. And there were the laminated pictures and handwritten letters and candles that had been placed gently along the sidewalk.

Across the street, a tall and tired maintenance worker pushed a large plastic garbage can on wheels. He worked slowly but deliberately as he pulled each of the bouquets from the fence and threw them into the garbage can.

I walked south along the edge of Ground Zero and turned west along its southern boundary. The entrance to the building where I worked was at the southwest corner. I saw the men dressed in their leather combat boots and their black combat military fatigues who were guarding the steel skeleton of what was never to become the new Deutsche Bank building. They were the same fatigues that we had worn in the Marine Corps except that they were midnight black. Something about the way they were dressed and the way they moved felt sinister to me.

Along this part of the path, scaffolding had been constructed. The walkway between the southern edge of the hole and the steel skeleton of the Deutsche Bank building was now an enclosed tunnel, with large planks of wood on the ceiling and on the walls. People had carved messages to the dead into the walls. Others had written them with markers. Each night when I got to this part of my walk to work, I began to walk more quickly so that I could not read the messages. But each night I stopped and turned and read them. And on that night, when I read them, I cried.

I continued the rest of the way through the tunnel and up the stairway that led to the entrance of One World Financial Center. Through the large glass revolving doors and into the cavernous lobby and the antiseptic world of corporate profits and polished marble floors and high cathedral ceilings.

I tried to compose myself in the elevator, but then I thought about Beth. Beth Anne Quigley.

That morning, you went to work at your trading desk on the 104th floor of the North Tower of the World Trade Center. Checking the trades from the day before and scanning the day's news, not knowing that the planes were already headed your way. But I tried not to think about what they did to you. I tried to think about those days in sophomore year when I sat next to you in Ms. De Roos's Spanish class at Red Bank Catholic High School. I tried to think about your smile and how the sunlight would come through the windows and shine onto your long brown hair that flowed straight and young and beautiful as a cool mountain stream. And I would always think of the skits we all had to do in Spanish for the class and how you did a little dance during yours and how we all laughed so loudly.

I remembered that terrible day in 2001, when we were already well into the first month of our six-month routine deployment. We were the Marines who were out on patrol in the world, ready to go just in case something happened. We'd just spent three days in the Australian outback conducting live-fire training. The heat was brutal out there but the training was good because we'd pulled the howitzers off of the ships and fired live artillery out among the desert mountains. We'd practiced coordinating with the Cobra gunship helicopters so we didn't accidentally shoot them out of the sky as we all pounded the same target—they with their rockets and machine guns and we with high-explosive shells. That day, we were young and ferocious.

We had one night of liberty—a night off—in the frontier city of Darwin. On the northern coast of Australia, it is surrounded by thousands of miles of rugged outback to the south, east, and west, with wild blue ocean to the north. More like a large town, Darwin had the feel of a tropical version of what I had always imagined the Old West to be—slightly lawless, with wooden architecture that had warmth and character and with scenery that was naturally beautiful. On liberty, two thousand Marines and sailors from the Fifteenth Marine Expeditionary Unit would change into civilian clothes for one night of hell-raising out on the town. We were free for a night and not due back at the ship until the next morning. The Australians had held up signs that said YANKEE GO HOME and MARINES STAY AWAY FROM OUR WOMEN when we pulled into the port. We all laughed and then thought about all of the beautiful Australian women in the town. The bars would be packed. And the whorehouses. And the shopping malls and the Internet cafés and every other place that held any potential whatsoever of meeting some luscious young Aussie girls, with their long legs and their perfect accents—which is just how we had spent every second of the last two weeks on the ships imagining them.

After spending several hours at a bar drinking enough to try to get our name on a plaque on the wall for the amount of booze consumed in an hour, several of us headed to the local casino. Armed with nearly a month's pay, because we had been stuck on the ship for weeks with no place to spend it, and fueled by booze and youth, we were invincible.

I played an Australian version of craps. I was up nearly $400 and was eyeing a beautiful brunette across the table. She was watching my winnings grow as I rolled the dice, and I was trying to figure out whether or not she was a prostitute. And I was also trying to figure out whether or not I cared if she was a prostitute.

Then a tap on my shoulder.

"Sir, check out the TV over there. The World Trade Center is on fire," one of the Marines from my unit said in a concerned voice.

A group of us stood in front of the wall of TVs above the bar just off the playing floor and watched. The crowd grew as we tried to hear what the announcers were saying over the noise of the slot machines dinging loudly in the background.

"They said that a plane hit it," one of the Marines remarked.

When the Marine had spoken, most of us in the small crowd had turned to look at him. As I turned my head back to the TV, my eyes focused on the burning building.

And just as my brain had processed what the Marine had said, the second plane shot across the frame and into the second tower.

Everything frozen. Someone said "Holy shit!" and a woman yelled "Oh my God" in disbelief. A brief second to think—then the realization. Marines scrambling to get to one of the two pay phones outside. Mental calculations about whom I knew who lived and worked in New York City. Calculations about how far my parents lived from the city and what the implications were. I was in line at the phones with probably thirty people ahead of me.

"Honey, get the dog and head to your mother's house right now. The country is under attack." A concerned Marine barked orders to his wife through the cables under the ocean to California. *This is like a fucking movie*, I thought. *But it's not a movie. It's real.* No way I was going to get through with that line ahead of me so I headed back inside to find Tim Lynch and Vic Lomuscio, two of my buddies whom I was hanging out with on liberty. We decided to head back to our hotel room and try to call from there. As I walked back onto the playing floor to find Vic and Tim, a loud and commanding voice flooded the floor through a bullhorn.

"All Marines and sailors from the Fifteenth MEU, report back to your ships immediately. Liberty has been canceled. All Marines and sailors from the Fifteenth MEU..." It was a detachment of Marine MPs and Navy Shore Patrol. They were dressed in uniform and carrying billy clubs. Everyone in the detachment wore armbands that said MP or SP on them.

We headed back to the ship in a cab that we shared with a captain whom I didn't know. He was one of the Cobra gunship pilots.

"Do you realize what this means for us?" he asked. None of us answered him.

As we approached the port, the Marines and sailors who had been stuck guarding the ships for the one night of liberty were now in full battle gear and carrying rifles and shotguns. They obviously had been set at the highest-level threat condition after the attacks and would shoot to kill. The look of war was already in their eyes. There was even a guard posted in full battle gear outside the ship captain's office—a young Marine, the last line of defense deep inside the bowels of the floating city.

Marines from my company—Charlie Company—were gathered in a group on board, waiting for the rest of the guys from the unit to drag themselves back off of liberty. Marines coming back to the mother ship in groups of three or four. Marines in various states of drunkenness, from the nearly sober to the nearly standing. But even the ones who couldn't stand so well and swayed slightly back and forth in the formation knew what this meant. Because we were currently the nation's forward-deployed quick-reaction force.

We stood next to the helicopters in the hangar deck of the USS *Peleliu* in our civilian clothes, just underneath the flight deck of the ship specifically designed to carry Marines and the aircraft that shuttle them to war. And as we stood under the bright lights next to the large gray helicopters with folded rotors, I thought about what the Marine had said to his wife over the pay phone. I thought about my brother Dan and my cousin Missy in New York City and how they both worked in midtown. Were they in danger from more imminent attacks that were about to hit the city? And I thought about when Major Russo had said, "I don't know, gents... but I feel like something is going to happen on this deployment," a few weeks before we steamed out of the naval base at San Diego. I thought about how before we had left, I had fought for the artillerymen to get a turn training through the mock urban-warfare town at Camp Pendleton, because throughout history some of the artillerymen always seemed to get turned into infantry when things got bad. I thought about Pearl Harbor and the Marines of the Pacific in World War II and how when I was a young boy, my mom gave me an old black-and-white photo of my great-uncle and his buddy as Marines kneeling over Congressional Medal of Honor recipient John Basilone's grave on Iwo Jima. I thought about the brunette who had been standing across the craps table and about the case of beer that we had left back in the hotel room. I thought about the people in the towers and tried to imagine the horror. The horror as the building swayed before they went down. I thought about them knowing that they were going to die. Then I thought about who might have done that to them. Whoever it was, I was hoping to be able to take one of their goddamn heads and stick it on a stake somewhere.

One night, a week or so after we pulled out of the port in Darwin in a hurry, I sat at the small metal-frame desk built into the wall of the forty-year-old troop-carrying ship. It was just before they shut off the ship's nonclassified e-mail system because we were about to head into the Arabian Sea. I opened an e-mail from Sheila Ochotorena—an old friend who had gone to both the same high school and the same college as I. "Beth Quigley and Pete Apollo are gone. They were both in the towers when the planes hit," her e-mail said.

I had to read it a second time to fully understand the words.

"Beth Quigley and Pete Apollo are gone," I said aloud.

We'd known them both in high school. And I sat silently at the metal desk in the cramped Charlie Company First Battalion office with the aluminum walls lined with the training schedules and rosters that held the names of young Marines who would soon go into battle. And the small light on the ceiling let off a glow that was hollow and cold. On a warship now in a time of war that was floating and steaming and cutting its way through the deep black water toward Afghanistan. I closed the e-mail and switched off the computer and the office light. And as I walked alone down the damp and dark gray corridor back to the officer berthing rooms, I thought of only one thing. *Beth Quigley and Pete Apollo are gone.* They were gone, but as long as I was still here, I would fight for them.

It was an odd feeling, thinking about these private things and the people you'd known who had been lost and about serving with honor in uniform in some distant dangerous place—while walking down an overlit Refco corridor in some downtown financial office building. Wearing cheap khaki pants and a button-down shirt and walking past paintings that were worth what I might make in twenty years. Past offices where I would get a glimpse of one of the fat cats dressed in a custom-made English shirt and suspenders and $700 Ferragamo shoes, sitting alone at a desk in a corner office and typing something at the computer. They would look at me with disdain. They would not smile and they would not say hello. I was a worm. A peon. I could sense the bad energy coming from them. Like they were hiding something and were angry that I saw them in the office so late.

So every night I spent eight hours, from midnight until eight a.m., taking calls from traders who worked for hedge funds all over the world. As the earth spun and the days shifted across the oceans, the traders would play the commodities and stock index futures markets before the cash markets opened. They bet big and they lost big, and sometimes they won even bigger. They would call from places like Bermuda or the Cayman Islands or Hong Kong. "Hurry up and get the trade done. What the hell is wrong with you—are you a fucking idiot?" they would say through the phone.

I would bite my tongue and write the order down on the ticket pad and enter the trade into the computer system. There were three of us on the desk each night. One of the guys had been there for years. He was kind, and he looked much older than his age. He was divorced and was devoted to raising his son.

"Someday I will go to Italy—to Tuscany—to die," he would say. And he would say it in a way that made you realize that he was serious and that his life was in such a state that the end was the only thing that he was looking forward to.

He would say that when the hedge fund traders were being harder on us than normal, usually because they were losing money. He was an old man who had long ago given in—so that he could support his son. And he knew that each night for the rest of his life, he would take the orders and type numbers into the trading system and take abuse from millionaires.

Some nights, when the clouds were low, they seemed to mix with the floodlights and the dust that rose up over the Ground Zero construction site. And I would sit at one of the windows that ran in a row just behind the long Formica trading desk. I would look out over the canyon of the site and think about Beth, and Pete Apollo, and Afghanistan, and Iraq.

To pass the long nights, we would have conversations about anything that popped into our minds. The same type of conversation that men in fighting holes sitting in the cold night desert in Afghanistan have. The same types of conversations that men stuck on oil rigs out in the middle of nowhere for months would have. Anything to pass the time and to make it seem like you are not actually at work. Around six or seven a.m. one morning, Frank came in to catch up on a few things before his shift started.

"Were you guys here on September 11th?" I asked the guys on the desk.

"I was here that morning. I actually saw the shadow of the plane go across those buildings right there."

Frank pointed to the row of buildings outside of the window. When he did, his eyes had the hollow look of a veteran.

"We all ran over to the windows and looked out at the tower just after the first plane hit. Maybe a minute later, one of the funds called in and asked me if we could see the towers."

He stood up and walked over to the windows.

"I told them that we could. They asked me if a plane had hit it. I put the phone down, ran back over to the window and took another look, then got back on the phone and told them—yes.

"Then they told me to sell fifty lots of S&P 500."

By selling the S&P 500 futures, the hedge fund had just made a massive bet that would potentially pay off in the millions. By selling the futures instead of buying them, they were betting that the market would drop after the news had spread that the tower had been hit by an airplane. The funds had no idea just how profitable bets based on the deaths of thousands of innocent people would be.

So in the same moment that innocent people were dying, or figuring out that they were trapped and would soon be dead, these guys saw an opportunity to make a buck. And I wouldn't be surprised if, as we rolled across the border into Iraq, risking our lives and knowing that some of us weren't going to come home, these same motherfuckers were probably betting on the price of oil going up.

On the morning of October 28, 2004, just a few days after Frank told me that story about the hedge fund calling on the morning of 9/11, a report aired on the news on the TV attached to the wall at the end of the trading desk. Rudy Giuliani had made a remark that angered some people. In the news clip, they showed the interview with NBC where he made the comment. I had not seen it before. When the interviewer asked him about the soldiers being unable to find any weapons of mass destruction in Iraq, he responded, "The president was cautious. The president was prudent. The president did what a commander in chief should do. No matter how you try to blame it on the president, the actual responsibility for it really would be for the troops that were there. Did they search carefully enough? Didn't they search carefully enough?"

When he said the "didn't search carefully enough" part, he lifted his hands slightly and wiggled his fingers as he sat in the chair. Making judgments about the troops from the safety of the cool NBC studios. Making judgments about those whose flesh was torn by shrapnel when the IEDs detonated. Those who risked it all as they patrolled the deadly streets in the 130 degree heat.

"I want to break his fucking fingers and punch that mother-fucker in the face. I am about to rip this fucking TV out of the wall and throw it out the goddamn window," I yelled. There were five or six of us on the desk at the time, as we were about to switch over from the night shift to the day shift. They all looked at me, eyes wide, sensing that I was dangerous.

I said nothing more and left the trading desk. I headed to the bathroom on my way to the elevator. My hands shaking. I was sweating as I turned the water on to splash it on my face. I was alone in the bathroom. I wiped the water from my face with the coarse paper towel from the gray metal dispenser by the wall. I looked into the mirror.

I was enraged at what I'd just heard. But as I looked deep into my own eyes in the mirror, I finally admitted to myself that the reason no one found weapons of mass destruction in Iraq wasn't because we didn't search carefully enough.

It was because they weren't there.

I began to tremble a little more strongly. Not just my hands but my legs, too. My stomach hollow and a lump in my throat. My hands now numb and not working so well. My arms went weak and I felt like I was going to vomit.

I wondered if it was just all a myth. If I had fought for my country. If I had made innocent American citizens more safe. Or was everything that I had ever believed in just complete and utter bullshit? A commercial for politicians? An easy fuck for the military-industrial complex?

I headed down the elevator and back out into the corridor around Ground Zero. It was morning and people were on their way to work, lost in thought and clutching their coffees and their *Wall Street Journals*. I walked past the part of the corridor with the wooden planks for walls with the messages to the dead carved into them. I didn't stop to read them.

And so I became a nocturnal creature. An animal that was slowly dying. My insides succumbing more each day to the dark cancer that was growing inside of me. The cancer that was the aftermath of the war. The cancer that fed on my light.

When I woke up at eight p.m. on the day after Halloween, 2004, I noticed that I'd missed a call from Tim Lynch, a close buddy I had served with in Afghanistan almost three years before and one of the guys I'd been out drinking with in Australia on the night of 9/11. I checked my voice mail.

"Hey Mike, this is Tim," he said.

He took a deep breath.

"I've got some bad news. Uh...give me a call when you can."

I could tell by his voice that someone was gone. I sighed quietly, wondering which one of us was dead. As I pressed the Call button on my cell, my mind flipped through names of buddies who were over there.

"Hey man, what's going on?" I asked, already knowing most of the answer.

"Hey, Mike. Unfortunately...Matt was killed in Iraq yesterday."

Matt was his little brother.

The shrapnel had hit him in the neck just above the protective collar on his flak jacket. He had been able to exit his vehicle, had taken a few steps, and collapsed on the side of the dusty Ar Ramadi road. They had been out clearing the road of improvised explosive devices (IEDs).

The last time I saw Matt was in San Clemente back in 2001 or 2002. He was always smiling. We were a bunch of young twenty-three- and twenty-four-year-old Marine lieutenants drinking beer. Just like we were at some off-campus college party. But we weren't.

Matt had been a swimmer at Duke and was a natural Marine leader. He did his first combat tour as an infantry platoon commander. Upon his unit's return to the States, Matt was immediately ordered back to Iraq as a combat casualty replacement. He would take the place of another lieutenant who was killed in a unit that was still in Iraq, thus returning to the war while his original unit was still back in the States. After completing that tour successfully, he rotated back to the States again. His original unit was now set to cycle back to Iraq, and Matt volunteered to go with them. He didn't have to. He had just done two combat tours in the hell of the Sunni Triangle in eighteen months. But he went anyway. His father, who had also been a Marine officer, had told him that he was pressing his luck. Matt said that he couldn't abandon his men.

He just couldn't stay behind. He couldn't let his men face the madness, the horror, and the fear alone. If they were going to be there, so was he, because when you are an officer or a sergeant or a corporal, those who are under your command become your sons. Your brothers. Your best friends. And when you've fought together and face death together and risk your lives for each other, there is nothing that can pull you apart. Your souls become forever fused. Like armor. And those few sons and brothers and best friends quickly become the only ones you can trust. Because they are the only ones who know what really happens in war.

Tim asked if I would be one of the pallbearers for his brother's burial. Of course I would. It was an honor. It would be the last time that I would wear the uniform of a United States Marine.

I took the train from New York City to New Jersey a few nights before the funeral to have dinner with my parents and to get my dress blues, which I kept stored at their house. That night at dinner, the darkness was there with us. At the table next to us. In the corner up by the ceiling. In my mom's eyes as she watched her own son tell the story of some other unfortunate mother losing her child. I had the same feeling at that dinner as I did in the war as we approached Baghdad. Impending sorrow.

They listened as I explained what the next few days would entail. The funeral detail rehearsal. The wake. The burial.

And though it had been only seventeen months since I'd last worn the uniform at the wedding in California, digging up all the pieces to it felt like visiting a school that I'd graduated from years ago. The ribbons, the white cover and gloves, the captain's bars. These physical pieces were the same, but they now belonged to someone else. A past version of me who no longer existed.

The next day, as I drove across the Verrazano Bridge on the way to Long Island for the funeral, I noticed a spot along the guardrail that was dented. Like a car had hit it. And then I remembered the spot on the bridge over the Euphrates just south of An Nasiriyah. The spot where the guardrail had a huge hole in it. And the conversation with a master sergeant from a tank battalion several weeks later who told me what happened. A young Marine was driving using his night vision goggles the night we attacked the city. He misjudged the distance, thinking he could clear the edge. The tank dropped through the air and into the water. Flipping upside down and coming to rest on the bottom of the black river. They pulled the tank out of the water a few days later. As the crew compartment had filled with water, one of the Marines had removed his 9mm pistol from its holster. Not wanting to drown like the others, he had put it to his head and pulled the trigger.

I tried to imagine his thoughts and what it must have been like those last few moments for the crew. It affected me deeply. It disturbed me. And the fact that I was driving to a funeral to bury a good Marine who was the younger brother of one of my best friends suddenly became too much. Why was I alive and so many others dead? And why was I not happy to be alive? In fact, why was I alive at all? I should be happy. Thankful. But I wasn't, so I felt that life was being wasted on me. And then I felt guilty.

So as I drove across, watching the spans as they sped by my window, I thought for a few long moments and seriously considered pulling over to the side of the bridge. To jump off of that motherfucker.

As Marines have done in every war, we rehearsed for the funeral detail at a reserve base in Garden City, New York. We practiced our positions and movements so that they would be perfect, to give Matt the respect he deserved. Since leaving active duty, I'd forgotten the feeling of being part of something that was more important than myself.

At the funeral home, I was surprised and thankful to see fifty or so Marines who had served in prior wars and who had come to pay tribute. Some were old men from the local Marine Corps League who had served in World War II and Korea. Others were

94

Vietnam veterans who were part of an honor guard of civilian bikers who escort the funeral processions of fallen service members on their Harleys. There was something so comforting and true and sad about all of these men. They never knew Matt personally, but they had come to pay their respects. Each of them, regardless of age or which war they fought or who they were now, had the same somber face and shadowed eyes. At that moment, we were all the same. War had left its mark on all of us. By being there together, we were fighting back.

The line of those who were waiting wrapped around the building and out into the parking lot: high school and college friends, family members, Marines, strangers. As Tim, our buddy Joe Choi, and I walked into the funeral home in our dress blues, the already hushed group waiting to gain entry went completely silent. To them, we were heroes. We represented everything that was good about the country. They knew we would give our lives for theirs (and we would).

"Mommy, the short one has a lot of medals," I heard a little girl say in the unselfconscious tone that only little kids have.

On the outside, my uniform had ribbons for time served as an enlisted Marine and for tours in Afghanistan and Iraq. Because I had been in the Marine Corps longer than many of the other guys who were in uniform at the funeral, I had more ribbons and medals, most of which were for things that had nothing at all to do with the war. The little girl and her mom had thought that meant that I was braver than the other guys there. I wasn't. The short one did have medals, but he was a ruined man.

I paid my respects to Matt as he lay in his blues and thought of how brave he was to volunteer for that last tour when he didn't have to. Civilians just couldn't understand the personal risk he was taking by making that decision. He did it because he loved the men whom he had trained and fought with during his first deployment and, knowing that they were about to go back, he had to go with them. *They were his brothers.* I stared at the Bronze Star with Combat V and Purple Heart that were pinned to his chest. I swallowed my tears.

As Tim and I walked out of the funeral home prior to the procession, a photographer for the *New York Daily News* snapped a picture, using a telephoto lens, from a vehicle at the far end of the parking lot. A reporter approached us and respectfully asked if he could speak with us.

"We want to share Matt's courage with the world," remarked Tim.[2]

"I've got a lot of friends over there and I feel guilty," I told the reporter. "You think you're out, but the war never leaves you."

The church was packed. Sunlight filled the room. Matt's coffin lay at the center, the flag draped over it. We sat in the front pew on the right-hand side just as Marines, on-line, would man part of a perimeter. Our emotional battle armor had been peeled back by the loss and our time away from active duty. I wasn't sure how I was going to make it through this. I could no longer hold back my tears, and it felt strange to be this naked in uniform. I looked over at Joe and he was crying too, so that made it OK.

Mr. Lynch was about to give his youngest son's eulogy. He had been a Marine officer just like both of his sons had. But no one in the church could have been prepared for what he was about to tell us.

---

[2] Richard Weir and Bill Hutchinson, "Recall L.I. Marine Slain in Iraq," *New York Daily News*, Nov. 8, 2004, http://articles.nydailynews.com /2004-11-08/news/18283317_1_5th-marine-regiment-iraq-big-brother.

All during our son's deployments, I had been haunted by a specter of Marines in dress blue uniforms, walking to our door, bearing terrible news…and that specter was rooted in my past. You see, in 1966, I too was a first lieutenant, then serving a short tour at the Marine Corps District Headquarters in Garden City. One of my duties was casualty calls. That meant when a Marine was wounded or killed, I had to personally notify his next of kin. "I'll only be here three months," I thought, "I should be OK."

The next week, my colonel grimly dropped a Teletype on my desk. "KIA," it started. "Lieutenant, will you handle this?" he said. My stomach rolled. My duty that day was to break a mother's heart. I gathered two NCOs, got a priest, and drove to the Marine's home. His mother was getting out of her car…she had just returned from the beach…she looked at us…and dropped like a stone. We took her inside, neighbors came, someone called her husband. "Come home right now," was all he was told.

When he arrived, he told me that he had immediately punched the wall at work, and would have punched me, had he been at home. "I just would not have wanted to hear what I knew you were going to say," he said.

I told my colonel we had a dangerous situation and that someone would eventually get hurt. We had no standard operating procedure for these casualty calls, no SOP. "Write one, Lieutenant," he said, and I did. I specified NCOs for wounds...but always an NCO and an officer for a death. I put my heart and soul into it, trying to devise something which would give aid and comfort to the bereaved and protection to our Marines. Years later, I encountered Marines from that same office. And we discussed casualty calls, by then quite numerous. "It's no fun," they said, "but at least we have a really good SOP." "I know," I said. "I wrote it."

On August 31, Matt returned with his buddies for a third tour, and on October 31, he was killed by a roadside bomb. That same day, my wife, Angela, and I, still unaware, drove to the beach, to walk the boardwalk. It was a gorgeous day, and we spoke of how fortunate we were to have such fine sons and how proud we were of our two Marines. We passed the beach where Matt worked and again spoke of him, and then we returned home. I parked the car, we entered our house...just as that mother had done almost forty years ago, the day I broke her heart. The door was ajar, and as I heard Angela exclaim "Oh No!" I turned to see two Marines in dress blue uniforms, grimly walking towards us. One an NCO, the other an officer. Each wore the same stony mask I had worn years ago, and in an instant I knew our Matt was gone.... You see, I'd written that SOP.

How ironic that the pain I'd delivered so long ago to someone else was now visited on my doorstep, and stranger still that the procedure I'd then written to console others was now applied to us.

His words would later be read to Congress by Representative Steven J. Israel.

We got into the limousine for the funeral procession to the Long Island National Cemetery. The procession was escorted by the Suffolk County Sheriff's Department and by the Harleys. They shut down huge portions of the highway so that Matt could ride unimpeded to his final resting place. We passed a fire station. They had carefully parked two fire trucks with crossed ladders and had hung an American flag at the top. Around forty fire-fighters and paramedics stood in uniform and at attention as the procession passed by. I looked directly into the face of one of them from behind the glass. She stood, saluting. She was pay-ing tribute with every ounce of her being. They all were, and we could feel it through the glass as we sped by. *The human spirit is good. People really do care.*

Just as we had to do in war, those of us in the back of that limousine on that November day in Long Island would have to switch off our emotions temporarily, so that we could accom-plish the mission at hand: to guide Matt gently to his gravesite. *God, for Matt and Tim and Molly and Mr. and Mrs. Lynch and the Corps, I hope I don't fuck this up. Please, God, don't let me fuck this up.* Maybe the other guys were terrified, too, I don't know. But that steely reserve that you get in combat when people are shoot-ing at you came right back like clockwork. *Just grit your fucking teeth and do it, Marine, and don't fuck it up.*

We would be under the watchful gaze of several hundred on-lookers. The Reserve Marines from the Garden City unit would be handling the rifle salute. We would carry Matt. I was on the left-hand side in the front.

We took our positions behind the hearse and, on command and in tandem, turned in a perfectly synchronized facing movement, paused, and grabbed hold of the rails. Matt's coffin had a calm heaviness to it. I am not sure how, but I sensed that he was resting peacefully inside. He was our fallen brother, the six of us carrying him that day by the tree in the cemetery.

As the front man, I was the first to step up on the platform while still holding the rails. As the weight and momentum of Matt's coffin shifted against my weight, I stumbled for a second, but thankfully didn't fall.

After laying Matt on the platform, the six of us took our positions, at attention, in the formation. With each volley of the twenty-one-gun salute, every man there who had seen combat was, for a moment, back on the battlefield. Each crack more final than the next.

The priest spoke his words. It was now time for Tim to say his final good-bye to his baby brother. With his wife, Molly, at his side, he saluted slowly with his white-gloved hand, as Molly gently dropped a rose onto Matt's coffin. Tim paused, gave one last look, then slowly walked away.

The funeral reception was at a bar called the Maine Maid Inn. The place was built in 1789, the same year George Washington was inaugurated president in the shadow of the Trinity Church that still stands just across the street from Ground Zero. Hanging from one of the oak shelves behind the bar was a Purple Heart. The medal was a gold-trimmed heart of purple bearing the bust of General Washington and awarded to service members wounded or killed in action. It was the same as the one that was pinned to Matt's chest. As I stared at the medal, I thought *Tonight is going to be a rough one.*

The drinks flowed. More drinks. Day to night. Fewer people. More drinks. Pretty soon I didn't even know where I was. And then the tears. *This fucking war. God damn this motherfucking war.* Joe Choi grabbed me. He had my back.

"We need to get you out of here," he said.

———

It was a few weeks after the funeral. I awoke after just an hour or so of sleep—startled once again by some sound or memory or dream that I couldn't remember. I knew there would be no chance of sleep again before work that night. And I wondered why sometimes you could remember some of the dreams so clearly, even years later, while others were erased in just a few moments. At first you could remember a detail or two, then you could remember just maybe the outline or the places, and then you couldn't even remember that. You only knew that something was there, but you couldn't remember what it was because all the pieces had fallen away. When I thought about *another night shift* without having slept the day before, I was full of dread.

I thought about quitting that night. It was easy to fantasize and plan and imagine myself saying "Fuck you!" to the hedge fund traders on the phone and then flipping the bird with both hands and waving them both at the whole goddamn sterile building as I went through the door for the last time. But then I thought of how I would have to look in the face of the guy who wanted to go to Italy to die and how he was a worker bee just as I was. He was the one I'd be hurting by quitting suddenly, because he would have to carry the extra load.

So that night I had the hollow and gray feeling that comes with insomnia. The same feeling you have at almost all times on the battlefield. My body and my mind remembered the feeling well. I watched the hands on the clock on the wall by the trading desk grind their slow circles. The slowness was maddening. Exhausting. Fuzz in the brain. Worried about making mistakes. Wanting nothing more than to sleep.

When the light started to come slowly to the sky in the early morning, Frank showed up for work on the desk for the day. I pulled him aside, and respectfully gave him my two weeks' notice.

But what I didn't realize was that without something like a steady job to absorb the energy, I would be left alone much of the time. Alone time for a veteran who is struggling becomes dwell time. Dwelling on the past. Dwelling on the reasons or the situations or the circumstances. And the dwelling begins to slowly solidify. Transforming itself. Feeding and sucking on your energy. Changing your brain chemistry. Your beliefs. Your perspective. Turning the world the same ashen color as the eyes of the dead children along the road.

Chapter Five

MEREDITH AND I SAT facing each other at a table with a red and white checkered tablecloth in a prix fixe Italian restaurant. The place felt just a bit touristy and was too brightly lit for me. At the other tables, couples spoke quietly.

"I quit my job," I said.

She looked concerned when I said it, and her body tensed up a bit. I knew I was already suspect in her eyes, because of what I'd said a few weeks before about heading back to Iraq, and because of the funeral, and because I probably looked terrible.

Now quitting my job would only appear to confirm what she already suspected. That I was taking another step down the ladder.

"What about paying the rent and buying food? What will you do for money?"

"I still have a little money saved up from all of that time I was deployed. You don't have to pay income taxes when you're in a combat zone, plus you get imminent-danger pay, so I was able to put some away."

I paused for a moment and, not liking to see her upset, changed the subject. I told her everything that had happened over the last few weeks with Sirk Productions, the company that was using my Iraq footage for a documentary. She listened intently and seemed to relax a bit as we discussed the film.

"They said that I'm going to need to go back out to California—to Camp Pendleton—to get signatures on a release form from all of the guys whose faces appear recognizably in the footage. They're going to cover the cost of the trip."

"Really?"

"Yeah, and I told them that a lot of the guys have probably gotten out of the Marine Corps, so I am going to have to do some digging to find out where those guys are."

Meredith and I talked some more about Kristian and Marc, and she said that she was looking forward to meeting them. I promised to take her by the production offices.

"I was thinking maybe we could go to the Whitney tomorrow and go check out some Edward Hopper paintings. *Early Sunday Morning* is there, and it's my favorite of all time, and I've never seen the real thing," I said.

"That sounds nice."

She smiled. I could tell from the way she looked at me that maybe she was starting to love me. But I couldn't love back, because a bunch of the cables that had always provided me stability and anchored me to the ground *had snapped*, and I was starting to wobble and sway a bit. And it is impossible to love when you are swaying and are not solid, because to stay upright you have to pull the shutters down and reinforce everything with concrete just to make it through the goddamn day.

The next week I was on a flight back out to the West Coast and Camp Pendleton and the life that I thought I had forever left behind. And as I sat on the airplane with the engines and the air humming around me, I realized that though I'd wanted to see my old buddies whom I'd fought alongside of, a part of me didn't want to see them. I wanted to talk about everything that had happened over there and the things that were happening to me back home, but I also didn't want to talk about any of them. I wanted to get the signatures on the forms and get out of there. But I also wanted to stay with those guys forever.

It's too soon, I thought. *More time needs to pass.* Because there is a certain amount of time that needed to pass before you see them again and it hadn't yet been long enough. The wounds were still too fresh. We needed time to grow a bit older. To learn things. To reflect on what happened. To put some distance between the war and ourselves. I knew it was still too soon, but I'd told Kristian that I'd get the signatures. So I went.

I walked into the headquarters building for First Battalion, Fourth Marines, Camp Pendleton. The building was drab and worn, a leftover from the forties or fifties. Inside the battalion's administrative offices, some of the same Marines I'd served with were still there, and they remembered me.

"Oh shit! Lieutenant Scotti, sir, how are you doing? How's civilian life treating you?" said one of the Marines who was sitting behind the desk.

"I'm good, fellas. How are you guys doing?"

"We're good, sir. We're getting ready to go play in the sandbox again. We deploy to Iraq in a few weeks."

I noticed a framed picture sitting on top of a filing cabinet with a set of dog tags draped over the top of the frame. The Marine in the picture was taking a long pull off a cigarette as he looked to his side at something that was out of the frame. He looked to be about twenty or twenty-one. The Marine sitting at the desk next to the filing cabinet saw me looking at the picture, and then he grew tense and his eyes went vacant as he looked out the window.

"Sir—that's Sergeant Straseskie. He drowned trying to save the pilots of a CH-46 that crashed in a canal outside of our perimeter. I think that was after you rotated home."

I stood silently in front of the picture and let the face of the Marine burn into my brain so I would never forget it. I hadn't known him, but it was obvious that this Marine and the one in the picture had been very close. You could feel it in the air, I could feel it in my heart, and I could see it in the eyes of the Marine behind the desk.

"He looks like a true fucking warrior," I said. He did.

"So I was wondering if Kyle Nickey or Eric Sibert or Tom Del Cioppo were still around the battalion." They were. And later that night, the four of us sat at a table in a restaurant on the boardwalk in San Clemente where the waves crashed directly beneath us and the sun set over the water. The three of them were just about to get off of active duty and were happy.

"Damn, sir, it's good to see you."

"Fellas, it's great to see you, too. And stop fucking calling me sir. I'm a civilian now." They would laugh and call me by my first name and then laugh some more because it felt so awkward to them after all those years of having to call me sir.

We talked about the guys we knew.

"Remember Waldo and his fly wars?" asked Kyle. "He would spend hours killing them. Slapping them with your *Iraqi Weapons and Tactics Handbook*, then there would be fly guts all over the book, and you'd get pissed off."

"Or how about the time Waldo went to take a crap during one of the security halts and he came running back two minutes later cursing because an Iraqi family appeared from nowhere and walked by him when he had his pants around his ankles," Eric added.

"Remember on those never-ending drives when you would give us advice on what to do when we went to college?" Tom asked. "Don't schedule any classes before noon if we can help it, because we won't go to them anyway. Make friends with upperclassmen and get them to tell you who the easy professors are, because the difference in the amount of work from a professor who has tenure and one who doesn't give a shit can be huge."

"And sorority girls," Kyle added. "I remember you talked about sorority girls. That depending on the school, becoming a frat guy can also be a mixed blessing. That after being a Marine and fighting in a fucking war, being a frat guy is going to seem like some sort of retarded joke. *But*—you have access to the sorority girls...and, well..."

"Ah...sorority girls," we all said in unison as we raised our beers.

"And, fellas, I think I also told you something else...something very important. Try not to be a fucking maniac when you're on campus. I ended up at the University of Miami literally seventy-two hours after I graduated from Parris Island when I was in the Reserves, screaming high and tight and all, and people looked at me like I was a lunatic—because I was a fucking lunatic. Grow your hair out, mellow the fuck out, and remember that you are surrounded by civilians—especially civilian chicks—and you live in their world now. It took me an entire semester to figure that out," I said.

"Or how about when the battalion started to run out of food? Remember that shit?" Kyle asked.

"Yeah, I remember. It was like the world's worst forced diet," I said.

"Remember on my twenty-first birthday when the colonel gave me a pack of Starburst? Which I'm pretty sure I shared with you, by the way," Kyle said.

"Oh yeah, I remember that. Yeah, you sure did," I said as I remembered that a pack of Starburst at that point in the war was about the greatest thing in the world. Just being there with those guys as we sat at our table on the pier reminded me of how glad I was that they were all still alive and breathing. And for a short time, the light that my buddies shined as we drank and talked seemed to scare away the darkness.

"Remember that picture we snapped of all of us during the security halt when we started to get skinny?"

"Yeah—I fucking love that picture."

I told them about the film. They were excited, and they quickly signed the release forms. But after several rounds of drinks, the energy shifted and things grew much more serious as they told me what had happened to a lot of the guys after I had rotated back to the States and out of the Corps. I had known about the dead. But I did not know about the wounded. The 81mm mortar platoon had taken a lot of casualties on patrol one day, very close to the time when I was at the wedding and had been thinking about them as they were on patrol in Al Hillah. Eric had taken a bullet fragment to the neck. He leaned over the table and showed me the scar.

Then they began to fill me in on some of the others. Marines, good Marines, had been discharged for doing coke and failing their drug tests. For others, it was crystal meth. Some of the Marines I had known were in jail. There were rumors that one of the most respected Marines in the battalion had found himself in a rough spot one night. The word was that he got pulled over while driving a government van and was past the legal alcohol limit. Two Marines I knew were discharged on 100 percent disability with PTSD. One of those couldn't stand to be driving on the road—any road—because he was terrified that something would explode underneath him. There had been literally dozens of DUIs among the Marines in the various units I'd served with. Two of my close buddies, one officer and one enlisted Marine, told me that their wives had cheated on them while they were deployed. The Marines in the battalions seemed different. Morale was different. The entire vibe was different. The battalion had been to a war and had fought bravely and with honor. And they were getting ready to go back to do it again. But it was clear that the deployments were taking their toll. And whether you were a Marine sitting in a jail cell because you had popped positive on your piss test or a Marine getting ready for your third deployment or a guy who had done his time and gotten out, one thing was the same for many of us: we had all fucked the same whore. And we had all caught the same virus.

The next night, my last in California, I went to dinner with some of the battalion officers with whom I'd served. Many of them were captains and majors and had families waiting for them, so they had gone home. Soon my buddy Mike Borneo and I were the only ones left sitting at a bar near the south end of the town. He and I looked like brothers, both of us with dark brown hair and olive Mediterranean skin. The bar was at the end of the town that was closest to the north gate at Camp Pendleton, and the bars and restaurants grew cheaper and more depressing the further south you went. When we were training before our deployments, we'd shoot artillery down in the valley on base, and the windows of the houses on the south side of town would rattle.

Mike and I had been deployed to Iraq as lieutenants. When you are lieutenants together, you grow together and fight and become men together, and there is an especially strong connection because you are the same rank. When you are the same rank, you have the same problems and responsibilities and fears. And you have to deal with all of the same bullshit from higher headquarters. And when you first start out as a lieutenant, you are just three or four years older than most of the guys who are under your command. The guys who die when you make the wrong decision. They aren't really much different from you, but they have to call you sir and look to you for guidance, and in their minds, they ask, "What now, Lieutenant?" when the bullets are flying and the radios aren't working and things are going to hell. Permanent things. And all because you went to college.

It was a weeknight and the bar was almost empty. The place was dark and worn, and whoever owned it had stopped trying.

"It's fucking great to see you, man."

"It's fucking great to see you too, brother."

"How was it over there after I left?" I asked.

He paused and the air was heavy. He stared straight ahead for a moment and took a sip of his beer.

"It was a tough fight. But we are Marines, you know?" he said. He filled me in on what happened. The deadly firefights in built-up urban environments, the rising insurgency, and the casualties, all in the brutal Iraq heat.

We talked about how our moms were speaking to each other almost every day when we were in the same unit in Iraq because we had put them in touch through the Marine Moms network and we were both from New Jersey.

He stayed in the Marine Corps and continued the fight. There was a reason the colonel made him platoon commander for the antiarmor platoon that screened out in front of the battalion—because he was the best. The colonel wanted the best out front, because Mike and his guys would be the first to deal with whatever was waiting to hit us. We sat at the bar and drank our beers, and suddenly there was a silence between us. Because he was going back in a few weeks to do it all over again almost from the beginning. He was going to face the artillery rounds buried in the road and the *click-click* of the detonators and then the burns and the screaming and the gunfire while I was heading back to New York City to worry about admissions committees and x squared equals an integer greater than zero. And the worst that might happen to me was that I wouldn't get into school or my savings would run out and I would have to move back in with my parents, but he or his guys could end up dead or as burn victims or invalids or bleeding on some roadside somewhere as they would rush and scramble to get the helicopters in time to try to save them.

My active-duty contract was up. And I could look in the mirror and say that I had done my time, but the truth was that I could've picked up the phone and said I wanted back in and I could've gone with them. But I didn't do that. I told myself that if they needed me, they would call me up from the IRR and then I would go. But deep inside I knew they needed every guy they could find. And so I said good-bye to my buddy whose job it was to drive first into enemy territory, and I boarded that plane back to NYC the next morning.

On the subway on the way home from the airport I watched a group of three people about the same age as me talking while dressed in tailored business suits. A woman with blond hair and diamond earrings and a blue collared shirt worn with the top two buttons open and a string of pearls around her neck. A tall, lean Indian man in a gray pinstripe suit. The third, a fat polished Pillsbury Doughboy whose chubby stomach you wanted to poke so he would go "Hoo hoo!" He had his curls and soft hands and fingernails and glasses behind which sat eyes that had never seen anything.

"I think the MD will remember me. I think he was impressed when I told him that I was at Goldman after Princeton," said the girl, referring to a managing director.

"Yeah, I got like fifteen business cards. I'm going to be up all night sending thank-you e-mails, but we have that accounting midterm tomorrow, and I still need to study."

They were students at some elite business school and had probably just come from some finance networking event for the investment banks. The air was full of their arrogance and their feeling that they were better than the rest of us in that subway car. I hated them because of it. And I hated the part of myself that wanted to be where they were. And I was sorry that Mike Borneo had to go back to fight again, and I was sorry for what the guys in California had told me about our brothers who'd lost their way, just as I had, and found themselves at the edge of the cliff staring into the darkness. They'd come home and thought the war was over, but now their luck was gone and they were fumbling. In exile. Like me. Wandering lost in the space between the war and the world they'd once called home.

So I stopped at a bar on the way home from the subway and drank alone until I was in the spirit world, and when I got back to my apartment, I surprised a man smoking crack in the hallway. I was just as surprised as he was, because I'd never seen anyone do that in my neighborhood before. The air smelled of burned tinfoil and crack cocaine. And the crackhead was just a little ashamed, but not so much anymore, because he had accepted his place in the order of things and was mostly just worried about whether or not I was going to call the cops. But the smell in the air in the hallway was similar to the smell of the vehicles burning and the dead on the side of the road.

Sleep comes fully clothed and with the laptop resting on my lap, as the guy who lives above me, a holdover from the sixties on rent control and paying a third of what I pay, does a bunch of blow and decides to rearrange his furniture or fuck his girlfriend or dance and whoop. And across the courtyard, a few floors above me, a puppy yaps and yaps and then cries out like the baby in her mother's arms I saw silhouetted against the moon and across the barbed wire as I tried to sleep in the dirt in the battalion perimeter just off of Route 7. The mother walking innocent and afraid as the tired and unsure Marine in front of her bumped into things and thought *I didn't sign up for this*, as he led her gently to the aid station. And the cries of the puppy cutting in the night as your eyelids got heavy and finally closed and that's all you ever really wanted. The silence and the quiet simple thoughts.

But then a few hours later, there was the heavy *thump thump thump* of my heartbeat. And as I awoke, there was for a moment a glimpse of what had been.

"*Check firing! Check firing! Check firing!*" And the voices seemed to bleed over from the spirit world to the world next to that cold brick wall and the neighbor that lived above who'd snorted too much blow and decided to rearrange his furniture. And the confusion and doubt of whether it had actually happened or had been another bad dream and I had actually reversed the numbers on the map by mistake. And that doubt and the wondering and the adrenaline in the pale hollow arctic desert that was becoming my life. Where sleep had been the only thing that I had left—but now they'd taken even that when they'd pissed on the oasis.

Mostly sober now but head pounding and throbbing and I was

113

the ashes that were left at the end. The last few warm sips of beer at the bottom of the bottle. The best part of me—the prime— had already passed. The clarity gone. And the meaning and the days fat with sunshine. Things were on the downward slope but I couldn't remember the exact moment when they had shifted quietly from the up to the down. But they were definitely on the down. And when they were, everything just seemed to gently roll that way no matter what you did. But I guess that was the natural cycle of things. That even a fish swimming strongly—but at the edge of the school—can be the one who gets eaten.

What was once just a gentle shift of my seesaw somehow greater lately when all things let go but still scratched and clawed the surface on their way down.

So this was how things were supposed to be. A prisoner staring at the cold gray walls—and the truth staring straight back. No matter who had ordered it or the circumstances—the truth always stares straight back.

So when you arrive in the lobby at the New Year's Eve party with the girl you love next to you and everything is OK—you see the young American girl, still a child, dancing young and free and innocent. And she was the daughter that maybe one day you were supposed to have. But what was left of the girl her same age on the side of the road and dead and splattered and gone—you ask yourself what the hell is the point of any of it anymore.

And you think about Beth and what the hell did she do to anybody as they were up near that top floor—but the windows were shattered and gone now and they all knew that the end was soon. The building had started to sway and then there were the noises. No matter how much they didn't want it to end, it was the end. So what do you say then at that moment? What do you say when you can't change the outcome and there is just the finality of it all?

This was it. This was how I went. So then you hope that the ones you loved *knew* that you loved them purely and truly. But there could only be the hope because this was it and you couldn't ever change any of it back. You had arrived at your end.

So you think about the last time you saw them and blink for a moment and remember. Then you turn your head to the left. And thoughts go toward the more immediate surroundings.

And as I lay alone and hungover, at the bottom, on the mattress on the floor, the room shifted. The ceiling seemed too far away. And the walls stood like pillars but they were against me. And it came from somewhere up there among the married and the normal and the happy. From up there where the sun still shined. It came over the top and down with the wind pulling some of it away in wisps because you always had to pay the price, but what was left came down heavy and unrelenting. And as I lay alone and hungover on that mattress on the floor, the blue cascade washed over me.

```
From: Meredith
To: Kristian Fraga
Sent: Wed Mar 30th, 2005 9:17 AM EST
Hi Kristian,

Could you please call me, or email me, when
you receive this message? I'm very worried
about Mike. Last night he told me about
some troubling things, in confidence. I am
uneasy betraying his confidence by reaching
out to you, but I think it's important that
```

I do. Plus, he told me that the only other person he has shared this information with is you. I'm not sure what to make of it all, and I'm not sure just how worried I should be, or if I should be worried at all. But I care about Mike very, very much— and I think you do, too—so I would appreciate your take on the situation. I hope that I'm overreacting.

Since I am disobeying Mike's explicit orders not to talk to anyone about this, I probably have no right to ask you to keep this email and your response a secret from him (and from your other friends at Sirk), but I'm going to ask you to keep everything quiet, anyway.

Thanks,
Meredith

Kristian Fraga replied:

Meredith,
I just got your email. I'm with you on this. We just have to be strong and figure out exactly what we can do to help him. I'm hoping he chills a bit now that he's back home but yeah, he's going through some intense shit and we're the only ones he feels close enough to talk to. I know he's a big

fan of yours, and you are somebody that he
cares about. I also know that he will listen to you.

If you want to talk to me or you think we
should get together, just tell me when and
where. Scotti's with me right now and he's
kind of out of it but better now than he
was yesterday. We'll just have to take it
one day at a time. He'll be okay, he's going through some shit right now that he's
having a hard time dealing with but I have
faith in him. We'll get him through it.

If you need to reach me any time, call me
at the office or on my cell.

Kris

From: Meredith
To: Kristian
Sent: Thu Mar 31st, 2005 10:09 AM EST
Subject: Re:

Kris,
Thanks for writing back. I saw Mike last
night, and he seemed more upbeat, so that
made me feel better. There was still some
talk about suicide, but he didn't seem as
focused on it as he had on Tuesday night.
But I'm not sure what's going to happen

if he doesn't hear positive news from
NYU.

I guess the best thing right now is for
both of us to keep on being his friends
(for the record, he thinks the world of
you, too), and to keep our eyes and ears
open. Mike's a great friend to me, so I
hope that I can return the compliment.

Please keep my contact info nearby, and be
in touch if you ever think there might be
trouble brewing. I'll do the same.

—Meredith

The night we officially signed the contracts to make the documentary film, a group of us went out to dinner. Up until that point, Sirk Productions and I had been working without formal contracts between us for licensing the rights to my footage, and now that things were official, the guys wanted to go out and celebrate. There were two other people with us in addition to Kristian, Marc, and me. Andrew Torkelson was the intern I'd met in the hallway at NYU's film school who'd introduced me to Sirk Productions. John Sikes, who was also a partner at the production company and who looked like a younger version of Sean Connery, would be an executive producer on the film. Dinner turned into dinner and drinks, which turned into more drinks. Around midnight, Kristian flagged down a cab.

The yellow cab, a Chevy Caprice with its white For Hire sign illuminated on the roof, pulled over to the east side of Second Avenue, facing south, halfway down the block. Kristian approached the driver's side of the car. He spoke to its angry-looking driver, who was of Middle Eastern descent, through the window. John Sikes and I stood a few feet away from Kris, near the left rear wheel well of the taxi. Marc and Andrew stood watching from the curb.

"We're headed to Scores on the Upper West Side," Kristian said to the driver.

The driver glanced back at John and me, then at Andrew and Marc. "How many?" he asked.

"Five."

"Too many."

"How about if we pay you extra?"

"Too many!"

"C'mon, brother. Can you help us out?"

The driver's eyes turned angry and he starting yelling—quite loudly—at Kristian in Arabic. As he did, his foot pressed down hard on the accelerator and the cab jetted forward quickly. The angle of the tires was such that as the driver sped away, the back end of the car swung outward to the left, hitting both John and me.

I lay on the pavement on my back, looking up at the black sky through the haze of the lights from the bars and the apartments above them. For a moment, I did not know what had happened. John Sikes lay next to me and I could see him lying crumpled, on his side. I glanced over at him, and with both palms pressed flat against the ground, I pushed the upper half of my body up. As I did, the watch that my mom and dad had given me as a present slid off my wrist and onto the street, the links of the metal band snapped in pieces. I looked back at John lying on the road, then back at my watch, then to the east and down the street.

The cab was caught at a red light just half a block away.

I popped up onto my feet and ran toward the taxi.

"Sikes is down! Sikes is *dooooooown!*" I screamed.

In just a few seconds I was at the driver's door. I knew that look of hatred he had in his eyes when he was arguing with Kristian. It was the look of an enemy. I pulled upward hard and fast on the black door handle. The door swung open like it was made of plastic. The cabdriver turned his head to the left. His eyes searching for a second. This Middle Eastern son of a bitch was going to pay for what he had done. *Left hand grab hard onto his lapel for leverage.* The handful of thick fabric twisted in my clenched fingers and pulled toward me. His body lurched a few inches outside the door as I pulled. *Right hand in fist. Lean forward slightly and take a small step toward the front of the cab so that the angle of attack is more head-on. Strike hard with strong right-hand fist.* Full power. Death power. Rage power. Wrist straight and aligned with the knuckles of the index and middle fingers. *Tink* as a tooth shot from his mouth and bounced off the inside of the windshield and onto the dashboard. *Strike again.* Blood and saliva ran from his mouth and down onto his chin. *Again.* Something popped on the left side of his face near the eye socket.

Die you son-of-a-bitch cabbie fuck. Please die. A squeal came from somewhere deep inside of him, like the rabbit I shot with a BB gun when I was a kid. I had felt bad when I was a kid, but now the sound seemed only to fuel my rage.

So this is what he got. This is what this *motherfucker* got because I had just seen Tim Lynch in his dress blues salute the flag-draped coffin of his little brother. This is what he got for the fact that Beth Quigley and Pete Apollo knew that they were going to die in the North Tower after the planes hit. For the Iraqis whose bodies we had ripped to pieces with 20mm, their mouths open as if in protest of their condition. For Jason's hand, Billy's arm, my sanity, and the tank crew that drowned to death at the bottom of the Euphrates after they drove off the bridge that night. And this is what he got for there not being any fucking weapons of mass destruction. No fucking weapons. *No fucking weapons...*

Then a whoosh, and my eyes saw only legs and feet. My arms pointed straight up to the sky and my chin pressed hard against my chest. A hard hugging force on my back and against my armpits and on the back of my neck. Andrew had me in a full nelson, a wrestling move meant to immobilize. Much larger than I, he dragged me back to the sidewalk. I did not fight it. There was no point.

Marc ran from the sidewalk to my left and out into the street.

That son of a bitch is going to help the enemy. Traitor!

Marc, screaming and cursing at the cabbie, grabbed his left leg and began to pull him out of the cab. Marc held the left leg close and twisted his body as he pulled the leg hard, and the lower half of the cabbie's body was now out. His upper half was tangled in his seatbelt. *Marc is no traitor—he's a goddamn killer! Outstanding!* Kristian grabbed Marc and put him in a full nelson. He dragged Marc to the sidewalk next to me, and we both hung there in the grip of our handlers. He looked over at me, and I nodded at him in acknowledgment of the fact that he had backed me up at the moment of truth as we'd stood up for John, who was still recovering over on the sidewalk. That was something I wouldn't forget.

A crowd had now gathered. A guy of about twenty ran up and kicked the back left side of the cab. Another onlooker reached into the garbage can at the corner and starting throwing handfuls of garbage onto the windshield and hood of the cab.

"You fucking cabbie!" a voice yelled.

Someone else in the crowd kicked over the garbage can and the garbage fell out onto the street.

The cabdriver, looking dazed, slammed his door shut and ran the red light.

"We need to get the hell out of here!" Kristian yelled.

John Sikes was now up on his feet.

"You OK, man?" I asked him.

"Yeah, I'm good. Here's your watch," he said as he handed me the pieces.

"My apartment is a block away."

The five of us walked, quickly, through the crowd. Within ten minutes, we were safely in my apartment building.

After what seemed like hours but was probably in reality more like thirty minutes, we grew restless.

"Let's get out of here. This is fucking boring," somebody said.

We headed back out to a place called Off the Wagon. The last thing I remember was playing beer pong in the upstairs loft of the bar with the guys from Sirk and a bunch of drunk college girls on vacation from Nebraska. Or maybe it was Minnesota.

Part II

PURGE

Chapter Six

I AWOKE ALONE in my apartment to the hammering in my head, the dryness of my mouth, and my bloody, throbbing knuckles. All reminders of what I'd done.

I am too old for this shit. Twenty-eight—and at the same time I'm applying to graduate schools, I'm also beating the shit out of cabdrivers in a drunken rage. If they had put the cuffs on me, my plans for grad school and everything after would've been finished. Because the jobs I'd be going after are the type that require fairly extensive background checks, and an entire world would suddenly be forever off-limits.

Things like what happened the night before were relatively common in New York City, and if I was going to be arrested, it would've already happened. The anonymity of the city had saved me. And luck. Luck and the universe had spared me from any cops being on that corner or down the street. And on Fridays, in that neighborhood, there were almost always several of them.

Over the bathroom sink, I poured hydrogen peroxide over the bloody knuckles on my right hand. There was a tooth mark from the cabbie's mouth. The peroxide bubbled and frothed where it came into contact with the open cuts. It stung for a few seconds, but then the pain went away quickly. As I stood in the bathroom, tired, hungover, and slightly indifferent, I wondered how many guys from how many wars went through this shit. How many of them tried to fight the darkness after they got out, but lost? How many drank themselves to death in some trailer out back? How many stepped out into their garages and put shotguns in their mouths or ropes around their necks? Or how many ended up living for the next fifty years wishing that they'd never made it back?

I'd been given a free pass. And I got the sense that it was to be my last one. But I'm not sure how much I really cared about that. Because nothing made sense to me anymore. I'd volunteered to go to Iraq because I thought it would help to stop someone from doing something like spreading nerve gas in the subway system in New York City. Something that took innocent American lives. *Not so that the fucking Iraqis could vote. I didn't give a shit if the Iraqis could vote.* Then I thought about the weight of Matt Lynch's coffin in my hand. And how I'd said, "Fuck 'em. Let 'em burn," as we drove north along Route 7 past the burning buildings with the Iraqi soldiers inside. The ones that I'd just hit with artillery. I had said those things because Beth and Pete were gone. But maybe I was starting to wish that I could take it back, because now I knew that the guys in the buildings that were burning in Iraq had nothing to do with September 11th.

And I thought of the day when I was eight or nine and my mom and I walked to the Memorial Day parade in our hometown. She'd given me a small American flag to wave, and I held the wooden stick in my hand and waved it as hard as I could when the veterans walked by. But then I remembered that day in the bathroom at work and thought that maybe all of these things that I'd believed in for my whole life *really were* just a myth. And maybe it should've been me that came home in one of those flag-draped coffins. Because any one of those who'd fallen probably wished they could've traded spots with me. To be alive. But what I was living wasn't really a life. It was going through the motions in some sort of emotional prison.

So maybe I should just raise my hand and say, "Fuck it. I've had enough. I'm done. I give up. They win."

And maybe I should make it look like an accident. Put on my Ironman watch and my running shorts and an old Marine Corps T-shirt. Slip my iPod into its holder and over my bicep. Go for a run. Right into the path of a bus. That way my mom wouldn't know. But she would know. So maybe I would just fly to California and take a cab to the Golden Gate Bridge. Walk out to the middle of the span, take off my shoes, and rest my driver's license gently on top of them. And just before I did it, I would think about the first person who had done that off of that same bridge, right after they'd built it.

A veteran from World War I.

I showed up an hour or so later at the Sirk Productions offices on West Thirty-first Street, just south of the Empire State Building, for a meeting. Kristian looked at me as if he were looking at the dead.

"Are you alright?" he asked, sounding genuinely concerned.

"Yeah, I'm fine. Why?"

"How's your hand?"

I looked down at my hand. It was swollen, and you could still see the cuts and tooth marks.

"It's fine."

"You sure you're OK, man?"

"Uh, yeah. I'm fine."

"You left pretty quickly last night. You were saying something about the flight home from Iraq, and then you just left the bar without saying good-bye to anyone."

I didn't say anything.

"You were talking about how no one clapped when the plane took off from Kuwait. How you had your video camera out when the plane took off because you thought that everyone was about to clap, but there was just silence."

And when he said it I remembered as the plane rolled down the runway and we gently lifted off and there was no sound but the hum of the jet engines as the bright Kuwaiti desert sun made everything look overexposed as it shined through the windows. The video camera on my lap switched on with my thumb ready to press the Record button because all of us on that plane had made it out alive and were going home and I thought that everyone would've cheered and clapped and whooped as the plane lifted off. But the faces around me were faces of men who were beyond exhausted. Some men with their eyes closed. Some just staring blankly at the back of the seat in front of them. So we'd made it out alive but then maybe we thought of the ones who hadn't made it or of our buddies whom we were leaving behind. I switched off the video camera and stuffed it into the seat pocket in front of me.

Kristian said, "That was just like the other voice mail you left me a few weeks ago about how they played the theme from *Lawrence of Arabia* over and over again on the radio when you guys were in Kuwait waiting for the war to start—and how there were other guys in your unit who also had cameras."

"None of those stories are anywhere in your footage or in any of your journals," he said. After a few drinks, usually when I was alone in the early morning hours at some bar or in my apartment, the stories and the thoughts and the memories would start arriving silently out of the fog. I had started to trust and admire Kristian greatly, and I would sometimes use his voice mail at three o'clock in the morning as my unfiltered notepad. I knew that stories like these were what he wanted to hear and I was lobbing him the football just before I got pummeled because I was starting to trust him. I needed to talk to somebody I trusted, but most of the people whom I trusted at that point, like my parents, would worry about me. And the last thing I wanted to do was to hurt them. I'd put them through enough worry already.

"I feel like what I know about your time in the war so far may be just the tip of the iceberg. If we are going to make a good film—a film that will endure and show the world the truth—I need to know everything. And I think we need to get everything you know and thought and felt in one place. On one document. And you are going to need to continue to trust me."

"Like a purge," I said.

"Exactly."

Kristian had reviewed every second of the raw footage I'd taken and read through the notes and journal entries I had scribbled in my waterproof battlefield notebook. He read every word of what I had written at the Western Hotel in Colorado that first summer after the war. And he slowly began to understand the mind of a Marine before and during combat. Many of our discussions would stretch into the early hours of the next morning.

But he was right. There was more that I was holding back because I just didn't want to talk about it. You weren't supposed to talk about it. Because that's what veterans did. They stayed silent. But that afternoon, the day after I'd smashed the teeth of a cabdriver, some small part of me *did* want to talk. Some small part of me needed to tell someone. To have someone else share the load that was slowly crushing me.

"It would take fucking forever if I have to sit and tap away at the goddamn keyboard and stare at a screen. It would take months."

"We can help you. You can have anything you need. We've just hired a new intern who is going to be working for us. Her name is Camille. We call her CC. She can help you."

In the back room of the Sirk Productions offices was a box that held nearly everything I'd been able to gather that related to the war. They'd asked me to put everything together and bring it to them when they first started the project, so that Kristian could go through it all. In it were all the letters I had received in Iraq and Afghanistan, which I'd saved in ziplock bags, printouts of all the e-mails that I'd forwarded to myself from the ships on the way over, the pictures from all twenty rolls of film I had shot, and the digital videocassettes that held all of the footage I had taken.

Kristian and I talked about it a bit more and came up with the idea that I would just speak my thoughts aloud and neither try to make them perfect nor fight them—just puke them all up as they came. CC, the assistant, would type them all onto the page. Kristian already had a list of specific segments of footage, pictures, journal entries, and e-mails that he wanted to know more about. He could sense that these things had greater meaning, and he wanted to dig.

Kristian and I walked to the back of the hallway connecting their offices to a narrow editing suite that they called the war room. It had editing machines and a wall of windows with black bars across them that looked through a fire escape and over an alley that was really a canyon of despair.

"Mike, meet CC. CC, this is Mike Scotti."

Camille Cappola, or CC, was the production assistant they'd hired for the preproduction phase of the film. She was twenty-two years old with long, wavy brown hair and large brown eyes. CC was a communications major at Hofstra University, studying TV and video production.

"Hi, Mike. It's nice to meet you," she said in a friendly, youthful voice.

"Hi," I said, feeling kind of overwhelmed that I'd just agreed to do this, and now meeting the person to whom, five minutes later, I would be baring my soul.

There was a cold twelve-pack of Coors Light in the office refrigerator and a pot of coffee ready to go. Kristian twisted the tops off of three of the beers.

"Before I turn you two loose, I want you to take a look at something," Kristian said. His energy changed. He grew serious and I could sense the shift and I suddenly felt scared and unsure so I guzzled my beer. Kristian pressed the spacebar on the editing machine and a scene started. The eerie music that came through the speakers made me feel more uneasy. It had the essence of the calls to prayer that they would broadcast over the loudspeakers from the mosques in Iraq. Then came footage of Marines I'd known and quick jumps to other pictures. Footage of vehicles burning and flashes of mangled corpses. Machine-gun fire and all the rest. At first I felt the uneasiness, but after a few seconds I just wanted the ground to come up and swallow me. To erase me. But when I saw the look on CC's face, the look of horror and disbelief as she saw the footage for what was obviously the first time, I no longer felt ashamed for the water that was accumulating in my eyes. It felt strange to be so naked and vulnerable and destroyed in front of someone whom I had just met. And Kristian's editing and the music he chose were so goddamn perfect and sad and terrible and beautiful at the same time that I couldn't stand it. After a few minutes, when the scene was finished, I walked out of the room and got another beer and twisted off the cap.

"I'm sorry, and I know this is going to be tough for you, man, but I needed to bring you back," Kristian said.

"This is how it is going to have to be," I said as I stared straight ahead.

He put his hand on my shoulder.

"You good, brother?" he asked.

"Good enough."

Kristian handed CC the list he had started to compile, and she clipped it into a clipboard that had been sitting on the table. CC and I exchanged small talk for a few minutes and then decided to begin.

CC picked up the clipboard.

"Item 1. Little girl's brain lying on the side of the road," she read aloud. The strain on her face was obvious. She read a reference number off of the checklist and then scrolled through some images that appeared on the screen in front of us. She stopped when she got to the shot of the small pink brain in the dirt in Iraq.

I began...

I think it was about two weeks into the fighting. We were south of the town of Al Kut, Iraq. We came across a taxicab that had been traveling south on Route 7. It had been raked by machine-gun fire. It looked like the car had failed to stop at a roadblock. There was no one else around, but it was clear that it had been over in just a few seconds.

The taxi was sitting there empty on the east side of the road. Bullet holes in the windshield. The right rear window was blown-in. There were tire tracks the car had left in the dirt as it veered off the road. There were no bodies inside. But what we did find was something that none of us would ever forget.

It was obvious that a child, a girl, had been in the backseat. Strands of her long black hair and pieces of her skull were crushed into the window by the force of the bullets. Half of her scalp had been flipped over the outside of the left rear door. Her brain matter was sprayed, in chunks, throughout the interior of the car. There was a pair of pink baby sandals with yellow and green flowers on them, covered in blood, in the backseat. I scooped up the sandals and brain matter and picked the hair and skull fragments out of the window. I noticed a piece of flesh outside of the vehicle. It was a small brain. I'm not exactly sure why, but I buried the little girl's pink sandals by the side of the road. Jeremy Davis, a corporal from Buda, Texas, who was with me, buried her brain.

It seemed like the right thing to do.

CC looked at me when I finished telling her the story and saw that I was visibly upset. She gave me a reassuring half smile that said it was going to be OK. It said that even though she couldn't know firsthand what it had been like, staring at the picture of the little girl's brain and hearing me tell the story was close enough. The words came quickly to me, and when she finished typing what I'd said, she took a deep breath, picked up the clipboard, and read aloud.

"Item 2. Surrounded," CC said and again she scrolled through the footage until she reached the correct clip. She pressed the spacebar on the editing machine, and together we watched a few seconds of video. The memories came rushing back.

"We have enemy headed this way!" screamed Major Casado, the operations officer for the battalion. I was standing in the large roof hatch of our vehicle with the camera pointed below to where he was sitting inside, in front of the radios. He was yelling to the assistant operations officer, who was standing behind me. "Tell Apocalypse to tighten up the position and pull back in to the southeast." We were just outside the city of Ash Shatrah, Iraq. A lone infantry battalion fifteen miles north of any other friendly units.

The sky began to turn orange, then amber. What was happening? Was the world ending? "No, it's a dust storm," someone said. The dust and wind whirling. Fine powder into teeth and mouths and ears. On hands and in eyes and into the bolt carrier group of your rifle. Into the air intake valves of the engines of the aircraft that dropped the bombs and fired the rockets that gave us life. The sun became a spot. A perfect circle. You could look directly at it, but your eyes didn't burn.

I heard the sounds of .50 caliber machine guns in the distance. Just beyond a sparse tree line and across a field a few hundred yards away. It was Mike Borneo's platoon. Both handsets were clipped to my helmet strap, and my rifle lay at the ready, resting across the top of the hatch.

Then a heavy burst of gunfire. *Jesus, that was a long burst of .50 caliber*, I thought. Another. Rifle fire. Then lots of machine-gun fire. And AK-47 fire and then something that sounded a bit heavier—like an RPK Russian-built medium machine gun. A distinct difference in the sound between our weapons and the enemy weapons. Another long burst of .50 caliber fire and then *thump-thump-thump-thump* as the Mk 19 automatic belt-fed grenade launchers started. The fight sounded ominous.

You could hear the fear in the length of the bursts.

"Elements are in contact with the enemy. The volume of fire is increasing," were the only words that came out of my mouth as I narrated the video. The words sounded weak from fatigue. I was worried about Mike Borneo and his boys. He was one of my best buddies.

Already thirty or so hours without sleep and now the enemy was starting to attack us again. Then I sank back into our vehicle. Everyone knew that we were about to get attacked and that the calls for fire would come. But what we didn't know was that this time we would even have to make some ourselves.

You could hear it. Stalking closer. Alpha Company. Bravo Company. Then Charlie Company. Each unit along the line began to fire as the enemy attacked. They were probing us. Searching for our weakness. We were in a cigar-shaped defense along the sides of the road. The Marines began to dismount from their vehicles to dig into the earth. They dug so that the earth would stop the bullets. They dug so that they'd be ready to stand and fight.

I sat two seats away from Major Casado. He was a man of few words but an iron mind. As the battalion operations officer, he had an unending number of things to worry about at all times. There were other people whose job it was to worry about things like communications and logistics, but because the operation and functioning of the entire battalion were always affected by everything else, much of the stress of that load ended up on his shoulders and in his mind. The location and movement of the three 250-man rifle companies, the weapons company, and the headquarters and support company, combat engineers, artillery, mortars, fuel, ammunition, radio communications, broken-down vehicles we had left behind to be fixed, patrols, adjacent units, the wounded, the dead, regimental command and higher headquarters, water, the weather, intelligence, civilians, the laws of war, the terrain, the rules of engagement, translators, captured weapons, explosives, minefields, nuclear/ biological/chemical threats, and of course the enemy. Sometimes during the past few weeks, our massive convoy stretched for nearly thirty miles. And all of it enemy territory.

I admired Major Casado highly. I was certain that there were only a few men whose mind could've been stretched to the limits that his was. Most men, I imagined, would make disastrous mistakes or suffer some sort of emotional meltdown. Especially given that many of his decisions applied to life-or-death scenarios, and were made while under direct enemy fire and with only a bare minimum of sleep.

"Mortars are taking fire from the southeast. And Bravo Company from the west."

I listened as the Combat Operation Center, as we were called, built the tactical picture of the battle that was unfolding. At that moment, we were supposedly the northernmost unit in all of Iraq. Enemy territory. Indian country. We were now being attacked from nearly every direction. An odd feeling. Somewhat terrifying but also exhilarating. Primal. A group of men all the way up here fighting for their lives together. I wished there were more of us. There could never be too many of us, and we could never have too much ammunition. I started to wonder how all of this was going to end up for us. Would we all be dead in a few hours?

Tink. Tink-tink-tink. The bullets would strike the sides of our vehicle and bounce off the thin armor. The hulls of our vehicles were made from aluminum because the vehicles were designed to float from ships far offshore and swim through the water like boats and onto the beaches. They were not really the best for

driving hundreds of miles inland and fighting in urban environments like the towns and cities we were attacking. *I'm glad that's
just rifle and machine-gun fire*, I thought, *nothing bigger. This
shitty bolt-on armor can't stop too much more than that.*

With a squeak, the heavy door on the back hatch of our vehicle
swung open. The automatic weapons fire grew much louder as
the door opened. It was Colonel Dowdy, our regimental commander.

"The entire city of Ash Shatrah has been declared hostile.
Everything and everyone in the city is enemy."

The Marine Corps had just increased greatly the level of violence that we would now legally inflict from this road next to this
shitty, worthless town in the dust storm in this shitty, worthless
country.

In a few minutes, the squeaky door swung open again. The
sounds of the battle on the outside were still at the same level they
had been before. Lieutenant Colonel Mayer, the battalion commander, popped his head in the door.

"Major Casado, pass the word to the rifle companies to conserve ammunition. We've been burning through a lot of ammo
over the last twenty-four hours and we need to conserve. We
don't know when the next resupply will be."

There was a web of irrigation canals and ditches in the fields
that surrounded our defensive position. The enemy fighters
started to use them as protective cover to creep closer. Alpha
Company called in a "danger close" artillery fire mission, meaning that the rounds were supposed to land within four hundred
yards of friendly positions. Very risky, but it was a calculated risk
that they were willing to take.

"Grid Papa Victor eight seven two niner four three... *danger
close*, over." I tried to speak as clearly as possible through the radio

handset to the Marine on the other end who was with the cannons fifteen miles behind us. I started to lose power on my radio.

"Say again, Palerider, over," he responded.

Not a good time for this to be happening. Not good at all.

Then Kyle Nickey, whose job it was to coordinate the jets and helicopters, pounded the ledge above his knees with his fist one time—but hard. His radio, always temperamental, also began to fail.

"Not again, you fucking piece of shit," he said to his radio as he removed it from its console and tried to fix it.

One of the communications Marines assigned to our vehicle tried to fix my radio problem as I waited and hoped. Critical minutes at the worst possible time—in the middle of a heavy enemy probing attack.

After two or three long minutes, my radio began to come back to life, and I got the rest of the call for fire through, and then two more quickly after. The enemy fire started to increase. Alpha Company let me know that there were now civilians seen milling around in the impact area. *Perfect, just what we fucking needed.* Within a few minutes I had four fire missions going on simultaneously. Four artillery barrages that would be arcing through the air and landing at four different areas of the battlefield, all close to friendly positions.

It started to rain, and I pressed the radio handset to get radio checks from the howitzers and from the three forward observers scattered along our defensive perimeter. I was beginning to become paranoid that we would suddenly lose radio contact with them in the middle of multiple fire missions. What if someone needed to call Check firing! to stop our artillery from hitting friendly troops?

The young Marine who was in charge of the defense of our

vehicle started to fire his machine gun. The enemy were close. *Gut those motherfuckers.* I wished that I was still a corporal in the infantry so I could get behind an automatic weapon and spray death. Instead, I was chained to that goddamn radio. We were in the command vehicle for the entire battalion of 1,500 Marines. Normally the battalion headquarters would be set up farther behind the lines to offer some protection to the nerve center of the entire combat operation. But in a mobile war like the one we were fighting, everywhere was the front line, and we were just another vehicle mixed in among the dozens of others in the rifle companies.

Except that we *looked* like a command vehicle, different from the rest, because we had seven or so extra antennas sticking out of us. And everybody—including the enemy—knows that on the battlefield you kill the command vehicle first. There had been jokes when the war started that if we ever needed to shoot the weapon that was now firing off of the front of our vehicle, things were not going well for us.

"Dude, we are like sacrificial lambs here in this vehicle," said Captain Evan Wahl, the always mellow air officer whose pilot call sign was Waldo. We all started laughing, but Waldo wasn't laughing. He was dead serious, but that made us all laugh even harder. Because we all knew he was right, and there was nothing we could do about it but laugh. There was no place for us to go. No hills to park the vehicle behind. Just a muddy road and the muddy fields with ditches and the enemy in them. Totally exposed. And individually at that moment, we were somewhat helpless to fight back with our personal weapons, because we were seated inside the aluminum vehicle manning the radios instead of standing with roof hatches open and our rifles pointing outward.

"Sir, maybe we should move the vehicle," Waldo gently suggested to the battalion commander, who was at this point standing all the way forward in the vehicle with his head exposed through the commander's hatch.

No response.

"So I guess that means that we are not moving the vehicle," he said to the rest of us seated in the rows in front of the radios.

We laughed even harder, but it was nervous laughter, because we were starting to really wonder if we were going to die.

Then a ripping crash outside the vehicle. The laughter stopped. A mortar. Somewhere in one of these fields was a man with a set of binoculars who had identified us as his target. If he and his mortar-squad buddies were any good, they would bracket us, quickly correcting and adjusting a series of single rounds like the one they'd just fired, until they got the range correct. Then they would release the mortar barrage, and a shell would hit the unarmored aluminum roof of our vehicle and that would be the end of us.

Fuck this, I thought. *Time to obliterate some Iraqi mortarmen.* I keyed the radio handset. Ready to unleash the full combat power of the Marine Corps upon them.

"Cobra Cobra, this is Palerider. *Snowstorm*, Papa Victor eight six two niner niner fife, over."

The Marine radio operator on the other end read back the transmission to me correctly.

By calling "Snowstorm," I'd alerted the artillery that we were taking indirect enemy fire—mortars or artillery—onto our position. Almost immediately a well-trained Marine from the radar unit would comb through the data that his battlefield radars had been collecting by constantly scanning the sky above us. He would see the arc of whatever it was had just landed

near us. And they would see the spot where the arc had origi-
nated. Then they would fire a large artillery barrage onto that
spot.

There was gunfire all around us. But what I heard on the
other end of the radio was not what I expected. Gunfire. Lots
of gunfire coming through the radio handset as I talked to the
artillery, who we thought were safely set up far behind the front
lines.

"Cobra, this is Palerider.... Are you guys in contact with the
enemy? Over."

"Roger that, Palerider. Be advised, we are under direct attack
from enemy infantry. Alpha and India Batteries are engaged in
direct-fire mode. Bravo Battery will be shooting for you."

That meant that at the same moment the enemy was attacking
us, other enemy units were attacking the Marines who were fifteen miles *behind* us. Those Marines were now fighting for their
lives, just as we were. And it had gotten so bad that the com-
manders back there had ordered one of the six-gun batteries into
direct-fire mode. The giant howitzers, which normally shot toward the sky, would now be lowered, parallel to the ground, so
they could shoot into the faces of the attacking enemy. It was
during this fight that Captain Jason Frei, the Marine who was the
first to greet us as we stepped off the bus at Camp Pendleton a
few months later, lost his right hand.

Then there was a familiar voice on the radio.

"Palerider, we are going to take care of those mortars for you,"
said the confident voice on the other end of the line as gunfire
rang out in the background. It was Major Russo. I grinned and
felt joy in the middle of hell when I heard his voice. He had probably tapped the radio operator on the shoulder and asked for the
handset when he heard what was going on. He was always there

monitoring but wanted me to know that he was going to make everything OK.

A minute or so later, we could hear our artillery barrage landing in a field several hundred yards from us. I knew that we probably had just killed the Iraqi mortar squad that was trying to hit us.

I was glad.

To my left and right, respectively, were Kyle Nickey and Waldo, seated so close inside the vehicle that our elbows were overlapping. In front of each of us, the same thing—two large radios bolted to the wall, four inches in front of our faces. The small flat-surfaced working space that was just below the radios rubbed the tops of our knees. Our flak jackets and helmets were on at all times. None of us was able to move freely when we were seated at the radios like this.

We had been sitting in these seats almost continuously for days. Not a second of sleep. Only time to piss during the security halts.

This thing is a giant coffin.

It was getting to be night now, and the intelligence officer read a report out loud that there might be a regiment of Republican Guard tanks headed our way. *A regiment of tanks.* That was too many. We didn't have enough antitank missiles for that many tanks, and we'd lost the use of our Cobra gunships with their Hellfire missiles because they couldn't fly in the dust storm. When the enemy discovered that the Marines were attacking north along Route 7, they sent their forces south from the big cities like Al Kut to hit us. That was most likely who we were fighting.

Then everything else seemed to go silent as *we heard it* as it flew just over the top of our vehicle.

The sound of certain death.

The exhaust from the missile sounded like the fryer where they make the French fries at McDonald's.

There was a stillness. *A falling.* A pause for a few seconds as each of us processed what was happening. Somebody said it was probably a Sagger—a Russian-made antitank guided missile. It was designed to pierce armor and liquefy everything inside. And it was guided, which meant that whoever shot it was *steering* it at us. At the vehicle with the seven antennas on it.

My world was now a wet cardboard box. Full of heavy things like this vehicle and the regiment of enemy tanks and the rain that had come in the night. And I was waiting for the bottom to drop out of it. The next missile would hit us and everything around me would explode. The last thing I would ever see would be these two radios that were four inches in front of my face. I would hear a scream and feel the pain and then blackness.

Jesus, I hope I don't burn.

I stared at the radios and thought of the others who like me were stuck in their own coffin. Waiting for it. It is a bad feeling to believe absolutely that you are about to die in a few seconds. That somewhere in the flow of the next few moments, you *will* explode. The lieutenant in his dugout shelter underneath the trench at the Battle of the Somme in the fall of 1916. The artillery barrage hits and rages above as he watches the dust fall from the support beam on the ceiling. Waiting for the collapse that will bury him alive. The submariner in 1943 standing silently, his arms against the bulkhead, looking down, not breathing, waiting, praying, hoping that the next depth charge won't crush them all in the tube at 175 feet. Dreading the water and the crushing and the clawing. Or the gunner in the back of the B-17 bomber over Europe in 1944—plane hit, engine on fire, and *worried about that wing.* He had seen his buddy's plane spiral and whirl down to the earth with the crew still inside.

I thought of my family and was glad that they had no idea of the mess we were in. I thought of my brothers, Dan working at his desk in New York City and Dave in L.A. practicing in the mirror as he prepared to play his next part. Of my father talking to one of his worried patients, trying to break the bad news of the cancer gently and with hope. Of my mother carrying the mail down the hallway and thinking about her sons and looking at the picture of us smiling and happy in 1984. That hallway where we had said good-bye. That hallway and that last moment—the end of our time together. And I thought of third grade when a substitute teacher, Mrs. England, came in one day and said that no one could speak except in case of fire, flood, or earthquake. But Mrs. England, what if they're shooting guided missiles at us?

Well, I might as well get it on film when it happens. Maybe somehow the camera will survive and there'll be a record of how we went. I pulled the camera from around my neck, clicked Record, and wedged it sideways between the two radios. Then I forgot all about it. The camera recorded more of the *danger-close* artillery missions we called in, and more power problems with the radios, and the incoming fire, and our fear as we fought back against a determined enemy.

The hours stretched on, and no tanks showed up. At some point we exhaled.

We never figured out whether it was bad intelligence, or old intelligence, or whether the enemy was using psychological warfare against us, or whatever the hell else could've been the source of the report about the regiment tanks. But throughout the entire night, we fought against and obliterated the enemy fighters on foot in the tree lines and in the trenches in the fields around us. We hit them with tank fire and artillery. One nineteen-year-old Marine used his Javelin missile launcher to kill two BTR-60 armored vehicles that were heading down the road toward our positions. *The men inside exploded in their coffins.*

The next morning, with the light, I saw the drained faces of the Marines on the line as we prepared to move north. I watched as the light armored vehicles shot the specks of people in the sparse tree line with their 20mm Bushmaster cannons. Every few rounds a tracer would shriek red across the fields. And I watched the M1 Abrams tanks fire their coaxial machine guns into the irrigation ditches. And the cluster-bomb artillery shells with their *pop* and then the *crackle crackle crackle* and the white-and-yellow sparkle shower as the bomblets rained onto the fields around us.

It was sad and it was violent and it was beautiful.

Finally the shooting died down, as did, for the moment, the fear of our world suddenly exploding.

Chapter Seven

THE DETAILS OF MANY of the scenes from the war were still very sharp in my mind and watching the footage there with CC made them even sharper. Together, she and I watched the forty minutes or so of the uncut footage that the camera had taken when I'd wedged it between the two radios during the battle outside of the Iraqi town of Ash Shatrah. It was strange to watch the footage from the time that I thought we were all going to die. Watching that video again felt like returning to the scene of a crime. Not because we'd done anything illegal, but because my mind had tried to disassociate itself from those hours.

So CC and I continued through that first night. When we hit some of the very bad and ugly stories, her typing would slow and she would glance over quickly as if to check on me. To check that I was still there. And at first, when I got to the bad stories and the thoughts that went with them, when I was saying them out loud and describing them and reliving them, I worried that they would shear away pieces of me. Like shrapnel.

At the end of that first night, I walked the thirty blocks home. After ten hours or so of telling the stories to CC in the cramped editing suite, I needed some air. We'd worked all the way through the night and it was early morning, just before dawn. The streets and sidewalks were mostly empty. I was ex-

146

hausted. And underneath the exhaustion was the nervousness of the battlefield. The fear had found its way back into me. My eyes darted from alley to alley. Watching and waiting for the muzzle flashes from the windows. To the rooftops. Searching for Middle Eastern men with rocket-propelled grenades. A helicopter flew high above the city. The sound of its rotors reverberating off of the windowed walls of the buildings around me. Through canyons of glass and concrete. A fruit truck, on its way to make a delivery to some uptown market, sped by. There was a loud boom as the truck drove over the thick metal slabs covering a hollow construction hole at an intersection on Fifth Avenue. My fists clenched and I grasped at my right for the rifle on an assault sling that was not there.

While sleeping that day, I dreamt of an abandoned stone cathedral far up in the mountains. The mountains of the high desert in Afghanistan. The mountains of the western slope of Colorado. An undecided place fabricated in my mind out of necessity. A mind trying to make sense of it all. That remote mountain spot a door between two uninvited worlds that were now colliding. Intruding upon one another.

The air thin and quiet. The sky perfectly blue.

My rifle leaned against the wall behind me. The walls of hard stone and the floor of fine desert dust that would linger in the air behind us as we walked. The radio chattered in the corner with the banter back and forth from some Marine squad out on patrol. The bright desert sun shined through the bare window. Me in full desert battle gear. My tan boots the color of the deerskin wallet my mom and dad bought me in the Arizona cowboy town we visited when I was five. A tourist town where it was the cowboys versus the Indians. My first sense of what the world wanted us to believe about the good guys versus the bad. When as kids we would shoot each other with our fake plastic revolvers. *Pew-Pew. Pow-Pow.*

Cubby was there, in the cathedral. Sitting inside on a simple wooden chair in front of the window. Looking out over the miles of nothing in the desert bowl in front of us. Smiling as usual. And Major Russo was there, studying a map that hung on the wall next to the radio. And so was Tim Lynch. Quietly filling his magazines with ammunition. Preparing to take his grunts out on patrol through the Afghani villages far outside the safety of our perimeter. Not yet knowing that his younger brother had fallen.

On my knee sat a young boy. I did not recognize him.

"Daddy, do you have to go now?"

"I'm sorry, buddy. I have to go to work now."

The boy, who I guess was my son, was holding the worn and dusty American flag patch I'd bought from the ship's store the night before we flew into Afghanistan. I'd bought it so that I could carry it with me and eventually someday give it to one of my children. He hugged me tightly and looked away for a second at the rifle that was leaning against the wall. When he looked back at me, his dead eyes were black and burned and hollow. His teeth turned to fangs and he jumped at me, jaws snapping.

I awoke from the dream feeling shaken. I guessed that kind of weird shit was what the constant fear of death did to a person. The weeks and months or years of multiple combat deployments. Sometimes the fear was in your face, like when the Sagger missile flew just overhead and you could feel death's hot breath upon you. At other times, like during patrols, the danger was still very real but less apparent.

The constant fear was an assault on one's brain chemistry, as the neural pathways that carried the toxic and hard chemicals of fear and dread grew stronger. The needle was always either pinned in the red, when the bullets flew and luck and a few inches meant all the difference, or at half-mast in the yellow, when the enemy was hidden but you could still feel their presence lurking and watching everywhere.

And the aftermath, the price of all of this after you came home, was a ticket straight to the bottom of the sea. First descending among the shadows. Then down far past even the shadows and into the black where the mean creatures and the nightmares live.

I headed into the bathroom and splashed some water on my face, thinking about the dream and everything that CC and I had talked about. And as I stood there in front of the mirror looking truly into my hollow self, I came to a realization.

I really was fucked up from the war.

By doing things like beating cabdrivers, I was destroying myself. My own thoughts and my own actions had become the enemy.

It was as if I'd been slowly dissolving my brain in acid since I'd come home. The soft flesh and the meaning gone. So now just a metal skull with edges of bone sharp and evil and unloving. I had been sitting out there on the edge for too long looking out across the gray sky. Muscle and skin now hardened to stone and bleached and worn away by the elements as the cobwebs slowly accumulated in front of my dead eyes.

Officers and men who permit themselves to be surprised deserve to die, I thought. A quote from Marine Corps officer training. My favorite. You know the stakes of the game when you start to play it. But these things had snuck up on me. And I had let it all happen.

I can't live like this anymore.

So decide, right now, one way or the other.

I would feel ashamed if they knew I did it.

Make it look like an accident.

But they will know anyway.

So then say "Fuck it" and do the swan dive.

But I will destroy the lives of Mom and Dad.

Stop being a pussy. Stop whining. You are weak.

Fuck you. I am not weak. I am a Marine. I fought in two wars.

You are scared to die.

I am not scared to die. I'm scared of living like this forever.

That's where you're headed.

Then I want to die.

Good. You deserve to.

But it will destroy the lives of Mom and Dad. And I can't do that to them. I just can't.

Why do you want to die?

Because there were no weapons of mass destruction. And there is no joy. Just the rage. And the sadness and the faces.

So what.

What do you mean, so what? There were no fucking weapons. And that was the point of the whole goddamn war.

You didn't start the war. You just fought it. And volunteered to fight it a second time.

But it ended up being all for bullshit.

For you it wasn't. You believed what they told you. What they sold you. You did it for Mom and Dad and Dave and Dan and the people on the subway. And you did it for Beth. You did it for your buddies. And you didn't have to do it. But you did it. And you fought well. Like a warrior. And your honor is clean.

My honor is shit. Everything is shit.

No it isn't. When the chips were down you pushed them all across the table—like any Marine would. You fought with honor. You fought alongside the best. You denied the white-phosphorus artillery shells that would burn at 5,000 degrees when the young Marines requesting them were being too aggressive, so the deaths of the people they were shooting at wouldn't be so brutal. The deaths would be terrible but would maybe be quicker, and the people would not burn, as they would have from the white phosphorus. And you shut down the friendly-fire barrage that day in Baghdad. You saved lives. Remember?

Yes.

And Captain Griffin from Alpha Company shook your hand and looked you in the eye and said thank you. And Captain Moran said, "You saved the day, Scotti. You saved the day." Those are honorable things. They are pure. Purer than most things.

Remember when Casey's father called you and said, "Thank you for bringing my son home alive"? What could be more important than that? And the letters from the strangers after they put your address up on the wall in the Post Office while you were still deployed. Strangers thanking you and pouring their heart out for you and sending you packages. The letter from the firefighter who tore the patch off his uniform and mailed it to you saying, "We are with you."

And don't you remember the day on the ship on the way to Afghanistan when you had that odd conversation at lunch with that shady guy who reminded you of a younger version of Rumsfeld? The guy who wore civilian clothes except for his tan combat boots that were too big for him. And you didn't trust him because his energy was off and he said, "The joke in the White House is that boys go to Baghdad, and men go to Tehran." Remember how you didn't think much of it at the time except that it did seem strange? So it was all out of your hands from the beginning anyway. And you can spend the rest of your days grinding down and down until there's nothing left, or you can kill yourself and destroy the lives of the two people whom you care most about, or you can do what the vet on the trading floor told you to do—try to let it all go.

I don't know.

You are not weak. You are a fighter. You have just bloodied yourself. If you don't want to do it, then you are going to have to fight. Take things slowly. Think like a Marine officer. Outsmart the problem.

But how do you fight yourself when your own thoughts are the enemy?

The following night, Kristian, CC, and I sat at the conference table at the office around nine p.m., eating the Chinese food we'd ordered for dinner. We would start things in the early evening and work until the next morning, because the production offices weren't crowded then with corporate clients and deliverymen and people who were not working on the film. Plus, the three of us, and Marc also, all seemed to be night owls anyway.

And for some reason it seemed easier to tell my stories at night. My mind had begun to process all of the footage and memories that CC and I'd discussed the night before. And I was feeling both terrible and reflective at the same time.

"You know, I can remember almost the exact moment I became a veteran. I can remember exactly how I felt when the reality of *what war is*...just seemed to envelop me. Like you could feel the kick. It was weird. And what's even weirder is that it's in the footage. I captured that moment on video."

Kristian, eating his steamed chicken and broccoli with brown rice, paused for a second, and looked over at CC.

"Let's take a look at that footage once we're done eating."

So a few minutes later, the three of us sat in the editing suite and scrolled through the video. As I watched my memories flash by on the screen, I saw the faces of guys I knew who'd been wounded after I took the video.

It felt strange to watch them because in the footage they had no idea what was going to happen to them. It felt like I was looking at something that I wasn't supposed to be looking at.

"Here it is. This is the scene," I said. Then the three of us sat and watched, and I narrated as CC typed.

———

It was when we first popped our heads out of the vehicle after driving through An Nasiriyah. The Marines in the turrets had been shooting all the way through the city as our convoy rolled north in the night. Just a few miles north of the city, we halted, where the Light Armored Vehicle Battalion had screened out in front of us. In the morning light, we saw a field of maybe twenty corpses next to us. No one spoke about them. But we all looked at them. And we all felt them. Each of us alone for a moment with private thoughts. Some of the dead were on their backs, some on their stomachs, and some just kind of thrown in unnatural positions.

The Cobra gunship helicopters were flying in pairs, one behind the other, in slow circles, just below the low-hanging dark clouds that filled the sky. Shooting their cannons while they tried not to crash into the high-tension wires that ran along the side of the highway. I flipped the video camera on, started filming, and said, "You can still smell the burning fires, and it is a very distinct smell. It smells like...I don't know what it smells like, but it's very distinct. There's dead everywhere...this is fucking *war*." And you could even hear it in my voice on the tape, it was the way I said *war*. Like I'd finally seen the true horror.

At the time I shot the footage, we'd been awake and either driving or fighting for days at that point, and were beginning to feel the effects. It would be another two days before we got any real sleep. Everything seemed to have a gray tint to it, like some midwinter silver gelatin photograph. We could all sense that the enemy was just beyond our reach, hiding, waiting.

We talked about the different types of rocket-propelled grenade rounds. I wondered if the supply officer for the Iraqi Republican Guard had ordered the regular high-explosive rounds or the much more effective antiarmor rounds, complete with shaped charges that would cut through our amtrac with ease. I imagined thousands of them being handed out in the weeks just before the war to eager warriors who wanted to blow up the American Marines. And I imagined that one had my name on it.

Maybe I'd be blown to pieces and end up like what was left of the people we'd just seen on the side of the road. Maybe one would hit our amtrac. We would be standing on the seats inside, with our upper torsos exposed through the overhead hatches. My legs and balls would be blown off. Maybe shrapnel would take off an arm. Or the fuel tank would explode and I would be burned. Maybe I would get shot by a sniper, the round splattering pieces of my skull and brain all over Kyle Nickey. These were the kinds of thoughts that were cycling through your mind all the time, until they became just the normal state of being.

But now that the Cobras were there and it was daylight, it was a bad time to be an Iraqi soldier anywhere near that road. Just a few minutes later, the Cobras spotted more troops manning heavy machine guns to the north who were waiting to ambush our convoy as we drove up the highway. The helicopters looked like sharks swimming effortlessly through the air. The enemy troops hadn't realized how exposed they were to airborne attack as they waited for us in their trenches. So, we watched as the Cobras took turns making gun runs on them. Really chopping them to pieces. Those troops died by the dozens.

———

And I remember seeing something very similar as to what happened to me, happen to this other guy. I saw the moment that an officer, a young captain just a few years older than me, became a veteran. The moment his eyes shifted and his energy forever changed. And when it then happened to me, because I'd seen it happen to someone else, I knew exactly what it was.

———

Our convoy halted about two miles south of An Nasiriyah as the fires burned along the cityscape. We were in the middle of the city dump, which stretched almost to the horizon, and there were millions of flies that swarmed over everything. The smoke and dust from the burning city and the stench of the rotting garbage filled the air around us. The cannon artillery cracked without warning as the Marines in the city called for supporting fire. We stepped out of the back of our amtrac among the fields piled high with garbage, and again the artillery cracked. "Wooo-hoooo!" yelled Major Casado after looking around for a second. His yell caused us all to pause and become completely present in the utter intensity and black energy of the moment. Six Army Blackhawk helicopters passed overhead. Each with a large red cross painted on its side. Each headed north to retrieve the broken bodies of young men.

Six is a lot of them, I thought.

Major Casado filled us in on what was going on ahead of us, and I scribbled notes in my palm-size waterproof notebook.

"Task Force Tarawa has taken over 50 casualties. They ran into a well-prepared defense set by the Al Fedayeen. Tanks, RPGs, small arms, and ZSU-23s [Russian-made antiaircraft vehicles] to defend the bridges. Our units in the city didn't have enough fuel to maneuver properly. The supporting artillery battalion is below 50% on ammunition. They purposely targeted our ambulance 'tracs. They are wearing black pajamas, and will fight until they are killed."

More reports surfaced from regimental headquarters and from BBC World Service that we listened to on the handheld shortwave radio that my parents had given me the year before. I was going to carry it with me on the yearlong around-the-world backpacking trip that I thought I was going to take when I got out of the Marine Corps. But that year there was to be no trip. That year, for me, there was only the war.

First Battalion, Second Marines, had been rammed by a fertilizer truck. They were still engaged in heavy fighting north of the canal that skirts the northern edge of the town. The Fedayeen were snatching civilians and forcing them to fight. Eight enemy T-55 tanks had been killed in the area, along with troop-carrying BTR-60s and other armored vehicles. BBC reported that U.S. troops had been taken prisoner and were being paraded on television. One of them was a female.

I knew that our families were scared right now. Glued to the TV, wondering if their child was one of the unlucky ones. An emergency resupply convoy drove quickly past us on the road. Trucks loaded with fuel and ammunition. Drivers wide-eyed and knowing that the speed of their arrival meant in a very real way life or death. Without ammunition the Marines to the north of the city would die. The drivers had learned about the emergency resupply in logistics school and maybe they thought *We'll never actually do that*, but now it was the first goddamn week of the war and they were already doing it.

Our battalion commander, Lieutenant Colonel John Mayer, spoke to us: "Our mission is to push through the city of An Nasiriyah as quickly as possible and to continue the attack up Route 7 towards Baghdad. There are two bridges that we need to cross. One over the Euphrates River that marks the southern edge of the city, and one over the canal that marks the northern edge of the city."

He paused and looked at me.

"Scotti, I want us to push a rolling barrage through the city."

"Roger that, sir."

"The battalion's movement will be at ten kilometers per hour [six miles per hour]. Plan to shift your fires to match that speed."

A technique developed in World War I—a war bloodier and more brutal than any previous war—the rolling artillery barrage is a wall of shrapnel and steel created by firing a large number of shells in a line simultaneously. Then, either at a preplanned time or at the command of the forward observer, the guns shift and shoot at a target a little further away, and the wall of steel rolls as the guns shift. The infantry "pushes" the wall; that is, they would follow just behind it. Terrified enemy soldiers left in the rubble might think it's over but then would immediately face machine-gun and rifle fire and hand grenades and bayonets and whatever else we could think of using to kill them.

I spread my map on the hood of a Humvee and studied the route we were to take between the two bridges. As I marked the spots for the linear targets that would form each section of the wall for the rolling barrage, a young captain from the regiment came up behind me.

"Lieutenant Scotti, what are you doing?" he asked.

"Sir, I'm setting the linear targets for a rolling barrage along our route—for when we push through the city."

"You can't just fire artillery into a city like that."

"This is what battalion has asked for, sir."

The look on his face at first was disbelief. Then confusion. Then pain. I watched him become, at that moment, a veteran. I watched him as his brain recalibrated itself. He realized that this was not summer camp. Not a fucking game. This was a war. And the helicopters that were flying over us with the red crosses on the side were going to pick up dead and wounded Marines. And yes, we were about to shoot artillery into a real live city with real live people in it. And some of the people were the bad men who were against us. And some of them were the people who just lived there. Scared and clutching their children and hiding under the kitchen table. But that wouldn't save them. Not from our artillery.

The captain looked at me, his brow furrowed, then turned his head and gazed out over the burning cityscape. He paused for a moment as if he was going to say something, then quietly went on his way to the next vehicle in the column.

Later, the colonel continued as he spoke with his staff: "If we get hit hard and we think the convoy is going to get bogged down, we will have to expend Bravo Company—dismount the Marines from the amtracs and have them push a few blocks into the city on either side of the road. Push the enemy back a bit so that Alpha and Charlie Companies can pass through. We can't afford to have the entire battalion sucked into a city fight. Our orders are to pass through the city and continue to push north," the colonel said in a commanding tone as our artillery cracked intermittently behind us. The shells arcing above our heads and blasting the city of An Nasiriyah to rubble.

It was the way the colonel said the words *expend Bravo Com-*

pany, so matter-of-factly. There was a straightforward professionalism to his tone. He was a great leader so he obviously understood the gravity of what he was saying. He *knew* what it meant. That many Marines would die. It was the calculated call that he would have to make to save the rest of the battalion if it came to that. I always admired him for that. I am not sure if I would have been able to make that call if I had been in his shoes. Even though it was the right one.

A few days later, I ran into one of the company gunnery sergeants, and he told me that during one of the firefights of the last few days, a young Iraqi woman had gone into labor near one of their checkpoints. When the doc got there to help take care of things, another lady had brought her baby, hoping to get medical attention. The baby's hand had been ripped to ribbons by shrapnel.

He also told me that he thought it was so strange to see young Marines manning the checkpoints and talking about video games. And some of the Meals Ready-to-Eat that we lived off of had powdered flavored drink mixes in them that were meant to be dumped into your canteen. Marines would tear the tops off the powder packets, add just a few spoonfuls of water, and mix it all into a purple or red or green sludge with the brown plastic spoons that came with the main meal. Then they would eat the sludge like pudding.

The Marines would be sitting at the checkpoints with their eyes glued to the road and their automatic weapons resting at the ready on their bipods. They would be eating their concoctions of cherry pudding or grape pudding or lemon-lime pudding and talking about video games and how nice their high school girlfriend's tits were. Then a vehicle would come barreling down the road, and it wouldn't stop. And the Marines would fire a burst in front of the vehicle to try to get it to stop. But sometimes it wouldn't stop, so the Marines would have to spray the vehicle with bullets and everyone inside would die violently. They would then investigate the vehicle and take whatever action necessary, but then they would eventually go back to manning the checkpoint with their eyes glued to the road and their automatic weapons resting at the ready on their bipods. Eating their concoctions of cherry pudding or grape pudding or lemon-lime pudding and talking about video games and thinking of how nice their high school girlfriend's tits were.

"What happens, CC, is, in a war…with these young guys, and me included, I guess…well, you just lose your innocence. And I don't think that you can ever get that back once it's gone. There are all of these things that happen in a war that just strip it all away. Of course there's the killing. That's the biggest. And the second biggest is the fear. Fear of being ripped to pieces or fear of fucking up and getting your own guys killed. And then there is a new type of fear when you realize that there is someone out there, hunting you. Some living, thinking human being who wants to see you dead and hang your limbless corpse from a bridge. And that is just such a foreign feeling to most people—that moment when you look out into the night and realize that the boogeyman is real. And the only way to not become the prey is to become the hunter.

"And then there are all these other things, horrible things, that happen. Things that can happen in an instant, or things that you hear have happened to other people just up the road from you."

CC looked at me kindly, and I felt at ease, so I decided to keep going.

"Like there was this intelligence report we heard that just really disturbed me. It was in the first few days of the war as we fought north along Route 7 toward Baghdad. We spent most of the daylight hours with our upper halves exposed through the tops of the vehicle. Because we wanted eyeballs. We wanted as many eyeballs as possible constantly scanning everything around us. And then we heard an intelligence report that the enemy was stringing wires across the roads to decapitate Marines as we drove along, exposed on the tops of our vehicles.

"Stringing wires. Across the road. To slice off our heads.

"And I remember thinking that because I was shorter than pretty much everybody else, maybe the wire would *catch me in the mouth*. And there would be that half second when I would actually know what was happening to me. I would feel the wire slice through the corners of my mouth, where the upper and lower lips come together, and then through my cheeks and then all the way back."

CC was typing away, and from the look on her face, I knew she understood clearly what I was talking about. I continued.

"And then we got orders from Division Headquarters: Marines will not throw candy or anything else to Iraqi children from moving vehicles. Word was that somewhere in the country a Marine in a convoy threw some candy to a group of Iraqi kids gathered on the side of the road. When the Marine threw the candy, because of the wind or because he threw it wrong or whatever, it ended up in the middle of the street. One of the kids ran out to pick it up. But there was a vehicle behind the one from which the Marine threw the candy, and the child was immediately crushed beneath it.

"So here you have a situation where you have a dead child whose life has ended in one of the worst ways I can think of, and parents who will be forever devastated because they have lost their child, and the Marine who was just trying to be nice who was now going to have to carry the weight of that death with him forever, and the Marine who ran the kid over, who also has to carry that with him. And when you hear about these things that are happening on other parts of the battlefield, it all weighs upon you, because you, in some way, are a part of it all.

"And there were more stories from other units that we heard just after they'd happened. Marines being run over at night as they slept on the ground next to the large amtracs. The Marines catching whatever sleep they could but then suddenly ripped to pieces by the large tracks of the vehicle because the driver didn't know that those guys were sleeping there. We heard of two Marines who were killed when they had their heads crushed under the tires of a Humvee as they sat behind their weapons in a fighting hole. Word was that some of the Marines from that unit who had gone out on patrol were in deep trouble and fighting the enemy, and the Humvee was part of a quick-reaction force that was rushing to get to the guys on the patrol, and it ran right over the fighting hole. And we heard stories of Marines dying in helicopter crashes and of Air Force A-10s mistaking Marine amtracs for enemy vehicles, and strafing them with their 30mm cannons and just...just shredding those poor guys who were inside.

"Friendly fire is a whole different level of hell. It is just a pure fucking waste. You'd never know if it was the result of ignorance or mistakes or incompetence, or confusing combat conditions and exhaustion, or just bad luck. But think about the parents and spouses of those who are killed by friendly fire. They don't even get solace in the fact that their loved ones died fighting the enemy. Their loved ones died because somebody made a mistake. And think about the guys who are responsible for friendly fire and what that will do to their psyche for the rest of their lives. It's just... fucking bad. Probably the worst thing I can think of.

"Just before we pushed across the border at the beginning of the war, General Mattis, the commander of the First Marine Division, spoke to our regiment. He mentioned a quote that he attributed to Geronimo: 'In war, bad things happen.' He couldn't have been more fucking right."

I took a break for a few minutes to go use the restroom. As I washed my hands, I thought about how everything seemed to be coming into focus. I was beginning to get some perspective: like how nice it was to have a sink with warm running water to wash my hands in and not have to worry about getting killed while I went to the bathroom. When I got back to the editing suite, I mentioned this to CC.

"You know, even things like hygiene become terrible in a war. I remember when we were still in Kuwait, waiting and wondering if and when the war was going to start, there was this one really good-looking female officer who had taken the ship over with us. We all tried not to stare at her whenever we saw her because she was hot and there were very, very few women around. A beautiful woman in the middle of all that was like a goddess. She was married, though. In the military, adultery is a big no-no; you will get totally smashed to pieces by the military legal system if you're caught messing around.

"Anyway, she was stationed at Camp Matilda, and she came over to our grunt camp for a meeting or whatever. I saw her at the camp that day and was like, taken aback. She had caught a weird rash and had these big sores all over her face. Open sores with yellow pus. I don't know whether it was chafing from the wind or some bacterial infection or what, but the goddamn desert, the war gods, just fucked her face right up. Like a leper's. To the point where you didn't even want to look at her. And she was hot; she had been this cute girl. And I was just thinking, *How fitting was that?* This place where we were just ruined her within a few weeks. Stripped her beauty right off. You could feel her shame and embarrassment, and I remember thinking how terrible that must have been for her."

CC reached up and touched her face, and I could see her imagining herself in the woman's position.

"Even back before Iraq, back in 2001, when we were in Afghanistan, we had spent all that time out in the desert and hadn't showered in months. Then we got back to the ships and were heading for Australia and then home, and I remember, right before I took my shower on the ship, I took off my desert cammies. And as I did, I felt something sprinkling down onto the floor at my feet. It was several weeks' worth of flakes of my dry skin that I had shed inside my clothes. There was so much of it that when I swept it up, there was enough to make a small pile."

Every night was the same. CC and I would spend hours in the editing room watching the footage as I drank my beer to open the gates. It was clear that her heart belonged to another man, and that was good, because it made things uncomplicated between us. But CC had the soul of a mother. Like Meredith's, one that was warm and kind and unjudging. And because of it, it was much easier to open up. CC and Kristian had created a safe place for me to become *vulnerable*. To get it all out. To flush the dark water from my mind and get it out into the open.

I'd tried to get across to her what it was like to see those things that were rattling around inside of my head in the time after the war. The things that had come up from the depths during those moments when I just couldn't keep them away. The dead children. The looks on the faces of the crawling wounded Iraqis who knew they were probably going to soon die. The Navy corpsman trying to help them. The utter destruction of entire neighborhoods. The terrified families hiding. The old folks wandering, confused, through the gunfire. The hammering and ringing in your ears from all the firing. The boiling heat and the exhaustion. The fear of making a mistake. The slicing edge of the jagged steel shrapnel. The heaviness of air sharp with danger. The squawk of the voices over the radios that meant the very real possibility of imminent death. The consequences. The physical vulgarity of dismemberment. The permanence of disfigurement. The shame of survival.

CC and I hit every line of the master list of thoughts and scenes and stories, which now stretched to over ten pages. I would talk and pace back and forth as the coffee and alcohol pulsed through my veins and she would tap away at the keyboard and write everything just as it came from my mind. She already had typed more than seventy-five pages of nearly stream-of-consciousness thoughts, and we'd been at it for only a few days. Stories would lead to other stories and memories, and then those would get added to the master list, so it was like we were caught in a current that was dragging us backward. Many of the nights ended only when the beer ran out and I'd be empty and too far gone as I'd close my eyes and rest my head on my folded arms on the editing table.

But then after that first week or so, something happened. I no longer dreaded our nightly sessions. I began to look forward to them. Because it felt good to know that there was at least one other person in my city who had a good idea of what I had been through. And after Kristian read through what CC and I put down on paper during the Purge, there were two people who knew. Then it actually felt kind of good to talk about these things.

I was a settler who had come to a new world and endured my first long winter. A settler who sensed that the weather was starting to change and for the first time knew that spring would soon be there and that he might actually live to see it.

I realized that all of those memories I feared, which had been sucking the life from me, were not as dangerous as I'd thought. They were still there, and they were ugly, but they had no teeth. They were part of a past life that I would never again have to live. As CC and I went through the footage and I spoke about it, their grip on me began to weaken.

As I sensed that the cold would break, I gradually felt something starting to grow inside me. It was barely perceptible at first, but after eight or nine sessions, I was more sure of it. It was not the war cancer. Something else—a sprout, or a small flower. With a stem that was growing more each day, bending and turning ever so slightly toward the light.

One night I thought of how it was the flow of chemicals through my brain that had made me like this. Just as how the harshness of the primitive combat conditions would wear away at physical things. How neighborhoods that took generations to build and people that took years to grow could be destroyed in moments by squeezing a trigger or keying a spring-loaded plastic button on the side of a radio handset and calling down screaming shells.

I knew it would take time to get better. But at least now I understood that something was wrong. I'd shunned the services at the VA hospitals, and I had a lot of mistrust of the bureaucracy of the VA in general. I remembered that lady at Camp Pendleton who gave the speech about the effects of PTSD. I remembered her indifference, her annoyance, her lack of empathy. And I imagined myself sitting in front of some bureaucrat who didn't care either way, trying to pour out my heart and soul. I knew there were good people who worked there, people who cared, who dedicated their lives to helping veterans, some who were veterans themselves, but based on what I'd seen at Camp Pendleton, I just wasn't willing to take that chance.

I slept days that first week of the Purge, and my dreams became much more vivid as parts of my mind that I hadn't used in years came back to life. I looked in the mirror and saw that my face was puffy and my eyes dark and hollow.

You look like you're fifty years old, I thought. *You and your brain seem toxic.* It was from too much booze.

So that next night with CC, I decided to skip the booze. And I decided to skip even the coffee. All natural, without any chemicals. And that night, our output was as good as on the nights when I had drunk the beer. I didn't want to look like I was fifty years old, because once you do that to yourself with booze, you can't ever undo it. *Booze only on the weekends from here on out— as a reward for the week*, I promised myself.

I drank water and felt strong, and CC joked that we were a fire team on a mission, and when she said that I felt like we were winning. I felt that the momentum of the thoughts and memories was enough now that we were with the current.

———

Kristian asked us to cover some of how it was like in the time just before the war. So I told CC a bit about what it was like just before we deployed and how combat changes a person forever. Just like aging and parenthood. The changes are permanent.

———

"The building manager in the apartment complex in San Clemente, California, where I lived while I was stationed at Camp Pendleton, had been a helicopter pilot in the First Air Cavalry Division in Vietnam. I lived directly above him for three years. Just before we shipped out for Iraq, he told me a story about flying helicopters in formation into a landing zone that was completely surrounded by the enemy. A few—his buddies' helicopters—had been hit with rocket-propelled grenades and had exploded in the air in front of him and then crashed violently to the ground as the formation descended into the zone to drop off the soldiers.

"'Those guys...those guys on the ground...they saved my life,' he said as he cried twenty-five years later.

"I didn't want to end up like him, his brain chemistry and his entire being cobbled together with medications. Always just one day from the end—one story, one drink, one flashback waiting to send him over. There was no more rage left in him. Only the sadness left now. A man made of tissue paper—like you could just poke a hole right through him.

"But he was brave. He lived through the pain and the memories of hell for two and a half decades. He woke every morning and got dressed and lived his life. And I now know, sort of, what that must feel like.

"But you know, being in the military, especially when you're young, can really alienate you from civilians. I felt it even before the war.

"There was one night just after the time when my building manager told me the story about Vietnam. It was the night when we first drew our desert pattern camouflage uniforms from the battalion's tin supply shack at Camp Pendleton, just a few days before we shipped out for Iraq. We hadn't had time to get our name tapes and U.S. Marine Corps patches sewn onto them. And without the names and patches, we were just more warm bodies inside uniforms that had been held in storage for years waiting for the inevitable desert war.

"After we had finished work for the day, I had headed home to my apartment. It was around ten p.m. on a Tuesday. We were set to deploy to Kuwait on Friday. My neighbors in the apartment a few doors down from me were partying. There were six or seven of them, all around my age, crowded into the front room of the apartment, with the front door wide open. They were the typical young Southern California skater/surfer local-types who absolutely hated Marines. I walked by the doorway in my desert camouflage pants and shirt and wide-brimmed boonie hat that was just a bit too large for my head. The light and their voices and the music from the stereo radiated out into the night. As I walked by the doorway, the conversation hushed. It was the type of pregnant pause that means that people are waiting for you to get out of earshot. One of the girls laughed loudly as she held the can of beer in her hand.

"'Ten four, good buddy!' she yelled mockingly just after I passed the doorway."

Why did they hate us so much? Maybe it was because we had to get these stupid haircuts every week. Or because we were not from Southern California. Or maybe it was because we got drunk in bars and started fights with their boyfriends, our young blood filled with testosterone and brought to a boil each week training with automatic weapons and high explosives and grueling twenty-mile combat-readiness speed hikes with eighty pounds of crap in the packs on our backs. In the movies about World War II, the ladies always wanted the men in uniform—the fighting men, who were *men*. But during the last fifty years, things had shifted, maybe not so much in the South or the Midwest, but definitely along the West Coast and to some extent, in the Northeast. Now the ladies seemed to ignore the men in uniform. The uniform and everything it represented seemed to repulse them. They wanted the surfers and the guitar players and the drummers. And the guys with the bags of really good weed who didn't disappear for a year at a time to go fight a war.

I walked to the door of my apartment. I put the key into the lock and turned the handle. I opened the door and flipped the light switch that had been partially painted over when they had repainted the walls before I'd moved in. The lights did not work. The power company had switched off the electricity on the wrong day. So I started to pack my gear by flashlight and by the small slivers of light, from the party down the hall, that shined through the window.

Chapter Eight

IT WAS AFTER MIDNIGHT, well into the second week of the Purge. CC and I had made very good progress that night and our two-man team felt strong. I looked through the list of stories that we were hoping to cover that night, noticing which ones were left.

"I've been thinking a lot about these next two stories. I've been kind of...reflecting on them for a bit. They're both from the notes in my journal—Item 102. *Missing chow* and Item 103. *The garden*. I figured we'd just head right into 102. Sound good?"

"Sounds good to me, Trashcan," CC replied, smiling.

It was the tenth or eleventh day of fighting in Iraq, and most of us were already exhausted. At one of the security halts, I walked along our vehicle column, speaking with some of the haggard, hungry-looking Marines. The shortage of food seemed to be the main topic of conversation. I spoke with a gunnery sergeant who was clearly agitated as he chain-smoked cigarettes.

"You know, sir, I get why there's no chow. Ammo and fuel take priority, and we are moving fast up this here highway. But I'll tell you, sir, something that is *really* fucked up. One of my rifle squads is missing some chow, sir. And you know, because we're running *real low* on chow, we know *exactly* how much we had left for the squad. And no one is sure what happened to it, sir, but all we know is that some of the squad's chow is missing. Now I don't know if it was one of these goddamn foreign translators that's ridin' with us who took it, or one of these Army soldiers that's attached to us, or one of these goddamn civilian attachments that always seems to be passing through our battalion, but I know that Marines don't steal from Marines and somebody's been stealing chow from my boys. If I catch 'em, I'll kill 'em, sir, I swear."

"Jesus, gunny," I said, in disbelief that someone would steal food from a squad of riflemen in the middle of war.

As I walked back to my vehicle, I thought of how I would hate to be the person they caught stealing the food. And I had visions of some dead outsider with a gunshot wound to the head after our next firefight. "Must've been a sniper, sir," the squad leader would say to the officer who came to the scene. And as I thought more about what the gunny had said, the rage grew inside of me. Someone had broken the code of the brotherhood of Marines. We were all hungry and all wanted to eat almost more than anything, but whoever had done it was weak and selfish and had taken the food from the young Marines who were fighting. And I remember thinking that if a Marine or a soldier had done it, I would gladly help beat the shit out of him. And if it had been one of the non-Marine outsiders, like a foreign translator or a civilian attachment, then just maybe it would be alright to shoot him in the fucking head during the next firefight and blame it on a sniper. At that moment, it seemed reasonable and fair.

I might've even pulled the trigger myself.

A glance from CC brought me back to the present. I think it was the look on her face when I said "I might've even pulled the trigger myself" that brought me back. It was clear by the way I said those words that the anger I felt toward the person who'd done it was still real and still inside of me. CC could sense that I really meant that I might've executed someone for stealing food. And her look gave me the perspective of what I had reflected on. That when a person is fighting a war, it changes them so that they become much more violent and lose a piece of their humanity. And at some point, thoughts or actions that are insane can become almost normal.

I continued with item 103, the next story on the list.

"CC, can you scroll to the footage that's just before the river crossing in Baghdad?" We watched a minute or so of the video together, and then I began.

It was morning just outside of Baghdad as our convoy crawled closer to the city with the sky dark and heavy above it. A light rain fell. As other Marines crossed bridges to our southwest, we were to open a second battlefront in the fight for the city. We stood with our feet on the tops of the swivel chairs in the back of the amtrac and looked through the palm trees that were so distinctive to the Fertile Crescent. They stood on the near bank of the Diyala River, an offshoot of the Tigris that flows along the eastern edge of the city. On the far side of the river were the outskirts of Baghdad. The trees had trunks that were thick and intricate and the palm fronds were long and bursting like fireworks above them. A buddy, Jerry Roeder, one of the bravest Marines I ever met, swam across the swift, muddy river. He was a combat engineer and needed to search the far riverbank for mines that could blow our tracks and to make sure that the angle of the bank wasn't too steep, or else our tracks would get stuck trying to climb up it. So he stripped off all his gear and armor and bit down on the 9mm pistol he carried in his mouth as he swam across the river wearing nothing but his T-shirt and pants and boots. There were enemy in the area, and firefights broke out along the line and later we sang "The Marines' Hymn" as we crossed the river in our vehicle while I shot white-phosphorus artillery rounds far downstream to confuse the enemy.

The cruise missiles were long finished now as our jets dropped massive bombs and the entire artillery regiment of fifty-four cannons shot simultaneously to mass on their targets. The entire regiment of cannons pounding and pounding. The fires and smoke rising and the ripping of the shells and buildings falling to rubble with the people inside.

And this one dog came running past us from the direction of the city. He was tan and a bit shaggy and had his head down and was running at full speed. He was running on his instincts and his eyes were terrified and he gave a brief glance up at us as he ran by. *Keep running, dog*, I thought, and a big part of me wished that I was going with him.

Our convoy halted and our vehicle pulled off the road just ahead of a large curve. We needed to pull off a bit farther to the right so our lone machine gun could see as far as possible down the road, which curved sharply to the left. The driver steered the vehicle farther off the road, then spun it to the left, pointing it toward the curve. We were positioned as well as we could be in this exposed spot. And we could see the buildings of Baghdad on the horizon much more clearly now.

But we were in some Iraqi man's backyard. He was clearly not a rich man, given the size of his house and the simple clothing he wore as he stood and watched us from his doorway. There was a child's bike leaning against the house just next to the back door. It was pink and you could tell that it was an old bike, but you could also tell that someone had been tending to it. Giving it the attention it needed to keep the rust from eating it away. Behind the house was a small vegetable garden with four or five rows of vegetables that looked to have been planted several weeks before.

When we spun to the left to position ourselves, we tore his vegetable garden to pieces with the tracks on our vehicle. On the ground behind us, crushed and mutilated plants and stalks of green and yellow and red mash that were now indistinguishable. I saw that the Iraqi man was still standing in the doorway of his house looking at us. There was no emotion in his eyes. Maybe because we were the ones with the guns. *I'm sorry*, I thought. You and your wife are here raising your children and growing your veggies and living a quiet life, and we have just destroyed your beautiful garden. But we needed this spot so that our machine gun could see down the road. I looked at him briefly, and for a few seconds our eyes met. I looked back toward the city.

And I felt nothing.

When CC finished typing, I thought for a moment and then told her what those stories meant to me. I'd been thinking about this during the days between our sessions.

"People are generally good, but when you put them into certain situations, the bad parts of them can come to the surface. This is especially true when you add the conditions of combat to the mix. Physical violence, fear of death, and fatigue will all wreak havoc on a person. And there is no emergency cutoff switch that allows you to quickly unplug yourself from who you were in the

175

war. You almost have to relearn things like compassion and a sense of humanity after you come home. At least, that's how it was for me. That cabdriver was probably just some father and husband trying to provide for his family. Yes, he did hit me with his cab, so some sort of retaliation might've been justified, but nothing like what I'd done to him. If they hadn't pulled me off, who knows how far I would've taken it? The same holds true for the person who was stealing the squad's food. Some sort of punishment would've been in order. But thinking back now on my thought processes and what I saw as a just punishment, it all seems insane. But in the war, it just didn't seem that bad. That's what being around all that violence and killing and fear does to you. As for that Iraqi guy's garden, that was terrible. We had no choice at the time, but looking back, that's one thing that I wish we hadn't done. I understand why we had to be there, but I still just wish to hell we hadn't done it."

I paused for a second to gather my thoughts. CC watched, waiting to type.

"I am not becoming a pacifist. Some wars need to be fought. World War II was one of those wars. But then there are the cowboys, with their bullshit bravado, their false toughness more dangerous than any weapon, their power and their desire to push the button. Guys looking for a fight, like schoolchildren. Sending the loyal and brave youth who love their country into battle, where they kill and forever lose their innocence. Like the young Marines eating their lemon-lime pudding at the checkpoint. Like that gunner in the tank watching the expressions of agony on the faces of the men he was machine-gunning to death through his infrared sights. Or like a young artillery officer who thought that by shelling a country he was preventing another 9/11.

"And there was this one conversation that I heard over there that I just can't get out of my mind. It was the day before we were set to attack the town of Al Kut, Iraq. I stopped by to top off two of my canteens at a large metal tank the size of a cow that had spigots on the sides. It had large rubber wheels and was towed behind one of the trucks in our convoy. Everybody called it the water bull. Two young Marines were talking as they filled their canteens on the side opposite from where I was standing. One was tall and skinny and carried an M16 rifle. The other was short and stocky and carried a squad automatic weapon (SAW, an assault rifle modified to serve as a light machine gun). They were both about nineteen.

"'You ready for MOUT tomorrow?' the one with the SAW asked the other as I was walking away. MOUT stands for military operations in urban terrain. City fighting. They both knew what that meant—that the fighting would be the worst type and that we would lose some Marines. And we all knew that Al Kut was a city of at least a couple hundred thousand people.

"And those two Marines seemed so young and so ready and you could sense that they were just as scared as I was. But they faced their fear like men. Like warriors. And at that moment, I loved them and was proud to fight alongside them, and then I was no longer afraid to die.

"But it can be difficult sometimes, CC, for a veteran. Because you have memories like that moment in your head, and you know that there are young guys over there like those Marines talking by the water bull. And they are just so brave and willing to die for this country and risking it all *every day*. Like, right now, as we sit here, Marines somewhere in Iraq or Afghanistan are in a firefight. They are scared and they are fighting bravely and some of them are hurting because they have been wounded. But then you come home and you see that the war is just in the background, and everyone is just kind of going about their business. Like the war doesn't even exist. It can be really difficult when you hear people complaining about stupid shit and whining all the time about trivial things. Or just acting in general like assholes, you know? Like this guy at the deli today who was freaking out and screaming at the girl behind the counter because she put onions on his sandwich. And she was almost in tears because of the way he was yelling at her, and it makes you wish sometimes that you could've defended only the good people, not the shitty ones. But that's not the way it works. Because when you put on that uniform, you have to be willing to die for whatever they tell you to die for. To the people doing the fighting, the underlying cause gets kind of washed away when the bullets are flying. You're just trying to kill the people who are trying to kill you."

During the fifteen days of the Purge, Meredith and I would take day trips on Saturdays to various neighborhoods around New York City in the afternoons, before I headed into the office to work. There was something special about living in Manhattan, and she was plugged directly into it. We weren't officially dating and usually saw each other only once every few weeks or so, but when we were together, there was a deep connection. One afternoon Meredith asked me if I'd ever been to Coney Island.

"I've never been there."

"Oh, I have to take you there. It's like a rite of passage."

"Alright."

After the long subway ride out from Manhattan to the southern tip of Brooklyn, I got my first glimpse of Coney Island. It was depressing. A shell left over from its heyday. Children's rides that looked abandoned. Most of the stalls and stands and stores along the splintered wooden boardwalk were closed and shuttered. Paint peeling off of walls. Garbage cans rusted. Vacant-looking people milling about, trying to force a good time.

They had this game called Shoot the Freak where some skinny guy would dance around in a face mask in a garbage-filled lot between two of the buildings on the boardwalk. You'd pay a few bucks to shoot the guy with a paintball gun. A group of young kids were laughing as they splattered the Freak with bullets.

Meredith and I walked slowly along the boardwalk under the overcast sky. The beach just past the boardwalk was empty except for a few seagulls pecking in the sand next to the garbage cans that no one used.

"You know, I have always wanted to come here. Thanks for taking me. Even though it's ugly and depressing, it's also kind of beautiful in a way."

Meredith smiled, happy to be the one responsible for the journey. Happy to drag me from my apartment.

Walking slowly toward us from the other direction was a man who looked to be in his eighties. He wore a red hat that said WWII VETERAN on it and had a small Marine Corps eagle, globe, and anchor insignia stitched onto the front in yellow. I stopped for a moment and shook his hand and said, "Thank you for your service, sir," and "Semper Fi," and at first he looked confused, but then he understood and I saw the lights and the memories go on in his eyes and he smiled before continuing slowly on his way.

"I think it's incredible how strong the brotherhood is in the Marine Corps," Meredith remarked.

I paused and thought for a moment.

"The Marine Corps derives its energy and discipline and sense of purpose from the generations of those who went before. When you become a Marine, you become a part of history. You have a responsibility—a very real one—to uphold the honor and traditions of the Corps. So even if you get killed, at least it happened when you were surrounded by your buddies, whom you were fighting for as a United States Marine. At least, that's how the thoughts went through my mind at those times when I thought that the end might be near. And it sounds weird to me to say that out loud now, knowing that Iraq had nothing to do with 9/11. 'Cause even though the politicians are the ones who decided that you should be there, to the Marines at the front, all of that shit is irrelevant. The Marine Corps, and the Marines who serve in it, are what really matter. And you know, becoming a Marine is the greatest thing that I have ever done. It's the thing in my life that I am most proud of."

Meredith smiled as we walked along. Then she spotted a small arcade that was open.

"I think that's the place that has a few Skee-Ball machines in the back."

"Skee-Ball? Excellent. I used to love that game when I was a kid."

"Well, let's go then," she said with a smile.

The next weekend, Meredith took me to another part of the city. She knew I was stuck, and she was trying to shake me loose. To get my blood flowing. To recognize the beauty of our city. And of life.

"Isn't it nice to get out of that stuffy apartment and that tiny editing room and enjoy this wonderful city that we live in? To just be outside? The city is so beautiful this time of year."

"Yeah, I guess you're right."

We headed far uptown to the northern tip of Manhattan. Fort Tryon Park sits high on the bluffs above the Hudson

Me, the proud Marine-to-be, saluting my Mom, circa 1980. (Courtesy Geraldine Scotti)

Happy days: Mom and I, with the BB gun my parents got me for Christmas, circa 1984.
(Courtesy Angelo Scotti)

Happy days: Dad and I on a summer trip to Bar Harbor, Maine, circa 1985.
(Courtesy Geraldine Scotti)

Enlisted-Marine recruit-training graduation, with Drill Instructor Sergeant G. Brady, Parris Island, South Carolina, August 1995. (Courtesy Geraldine Scotti)

Me, Dad, and my brothers Dave and Dan at a New Year's Eve Billy Joel concert at Madison Square Garden, New York City, 1999. (Courtesy Geraldine Scotti)

Marines of Regimental Combat Team One listen as General James N. Mattis (out-of-frame) speaks, Kuwait Desert, March 2003, seventy-two hours prior to crossing the border into Iraq. (Courtesy the author)

There's always time to take a moment during hygiene time for the "I love me" pics: Bill Wooddall, Tom Del Cioppo, me, and Kyle Nickey, south of Al Kut, Iraq, March 2003. (Courtesy Evan Wahl)

Billy, Waldo, and me posing in front of a well-shot-up mural of Saddam Hussein. Billy was wounded a few weeks later. (Courtesy Eric Sibert)

Lieutenant Colonel Joe Russo, Helmand, Afghanistan.
(Courtesy Master Sergeant Jeffrey Finnegan, USMC)

Captain Robert M. Secher, a.k.a. "Cubby," aboard ship in the Arabian Sea, returning from Operation Enduring Freedom, February 2002. (Courtesy Ismael Gallardo)

A market burns amid the chaos in Baghdad, Iraq, April 2003. (Courtesy the author)

Lieutenant Colonel John Mayer, Commanding Officer, 1st Battalion, 4th Marines and me somewhere along Route 7 in Iraq, March 2003. We hadn't slept in days and you can see, in our faces, the effects of the fatigue and combat conditions. (Courtesy Eric Sibert)

Members of our artillery detachment holding the flag that I carried in my pack and gave to my mom after I came home: Terrill Fox, Jiemar Patacsil, John Bridinger, Slade Rohrdanz, Casey Collins (standing); Sean Metz and me (kneeling), May 2003. (Courtesy Raul Nungary)

Heading up the steps to the airplane that would carry us home. The cheap disposable 35mm camera malfunctioned, giving the photo a dark and unfocused haze that was a hint of things to come. (Courtesy the author)

Captain Timothy Lynch
and Lieutenant Matthew
Lynch, Kuwait, 2003.
(Courtesy the author)

Captain Tim Lynch
and me leaving the
wake of 1st Lieutenant
Matthew Lynch, Ver-
non Wagner Funeral
Home, Hicksville,
New York, November
7, 2004. (Courtesy *New
York Daily News*)

Just a few weeks after I returned to the United States, looking skinny: me, Dave, Dad, Mom, and Dan.
(Courtesy the author)

At dinner, the night we signed the film contracts, just a few hours before the taxi driver incident: me, Andrew Torkelson, Marc Perez, Kristian Fraga, and John Sikes.
(Courtesy the author)

At the 2009 Rome International Film Festival, where *Severe Clear* was awarded a Special Mention by the Jury of Cinematic Excellence.
(Courtesy Geraldine Scotti)

River. There are well-worn wooden benches below the leafy branches of the large trees that line the top of the bluff. We sat on one as the breeze rolled gently over us and we enjoyed the view across the river to the Palisades, the cliffs on the opposite bank.

"I had no idea this was even here. It's like we're in a completely different country."

She smiled.

"You know, something that I've been thinking about lately is that in the Western world, what we do to earn a living largely defines, in the minds of others, who we are. So what do you do? is one of the first few questions strangers ask one another when they meet."

She was listening intently, as she always did.

"Like you...people would see you as a young assistant district attorney who lives in Manhattan. That is who you are. Just based on that, people would infer a long list of things about your personality, social habits, level of intelligence, economic level, and a whole bunch of other things. But right now, as far as life goes, I sort of feel like I am nobody. Especially in a city like this, where the first thing people look at is the type of shoes and watch you are wearing.

"It's like when you take off the uniform for the last time, you are actually giving up a large part of who you are. The drill instructors spent all that time in boot camp, breaking us down, then building us back up in the vision of the Marine Corps. So we actually became someone else. Someone better, more disciplined, with a purpose. And when we graduated as freshly minted Marines, we were like shiny new cars on the lot. And after the war and heading home on leave we walked through the airport looking sharp with our medals pinned on our chest. But then, just a bit later, we are driven off the lot, and we become civilians again, and then we are just like everyone else. The wars are fought by someone else. The action and juice and the excitement and danger are now someone else's game. And in this city, when someone asks what you do, you can't say to them "I am a Marine who fought in Iraq and Afghanistan," because that is what you *did*, not what you *do*. So I'm basically invisible here. I am just an out-of-focus shape moving slowly in the background."

"Well, the fact that you fought as a Marine in a war—two wars—is something that no one can ever take away from you."

———

Over the weeks of the Purge, I continued the conversation that I was having with myself about the question How do you fight yourself? Maybe what I really meant was How do you examine and heal yourself? Over the weeks of self-reflection, I slowly began to figure out how I was going to fix things. All that time I was alone after the war, what I needed was a place where it was OK for me to talk about everything that happened. A safe place to be vulnerable. But what I also really needed in that time just after the war was to directly enlist the help of others. To admit that something was wrong and to ask others to help me. To tell someone, truly and directly, all of the things I experienced in the war. To release the pressure that had been building inside of me all that time. And I needed to reflect on the loss of innocence, compassion, and humanity, which can so quickly get swept away in a war. Once I was aware of these things and thinking about them, I needed to start working on undoing the damage that the war had done to my brain chemistry.

———

It was the night of our last session during the Purge, and there was one last story to tell.

It was around the time we started to run out of food. We'd fought our way so deep into enemy territory in Iraq that the re-supply convoys fell too far behind. Many of the convoys were being attacked, and death was never far away from us, so the supply priority was ammunition, fuel, water, parts for vehicles, then food. Then mail.

A helicopter had been summoned to the front lines to carry a part that was needed for one of the vehicles. It also carried some more Marines who would join our unit as reinforcements. The pilot, who I'd imagined was as cool as Waldo was, had done something beautiful. He had grabbed a single bag of mail off the pile that was growing daily, miles to the rear of where we were. One bag was light enough that it didn't make a difference as far as his helicopter was concerned. And I was lucky. There was a letter in it for me. At that moment, the most valuable thing on earth: *news from home.*

I peeled open the letter just as the sun started to sink low in the sky above the Fertile Crescent. *It will be dark soon*, I thought. My filthy hands left smudge marks on the clean white paper of the envelope as sporadic gunfire rang in the distance.

The letter was from my friend Corie, from high school. She was the best friend of a girl I'd dated for three years, and her family and I had grown close over time. She told me about a birthday party they threw for the older brother of another high school friend. They were drinking on the front porch in the spring in Allenhurst, New Jersey. Sitting in the big chairs half a block from the beach and the beer was ice cold from the can and maybe just

183

maybe I would've taken one of the girls from the party up to one of the bedrooms in the house and her breasts would be firm and I would get lucky.

And as I read the letter, the gunfire started up in the distance again and I looked at the next town just on the horizon. *I don't want to go in there*, I thought. I wanted to be on the porch by the beach and then up in one of the bedrooms. But I was glad that there was still a world somewhere that didn't have babies with bloody ribbon-fleshed hands and pieces of children lying in the dirt on the side of the road. A place where there wasn't the fear and the hunger and the tired. The sad and the worry and the dead.

Each of us did a mental inventory of what we had left to eat in our packs. Each cracker a treasure. A main course, if you were lucky enough to have one left, was a feast that was almost unimaginable. We began to eat the creamer packs for the coffee. Drink the tiny half-ounce bottles of Tabasco sauce that were included in what had once been a full meal. The twenty-four-hour combat operations, the stress, and the constant hum of adrenaline through our young conditioned bodies had cost us a lot of calories. And those calories were just not being replaced.

There are people who are forced to live like this every day, I thought. Such a foreign concept to most Americans.

And a true definition of love is when you are starving and you have no idea when the resupply is coming and all you want is any type of food but especially cakes and cookies and candies and pizza and ice cream. And so you say fuck it I'm just going to eat everything I have left, which was just one main meal, so you tear open the olive-drab packaging and dip the brown plastic spoon into the chili and macaroni and it smelled better than anything you've ever smelled before. But then Kyle or Tom or Eric was sitting next to you and he was just as hungry as you were so you pass the olive-drab package back and forth until it is empty.

We were at an extended security halt, and from my pack I took a picture that my mom had sent me the year before when I was in Afghanistan. My mom and dad, my brother Dan, my uncle Bernie, and my cousin Ed were sitting at the kitchen table. On their heads, each wore a helmet from my collection that had been stored safely on the shelves of my childhood bedroom. On the table was a half-eaten chocolate birthday cake with white and blue icing. Stuck into the top of the cake was a small paper American flag on a toothpick. Everyone was smiling proudly. Dan and Uncle Bernie gave thumbs up. Mom and Dad saluted. The helmet my mom wore was the pride of my collection, an original that Marines had worn in World War II. It had a vintage camouflage cover on it with the tan, brown, and green blotches in the pattern worn by the Marines in the Pacific, and a simple eagle, globe, and anchor insignia stenciled on the front. As a boy, I had worn the helmet and imagined being one of the brave Marines who had stormed the beaches through the exploding shells and the machine-gun fire at Iwo Jima or Tarawa. She wore the helmet cocked slightly to the side, just as they did in all of the pictures from the war. Her salute was the kind that a dancer onstage would give, with her fingers separated and splayed outward. I smiled and remembered that when she was eight or nine years old, she used to dance in a small troupe on the boardwalks in Atlantic City.

Then I looked at the cake. There was a piece on the table in the foreground of the picture. It was moist and chocolaty, and the white icing was spread thick in swirls along the top of the piece. *Jesus, what a piece of cake!* I thought.

I felt around deeper in my pack hoping for a miracle. Some

forgotten piece of food like the $20 bill you find in your jeans after you've washed them. There was nothing but an empty package of crackers that had a few remaining crumbs inside. I folded and rolled the package, careful not to spill any of the crumbs, and put it in my pocket.

Our vehicle was parked in a field just off the highway. The rest of the battalion was spread throughout the adjacent fields. Rifle in hand, I walked fifty yards away from the vehicle and out into the field to explore some of the pools of water scattered nearby. I was careful to always stay within sight of our vehicle. The sun was very low now, and the sky was dark blue except for some large white clouds with fluff like mountains of pure cotton on the top where the sun shined on them brightly. And the bottoms flat and slightly gray where the weight of the world pushed up from below.

I sat on the hard clay at the edge of one of the pools. Behind it a lone line of telephone poles with a sagging wire trailed off into the distance. The pool was just a few inches deep. In it a small school of tadpoles hovered in the clear water. The tadpoles gray with purple and turquoise stripes shining in what was left of the sun. The colors so bright against the darkness of the green algae and the blackness of the mud bottom. *The closeness of death makes the senses sharp*, I thought, and I felt so very much alive.

In the distance, I saw a furry white creature slowly approaching from across the field. A dog. As she came closer I could see that she was mostly white with some tan fur the color of desert sand along her back and around her back legs. Her floppy ears and the sides of her head were also tan and she had a white line that ran from the top of her snout up between her eyes and straight down her back. Her fur was clean and she stepped gently on her paws but always deliberately closer to where I was sitting. She was beautiful.

I was squinting to study her carefully as she came closer, looking for the telltale strap around her body that would be used to attach explosives to her belly. The enemy observer hiding and watching in the distance and waiting for the right moment to press the button on his remote-control detonator. Just as we'd heard the mujahedeen did to the Russians in Afghanistan in the eighties. *If I see the strap, then I'll have to shoot her and hope that she's not yet close enough to wound me.*

She walked directly at me, unafraid. She was clean and fresh and beautiful. She sniffed my boot and licked my hand. I rubbed her behind her ears and pulled the folded and rolled package of cracker crumbs from my pocket. I unfolded it and put it on the ground for her to eat. I wondered if we had bombed her owner's house or maybe we'd hit it with artillery.

And in that moment I wished I could just drop my rifle into the Tigris and head back south along the highway. Far away from the city of eight million people that we were about to attack. I would take her with me and head back home and find a loving woman and together the three of us would move to a quiet spot somewhere to live.

To live.

To the fall in New England with the air clean and fresh and sharp. And the colors of the leaves on the mountains as bright as the tadpoles.

After a few minutes there at the edge of the pool, it was time to leave. To continue the fight toward the north. But as I started back to the vehicle, she followed. And until we finally started the engines and moved on a few minutes later, she sat quietly resting on her front paws folded in front of her. Just a few feet away from where we were parked. Watching over us.

———

When things were rough, I would always think about that day with that dog next to the pool with the tadpoles. But there was still the feeling of impending doom I felt about what lay ahead of us. Wondering if you would survive the fight in a city that stretched for miles and was home to millions. A fight where the defenders always had the advantage. But in those weeks of fighting ahead, for a few moments anyway, I was always able to put myself right back in that peaceful place. And that was the power of newfound perspective.

———

It took us two full weeks to get through all of the items on Kristian's list. By then, CC had over 250 pages of stream-of-consciousness thought in one long Word document. Each paragraph titled with the name of the story on the master list. A complete picture, broken down into sound bites, of one Marine's war. And at the end of the second week, Kristian, Marc, John, CC, and I all headed to the Irish pub around the corner to celebrate our accomplishment. As I sipped my Guinness in the crowded bar on West Thirty-first Street, CC told "war stories" about our time together in the editing room. And Marc and Kris and John laughed as I made fun of myself for being such a fucked-up Marine. The air was lighthearted and we felt like a squad who had just fought well in our first battle.

These people were my friends. They'd become members of the unit in which I fight back against the darkness. They were artists, like my brother Dave—those who live a life without material luxury but pursue a craft that connects us all as living, feeling human beings. I now felt connected to them in a way that was similar to the bond between combat veterans. And though they would never know the horrors of combat firsthand, they'd seen what I'd seen in the war. They knew what had happened to me. My stories. My most intimate and ugly moments. And they loved me anyway.

As I walked home later that night, I thought about how much better I felt because *I had told someone*. I had told them the things that were in my nightmares. And as I walked through the streets, the lights of the city seemed just a bit brighter, and the shadows in the alleyways, not so dark.

Chapter Nine

IT WAS JUST A few days after CC and I finished our sessions together. I sat quietly on a chair in the main office at Sirk Productions admiring the Art Deco design of the Empire State Building through the large bright windows that faced north. Next to me, on Kristian's desk, stood a small statue of Yoda. That day my energy was clean and good and overflowing the way a mountain stream in the Berkshires runs clear and swollen after a heavy autumn rain. It was almost too much energy, but it was the friendly type, and there was no anger in it.

Art Deco is my favorite, I thought, and it felt good to be alive and curious about things once again. To really *notice* and appreciate the design of the building and to feel its beauty. I wondered about the people who had designed it back in the twenties. Were they happy? Did they struggle with their own demons? Had they tried to quit smoking cigarettes, did they worry about running out of money, and how did they take their coffee? And I imagined the generations of lives that had unfolded in the building's shadow. Young couples holding hands, and glancing up at it, and smiling because life was so beautiful. I thought how over the decades there had been chance meetings in its elevators that had led to marriages and fortunes or divorces and ruin.

It was mid-April, 2005, just a month before my twenty-ninth

birthday. I'd started a daily exercise regimen that I followed religiously. There were long runs and sit-ups and free-weight sessions that reminded me how good it feels to build your body. It's one of those lessons that you forget when you become lazy but learn again when something moves you to get back into the gym.

The endorphins humming through my blood would carry me through the day. The longer or the harder you run, the more intense the glow. And when you push yourself extra hard, as I had that day, you shift into some higher level of energy and being, and you wonder how you had forgotten about this.

I drank as much water as I could. There was always a bottle by my side. The water kept it all flowing and lubricated and sloshing along to make sure that when you had to pee, it was always clear. When it was clear, you were well hydrated. When you were hydrated, your thoughts and your body were clean and strong. It was a lesson I'd learned firsthand at Officer Candidates School (OCS) several years before—the lesson that thoughts and emotions are linked to the chemicals in the brain that regulate them and that water is very important to that process.

One morning at OCS, when I'd just turned twenty-three, I looked out across the parade deck and saw the small red flag flying against the clear blue sky. It was still early, but it was already hot enough for them to fly the red flag. The air was wet and heavy and sweat soaked our uniforms. The red flag was a signal to our sergeant instructors that there was a high risk of heat casualties that day, so they needed to push us to drink water. At the time, I was ranked in the top 10 of the 180 or so officer candidates in the class, and the day before, I had let myself imagine for a moment that I would make it.

But something was off that morning. I was tired and felt depressed and I wanted to quit. I asked myself why I was putting myself through another Marine Corps boot camp when my buddies from college were sitting in air-conditioned offices and sleeping next to their girlfriends every night. It seemed strange, because I'd wanted more than anything to be a Marine lieutenant, but at that moment, all I wanted was to quit. It was as if someone else was thinking my thoughts for me. *I'm not going to make it.* The pain in my hip and my knee was going to get worse as the runs and hikes got longer. I felt I was made of glass. *It was a mistake coming here*, I thought. I regretted signing.

But then the sergeant instructors halted the platoon in the middle of the parade deck and had us all stand at attention on the asphalt. I could see the heat in waves rising up from the blacktop. The sergeants ordered us to remove our canteens from their holders and hold one in each hand with our arms stretched out straight in front of us. The sergeants walked through the ranks checking to make sure that each canteen was full. They were, because we had just left the squad bay. They ordered us to chug both until they were empty, and we had to hold the empty olive-green plastic canteens above our heads. I felt like I was going to puke, but my body absorbed the water quickly, and I swear I could feel it start to flow through my cells. And within just a few minutes, I felt strong, like a warrior again, as the water dissolved my negative thoughts. The water was correcting the chemistry in my brain that was imbalanced because of the heat and dehydration.

You are not your thoughts, I said to myself, as I realized how quickly, almost instantly, my entire outlook and perspective had changed. The dark, undermining thoughts that had seemed so real and tangible and solid as concrete just a few minutes before were quickly washed away by the badly needed water. *Thoughts are brain chemistry and because they come from inside of you, you think that they are you, but they are not you—they are just brain chemistry.* I didn't know it at the time, but that was the most important lesson I would ever learn. And it was one that I'd forgotten.

I talked with Kristian while he worked at the editing machine. "You know what, man? I've been thinking about a lot of things ever since we put everything down with CC."

"Oh yeah? What's up?"

"One of the things I've realized is that the battlefield *really is* the most unforgiving place on earth. It's the most brutal thing that a human being can endure, both physically and mentally. Because almost everything that happens there can profoundly impact one's life in some permanent way. And the impact can be either physically permanent, like death, loss of limbs, burns, or scarring, or mentally permanent, like the overwhelming regret or shame if you were the cause of friendly fire or responsible for the deaths of civilians or things like that. The pressure of this permanence and the nature of combat conditions stretch the human body and mind to their limits. Sometimes it stretches them beyond those limits and things snap and tear—like ligaments."

Kristian made a disgusted face when I said *ligaments*.

"And everything is extreme. Fighting units are always battling the elements. It always seems to be either 120 degrees in the summer heat in Iraq or 10 degrees in the winter mountains in Afghanistan. Heat, cold, sandstorms, dust, mud, snow, rain—all that shit—they all wear away at a unit's effectiveness and morale. Like we can never fight a war in some nice place like Greece or something. And combat loads regularly go to 130 pounds because of all the shit we have to carry, and the weight just crushes your whole goddamn spirit. There is never time for sleep, so you are never just tired, you are utterly fucking exhausted to the bone.

"And then you are also battling emotions. When a buddy falls, you are not just sad, you are fucking devastated, because he was like family—or closer—to you. Of course there's the fear, but CC and I already have gotten that down on paper. And then there are the instincts: your instincts become more finely tuned, because you are relying on them constantly."

"Like in your footage just before the ambush in Baghdad—where on one block there were all of these Iraqis milling around on the streets, and then you guys turn the corner and there is no one; all of the people have disappeared. You said, 'See how quickly we go from happy to...war' into the camera, because you could sense the danger, and then ten seconds later, the shooting started," Kristian said.

"Exactly. It's your instincts. The same as when all of the bugs stopped chirping in the grass in the fields at the Route 7 and Route 17 interchange just before the big night battle."

Kristian wrote down the word *instincts* on his notepad and circled it.

"The one with all of the tracers and RPGs," he said.

"Yeah. All of the bugs stopped chirping, and then it was just too silent. You could sense the energy in the air. We knew they were going to attack, so I took out my video camera and picked up the radio handset, and sure enough—*swoooooooooosh*—the RPG came flying right over us, right through the center of the shot."

"I love that shot."

"You can hear the *tink tink* of the AK-47 rounds on the vehicle armor just a few feet away from my head."

Kristian kept writing in his notebook.

"The other thing I wanted to tell you about was this book, MCDP-1, *Warfighting*. That stands for Marine Corps Doctrinal Publication number one. I think I might have mentioned it to you before, but I found my copy, and once I'm done reading it again, I'll give it to you. It's fucking gold. That's where I got most of these ideas from. It's probably the greatest thing ever written about the human element of war and combat, and they make all of the young Marine officers read it. But it's so good that I want you to read it too."

"Bring it in when you're done with it, 'cause I'd love to read it," he said.

———

The next day, I sat at home and flipped through the pages of MCDP-1 with a highlighter and pen. The edges of the small book were tattered and LT. SCOTTI was written across the back in thick black marker. I read through the faded and worn pages about things like *friction*—the countless factors and adverse circumstances that make even the simplest task difficult in combat—like the radios going dead in the middle of a call for artillery fire. Or trying not to mix up a six-digit grid coordinate while your hands are shaking, and you haven't slept in four days, and there are bullets snapping by your head. You can imagine the problems friction creates when two rifle squads are trying to link up at night in enemy territory without killing each other or alerting the enemy to their presence. Then there's *tempo*—the force of speed over time, which is a kind of combat momentum that can, itself, become a weapon. And *initiative*: by taking the initiative, you dictate the terms of the conflict, and you force the enemy to meet you on those terms. *Combat power*: the total destructive force you can bring to bear on your enemy at a given time.

I read about things like hitting hard and fast and sending a shockwave through the enemy. Breaking his will to fight and crushing his means of counterattacking. Gaining momentum through speed and shock and violence and fluidity. Attacking gaps in the enemy's defenses rather than hitting heavily defended areas straight on. Incapacitating the enemy systematically. The importance of morale, fighting spirit, perseverance, and good leadership. The use of surprise. Boldness. Stealth. Exploiting the enemy's critical vulnerabilities. The chaos and uncertainty that is inherent in war and the ability to overcome it and project your combat power.

As I read, I imagined what it would be like to apply these concepts to the world of business. To Wall Street, to investment banking or bond trading. To the recruiting process at graduate school. And to life in general.

I grabbed my notepad and wrote down a list of words: "Perspective. Instincts. Physical/Emotional. Extreme." They were reminders to myself. I wrote the words again—in large block letters on individual pieces of paper and taped them to the mirror in my bathroom. Each time I saw the word *perspective*, I would think back to waiting for impending death in the back of the amtrac in Ash Shatrah. Waiting to get hit at any moment by an antitank missile while staring at the radios. A hard feeling to describe until you have felt it, but at first there was the thumping of my heart so loud and strong that I could hear it in my ears and feel it in my gums, and then as the waiting dragged on, there was only the quiet dread.

And each time I saw the word *instincts*, I would remember the day that Kristian and I had just spoken about, just before the ambush in Baghdad, when I'd said out loud on camera that we were about to get attacked, and I would remember that my instincts are usually right. When I saw the word *extreme*, I remembered that I was sleeping on a nice mattress. Although it was on the floor because I was a slob and a lazy bachelor, it was still a comfortable mattress with sheets, and it was inside an apartment where there was no wind or dust or rain to make my life miserable. There were no bugs, and no one was shooting at me. *No one is shooting at me.* I could eat when I was hungry, sleep when I was tired, and go to the bathroom or take a shower whenever I wanted to. And this, in turn, would remind me again of the word *perspective*.

I had read a quote somewhere by the Buddha and copied it down in my notebook. I ripped out the page and taped it to the mirror underneath the other words. "The secret of health for both mind and body is not to mourn for the past, worry about the future, or anticipate troubles, but to live in the present moment wisely and earnestly."

Over the last few weeks, I had disassembled, cleaned, and reassembled my brain as if it were a rifle. A Marine's rifle is his best friend, and he must know the inner workings of it. The Marine must know where the carbon residue from the burnt gunpowder of the expended ammunition hides within that particular rifle so as to keep the weapon clean. The Marine must do whatever it takes to keep his rifle clean. The Marine must know its quirks, its strong points, and its weaknesses. Its capabilities and limitations and the proper employment of the weapon. So that when the moment of truth comes and the Marine squeezes the trigger, the weapon will fire cleanly and the bullet will strike its target squarely and the enemy will die.

I was dissecting myself. I had no choice, because the madness was still only a few weeks past, and I knew that it could come back, and if it did, it would be uglier and more powerful than it had been before. So I needed to do what I could to fight against it while things were in my favor.

The *physical/emotional* connection had been very clear to me for years, but for some reason living in cities, eating out in restaurants, and having warm water whenever you want it make one forget the lesson. The lesson is that the body and the brain and your emotions are directly linked to one another. Take care of the body, and it's easier to take care of the emotions.

When I drank at least four quarts of water per day, I felt five times better. I bought a Brita because I was spending a fortune on water but was afraid to drink it out of the tap because of the things that sometimes fell out of the faucet. What were those things, little black eggs?

When I drank more than two or three beers in one night, I felt depressed the next day.

When I ran sixty minutes or more at least three days in a row, I felt fantastic.

When I slept eight hours or more in one night, I felt rested; six and a half hours or less, I felt tired and unproductive.

When I ate fried food, I felt polluted. Like I had betrayed my body.

When I ate vegetables from the farmers' market, I had more energy.

When I ate candy that had corn syrup in it, I felt nervous and hollow within twenty minutes. Then I started paying attention and learned that in America, almost everything that is the cheaper version of itself has high-fructose corn syrup in it—pasta sauce, half and half, even bread. When I ate candy that didn't have corn syrup in it, I didn't get the nervous hollow feeling.

When I thought about the war and the president and Rumsfeld and the CIA and tried to figure out *who knew what,* I felt angry. But then I remembered that it was all out of my hands *from the beginning* and that I had fought with honor and done my job, and then I stopped thinking about all of that.

When I would feel the shadows and the faces start to creep up on me, I would go for a run or to the gym or to a movie.

When I spent at least twenty minutes outside in direct sunlight, so the sun would hit the back of my eyeballs, I felt like something had switched back on inside of me.

When the moon was full, I had weird dreams.

When I talked on my cell phone for more than thirty or forty minutes, my brain would hum and I would feel tired and out-of-sorts.

There were many observations that took some time. On days when I felt bad, I would look back over the few days before, to see what had triggered it. Was it something I ate or drank, something I did or didn't do, or something that I had thought? Was it the weather, the news reports, a phone call from a buddy, working on the film, or something that had nothing to do with the war—like waiting for the yes or no from the admissions committee from NYU?

I added other things to the mirror. A piece of paper with the letters PMA written on it. I'd picked up the term from my grammar school gym teacher, who was featured in *Sports Illustrated* for soccer coaching techniques that led to an unprecedented number of victories. His name was Art Abazia, but we used to call him Mr. A. "PMA all the way, baby!" he would say to us awkward, confused, angst-ridden kids. Positive mental attitude. The secret to unlocking everything. The fuel to push you past the shadows and the doubt.

I leaned my ribbon rack against the mirror just to the right of the faucet. The four rows of multicolored pieces of cloth that were meant to be worn on my uniform. Each ribbon a story. Each set onto the metal holder in order of priority. Seniority. The ones at the top, personal decorations. Reminders of who I was. Who I'd been when there was danger and things had purpose and meaning.

On the days when you feel like you're going backward, just fake it. Focus on the daily tasks and don't think about it. Just like they taught you in the Marines to fake the motivation when you weren't motivated, because nobody is motivated every day. So you say to yourself, *At least no one is shooting at me*, and over time things will become easier and then you will turn and be with the current.

At times I would run in the early morning hours through the deserted lower Manhattan streets. There was no traffic and there were no people to dodge. I would run and loop around Ground Zero and think of Beth. I would run through Chinatown—the real Chinatown—which stretches for blocks and blocks below the Lower East Side, and think about the immigrants fighting to scrape out an existence. I would run through Battery Park past the large metal globe sculpture that still bore the scars of when the towers had collapsed around it. And the Statue of Liberty in the distance with the salty spray of the waves coming up through the bulkhead at the edge of the water.

I would think about the gravitational pull of the moon on the earth as its light sparkled on the Hudson River. About Vic Lomuscio and Mike Borneo, buddies who were still over there, and *God, please let them make it home safe*. I would think about admissions committees and the rent and the fact that I needed to do laundry.

Early one morning when the run was a good one, I thought about what it was that I was trying to accomplish. My operating system had almost crashed a few weeks back. But I had used the momentum of the exercise and all of its bathing and cleansing properties, and the compassion of people who were now my friends, to reboot it. I had pressed a button and sent a shockwave of good chemicals through my system—just as an infantry battalion, when it's fighting the way it should be, sends a shockwave through its enemy. After the run, I climbed the stairs to my apartment and grabbed an index card and a marker. I wrote the word on the index card and taped it to my mirror underneath the other pieces of paper. And when I read it, my heart skipped a beat.

Reset.

My mom called me one day and said she wanted to tell me a story about my dad.

"Your father had an idea the other night of writing a story about what it's like for parents when their child goes to war. I think they gave him caffeinated coffee instead of decaf at dinner, because he sat down and wrote the whole thing as soon as we got home."

I laughed because whenever my dad had caffeine, he would always run around coming up with ideas for books and businesses and screenplays. And the ideas were almost always good ones. It made me happy that a sixty-seven-year-old man who was a beloved doctor and had been the greatest father that any boy could ever hope for—a man who had been working hard since he was just eleven years old, starting in his father's grocery market where his father was a butcher—could still have limitless energy and ideas and still find so much joy in the world.

"Send it to me, Mom. I really want to read it."

"OK, honey, I will. He wrote it by hand and you know how messy his handwriting is, so I'll have to type it up on the computer. Can you teach me again how to do an attachment on e-mail? I wrote down the steps the last time you taught me, but I still can never seem to get it to work."

"OK, Mom, I'll talk you through it."

> The unthinkable is about to happen. Our youngest child is going to war. He will be in harm's way, facing gunfire, rockets, and possibly toxic gases and deadly organisms. Yet preparation for the journey begins in almost mundane fashion, as if he was going off to college.

> However, the preparations do not deal with proper clothing to buy or which would be the best classes to take. He will have only one dress, Marine fatigues. And we won't be discussing which classes to take; we will be discussing, planning for, and promising to carry out his wishes. How to distribute his life insurance among his friends, relatives, and others he chooses. Written instructions on what to do with his personal possessions and where to find his car keys should he never again have a need for them.

> We listen to his instructions and list his orders as if we were going shopping, but our mouths are dry and we choke back the tears of mourning, which would be premature. Before we can mentally collapse from the burden, we are saved by his aspirations and plans for the "trip" to the Mideast.

In the likely event of a safe return, he will write a book about his war experience. Preparations include armfuls of books for the boat trip over, pads and pencils for the extensive interviews to follow—on this ship—during the war and after. Plans to speak with anyone who will respond, before, during, and after the conflict—on either side.

The trip over, forty days by ship, is the calm before the storm of war. Frequent e-mails, learning the geography, contacting the network of other Marine families, all to keep us busy. We reassure each other that it may all be a bluff, the war may never happen, but deep down we know it is inevitable. We are already in a war of terrorism, which destroyed the buildings and thousands of innocents. The building where our son might have been working had he not chosen to go to OCS and become a Marine officer.

Our great pride during his graduation from OCS is now tempered by the realization that Marines are trained to kill and be killed protecting comrades. There is a mixture of pride and sadness, knowing the group our son has joined is the first to face an enemy and die in the greatest numbers of any service.

Communication stops, and we assume that Michael is in Kuwait. The TV is now on nearly twenty-four hours per day. The uneasiness increases amid talk of suicide bombers, chemical and biological warfare, and the race with the seasons to avoid the brutal summer heat in

Iraq. The heat will make life nearly unbearable for the unshowered men and women who will be wearing their chemical warfare garb and donning gas masks with every alarm.

The TV becomes an addiction, along with the Internet, where my wife searches day and night for clues to where our son may be, trying to guess if and when the conflict will start.

Although there are no more e-mails and no hope of a phone call from our Marine, there are postcards written on the back of MRE (Meals Ready to Eat) wrappers, where no stamp is necessary. Though our fighting Marines don't pay taxes during the conflict and have free mail, the officers must pay for their food while aboard ship, something that we found incomprehensible. Even the postal workers of our small town look forward to the MRE cards.

Suddenly, the war really begins and the fear surfaces, fear for our son's life, his mental and physical health, and our peace of mind. The feeling that all will be well disappears as the newscasters announce movement of our forces from Kuwait to Iraq. The war is really on, and we know from his assignment that Michael will be in the middle of it.

The terror we experience with every death announced on TV is mixed with a form of guilt. As we listen intently to death reports, especially alert to the service (is it a male Marine?), the rank (is it a first lieutenant?), the station (is it Camp Pendleton?), we desperately wait for information to indicate that it wasn't Michael while trying to deny the guilt of wishing someone else's child dead.

It becomes difficult to think of anything other than the war, the suffering of combatants and their families, and our efforts to determine where our son is. There is an obsession with collecting information from newspapers, the Internet, network news, other Marine families, and every other conceivable source. The collected information is analyzed by us in our own inexpert fashion, and we map an imaginary route of our son, assuming that the implanted reporter was Dr. Bob Arnot; it turns out that our guess was correct, at least initially.

Forcing ourselves to assume Michael will return safe and whole, we fill a war chest for him. Daily we collect newspaper articles, Internet articles, and any other paraphernalia that will, in retrospect, be of historical interest. In spite of our optimistic assumptions and hopes, we cringe with every casualty, fear every ring of the doorbell, and hesitate to answer the phone, because it might be the president. We have heard that the president calls the family of every dead combatant within forty-eight hours. We do not want to see Marines at our door or hear President Bush's voice on our phone.

In a frenzy of patriotism and as an act of diversion, we buy a long flagpole and proudly fly the American flag, as well as the Marine colors. Prior to that, the flags were suspended from our porch, frequently flipping up to be trapped by the rain gutters during a windy wet storm. The feeling of patriotism compels us to talk with others, and in doing so we discover a whole new world among the familiar.

Men we had known for years who, unbeknownst to us, had been Marines in previous wars treat us like family. They seem to share our pride and grief and to join us in our suffering. People who were casual acquaintances behave like lifelong friends—being supportive and empathetic. Even strangers seem to know our son and care about his safety. We even find ourselves, usually reserved, beeping our horns and pointing thumbs up to those with flags on their cars or houses, especially with a Marine flag.

After no news for months and an almost constant instant adrenaline rush of flight or fight, it is over! An unexpected phone call from our son, sitting in the ransacked UN headquarters in Baghdad. Our response is a combination of tearful joy, relief, heart-swelling pride, and a dreamlike effect of surrealism. Could this be the little child we had such a short time ago?

After the emotions cool down, we begin to breathe easier, but we know the roller-coaster ride is not over. There are still reports of snipers, fanatics wearing explosives, and war accidents. Then there is the fear of emotional reactions in our servicemen, the result of war horrors, the sight and smell of death, the body parts, and the knowledge that they caused the deaths of other human beings.

Now that he is home, Michael is a lot thinner, more serious, and at first, more reserved than we ever remember him to be. A new life faces our son, and we are thankful that Michael is alive to pursue it and doubly thankful that the unthinkable did not occur, at least to our family. Our hearts go out to the families of those heroes who did not share our luck. This story is dedicated to you.

Rob Secher, my buddy who'd written me the letter that I'd received just before we invaded Iraq, called me one afternoon. It was great to hear his voice.

"Trashcan, I'm coming to New York City, and we need to link up," he said on the phone.

"Hell yeah, Cubby—definitely. When are you gonna be in town?"

"Next weekend."

"Sounds good, man. It'll be great to catch up."

I was excited to see Cubby, because it had been entirely too long since we'd had one of our excellent beer-drinking nights together.

That next weekend, I climbed the stairs to the second floor of the Old Town Bar. It was one of my favorites. The place was just north of Union Square Park and had not changed in almost a hundred years. The tin roof, the carved solid-oak bar with marble countertops, the tiled floors and the original urinals in the bathroom from the early 1900s that when you pissed in them you felt like you were back in 1916. You would rest your beer on top of the urinal and you could easily have been an artillery forward observer in World War I and your girlfriend who was waiting for you outside had one of those flapper haircuts.

Sitting at the worn wooden table with Cubby was his girlfriend, who was a student at the University of Pennsylvania Wharton School of Business, and a few of her friends. There were already two empty pitchers in front of them.

"Trashcan!" he yelled as he gave me a big hug.

"Cubby!" I yelled back, and there was the happiness of two brothers who had not seen each other in a few years.

We caught up on what everybody else was doing, guys who had stayed in and guys who had gotten out. Cubby and I talked about our best days, when we were two of the six or seven lieutenants who had served in Bravo Battery, First Battalion, Eleventh Marines, together under the command of the great Major Joe Russo. "To Fightin' Joe!" we said loudly as we laughed and raised our glasses.

Cubby had a certain energy that civilians just didn't have. He was still part of something bigger than himself, but it went beyond that. He loved the Marine Corps and had never wanted to do anything else. He'd spent four years as an enlisted Marine as a machine gunner in the infantry, then received a full college scholarship as part of a Naval Reserve Officer Training Corps. This was an extremely rare honor, as not many active-duty enlisted Marines were ever given this opportunity. Someone had seen the genius in him and had given him the chance.

Rob was always interested in the centurions of the Roman legions. When it came time for us to inspect the Marines, he would talk about things like *integritas*, which is what the centurions would say to their inspecting officers in formation as they smacked their armor just above the heart. Integritas referred to the material wholeness of one's character. And by saying this, each centurion was saying that his spirit was strong and that he was dedicated and ready to head into battle. That was pure Cubby. Cubby *was* integritas.

When he had rotated out of the battery, we had all pitched in to give him a plaque inscribed with his favorite quote, from Cormac McCarthy's *Blood Meridian*: "War was always here. Before man was, war waited for him. The ultimate trade awaiting its ultimate practitioner."

"Yeah, the Corps has its problems like anything else, but I am staying in mainly because I want to create something special—that same something that Major Russo had created in our battery. A unit where there is no bullshit, no stupid fuck-fuck games, no politics. Where the Marines are proud and happy, not miserable. The way it's supposed to be. Just like we were when we served in Bravo Battery."

Cubby was so serious about it and had such a pure and unselfish sense of purpose that I got goose bumps. I remembered exactly what he was talking about.

"Yeah, man, I hear you. Bravo Battery when Major Russo was the CO was as good as it can possibly get anywhere. His leadership, the vibe, the whole thing. I have never seen anything like it since—not in any of the other units in the Marine Corps and definitely not in the fucking civilian world."

There was no doubt in my mind that Rob would one day make an outstanding battery commander. He was as good as it gets. He cared more for his Marines than he did about his own career, and his Marines would immediately sense that. And they would work harder and longer for him, without being told to do so, to get the job done.

His time at OCS was going to end in a few months, and then he was to rotate back out to the Fleet Marine Force in Okinawa, Japan, which would put him into the lottery to head back to Iraq or Afghanistan.

The night seemed to go by quickly. It was a good night. A happy night. The first really happy night in a long time. The darkness that had already been greatly weakened over the last several weeks was now almost unnoticeable. But the time soon came for the night to end. Cubby told me that he had gotten word that he would most likely deploy to Iraq, as part of a team of Marines who would help to train the Iraqi military. It was a dangerous job, because they would be doing live patrols through enemy territory with their Iraqi students, some of whom were not the type of people you'd want to trust with your life. Some of whom might even be loyal to the enemy. But it was necessary if we ever wanted to hand their own country back over to them.

"Cubby—take care of yourself over there, man. Send me your overseas address as soon as you get it. I am going to send you a bottle of special mouthwash."

He smiled when I said it. *Mouthwash* was code for the booze I was going to pour into a Scope bottle and tape up tightly so it wouldn't leak. I would carefully place it in a care package along with smokes and Copenhagen and porn and candy and anything else I could think of that I wasn't supposed to send but his boys would like. When we said good-bye, I hugged him and said "I fucking love you, man," before I headed off into the night. As I walked through the streets, moderately drunk, I was glad that people like Cubby still existed.

One day on the way to the gym, just a few blocks north of the Angelika theater at the corner of Bleecker and Mercer Streets, I came across a pool of blood in the road. The blood, with some tissue, was in a patch on the west side of the street, just next to the row of parked cars that hugged the curb. The blood was fresh. *Isn't it somebody's job to clean this shit off the street?* I thought. I couldn't tell what part of the body the tissue was from. Somebody probably hit some NYU student who was riding a bike. Or someone listening to headphones had darted out from the small space between the two cars that were tightly hugging the sidewalk. The paramedics and cops must have just left, because the blood had not fully coagulated yet, and the pools of it were still shiny and slick. For a few seconds, I felt the tightness in my stomach and the *thump thump thump* in my teeth and the quick breathing and the lightness of my hands. And the buildings looked a bit foreign and that helicopter flying in the sky and the vehicles everywhere. And just for a moment, flashes of scenes.

But their sting was much weaker than before. Because the scenes—*my scenes*—were now sitting on a hard drive attached to an editing machine thirty-one blocks north of where I was standing. They were sitting on a few hundred pages in double-spaced Times New Roman 12-point type on Kristian's lap while he sipped his Snapple Iced Tea and took careful notes as he read them.

By telling Kristian and CC all the things that were in my head, I'd pushed them out into the light. Once they were no longer inside of me, they could no longer hurt me, because when the light hit them, they were not the same animals that they were in the dark. That is the magic of telling someone—anyone. That is the magic of talking about it and working through it and facing the fear. Because when you face the fear, you gain the clarity. And Kristian would turn it all into something that others would understand. Then the others would share the burden of it with me. And maybe those who'd also served who saw it would know that they were not alone in their darkness.

I walked half a block north to the New York Sports Club fitness center and showed the girl at the front desk my bar-coded key chain. As she scanned it, the computer beeped and the brown ringlets of her hair rested gently on her shoulder. She handed me a towel, smiled, and said, "Have a good workout," and I smiled back, happy to be alive and in one piece, and said, "Thank you."

As I lifted the weights in the gym, I thought of how a man needs to feel strong. When a man feels strong and his energy is good, he has the power of a thousand suns and a thousand gods and a thousand generations behind him. Others sense this in him and they want to know him and love him and be like him. And when a man feels strong, he allows himself to be vulnerable, and he has no shame, because sometimes even warriors need to cry, and the crying only makes him stronger. When his energy is good, he can look at old things in new ways and find the beauty in them.

But when a man feels weak or ashamed or impotent, he no longer feels like a man. His thoughts become feeble. Brittle. Fragile. He follows these thoughts and does things that make it all worse. And once this seal is broken, the black water begins to seep in, and he feels more ashamed and unworthy as he slowly, quietly, begins to rot.

And there is nothing that I can think of in the civilian world that can replicate war. Once you have fought in a war, it forever defines a large part of who you are. So I decided to turn the whole mess on its head. "Make chicken salad out of chicken shit," as Major Casado would say when everything had completely gone to hell on the battlefield. Use the experience of combat, the Marine Corps training, and the knowledge that one can choose victory over failure to my advantage. Make it a source of strength. Bend it and shape it and make *it* serve *me*. And when I need to, grab it by the throat until the veins pop out of it and then smash it into the wall. Stomp it to death with the heel of my boot, then use the butt of my rifle to smash anything that is left until it is dust.

And so my way forward was now much more clear. I was going to shove it down the throat of Wall Street. I was going to launch an all-out offensive. I would focus on my original plan and shift all of my energy into the mission. *Everything is a war*, I thought. And when you go off to war, you had better be strong. And you had better be ready, because the enemy most certainly is.

So, I prepared for battle.

Part III

UP

Chapter Ten

Date: Fri, 15 Apr 2005 10:08:23 -0400
From: Anika Pratt
Subject: Meeting at NYU Stern
To: Michael Scotti

Dear Michael,
My name is Anika Pratt and I am a member of
the admissions committee at NYU Stern. I am
writing to find out if you can come to
Stern to meet with me sometime next week.
Please let me know your availability to
meet during business hours. Thank you, and
I look forward to hearing from you soon,
Anika Pratt
--
Anika Davis Pratt
Director, MBA Admissions
NYU Stern School of Business
http://www.stern.nyu.edu/admissions
Downtown. Down to Earth. Down to Business.

A jolt of equal parts hope and fear hit me as I opened the e-mail. I spent a ridiculous hour pacing my apartment. Trying to decipher any hidden meaning in her message. Looking for the slightest sign of what her intentions might be and scrutinizing my response. Making sure the three sentences in my response were perfect.

I kept hearing my brother Dan's voice in my head. *Whatever you do, don't spell her name wrong!*

Just a few days later, Anika stood smiling at me, eight months pregnant, in the hallway that led from the reception area to the offices where the admissions committee and staff worked. Next to her on the counter in front of the receptionist was a cup full of purple pens with NYU STERN on them in white lettering. They were the kind of pens that you clicked with your thumb before you started writing. I wanted to take one of them, but I was scared that maybe I might jinx things.

The light in Anika's office was bright and clear and shined through the large window that faced north over West Fourth Street. She gave off the energy of someone who enjoyed her work and who genuinely liked other people.

She held the keys to the kingdom in her hands. The promised land. Where the golden sun bathed the fields with light. A world that was surrounded by the highest walls. Off-limits to most who try to enter. A place where a guy could make a million a year. Or two million. Or five. Some, even more.

This was my last chance. I'd applied to six schools, was quickly rejected by three of them, and wait-listed at two of the remaining three. And being on a wait list at an ultracompetitive school didn't offer much hope. So there was the pressure. At that moment the pressure of all of my future plans felt heavy upon me. And because it was all out of my control, I felt weak and that maybe I was going to implode from the weight of it. It would crush me, and they would have to scrape me off the floor. "What the hell happened to this guy?" the janitor would ask when he saw the mess in her office.

I sat in the chair trying not to look nervous. My heart beating hard. Maybe I'll just open a bar in Costa Rica or something. Or become a real estate agent and sell beachfront lots to rich guys from Wall Street. Anika walked over to her side of the desk, and with one hand holding on to the armrest of the chair and the other holding on to her belly, she gently placed herself into her seat.

"So, Michael, we were very impressed with your application. Tell me why you want to get an MBA, and why specifically you would like to attend NYU Stern."

I paused for a second and noticed the double chocolate Tasti D-Lite that rested on the desk between us. The beads of perspiration dripping down the sides of the waxed paper cup formed a small puddle on her desk.

Then I was surprised how easily the semi-bullshit-laden corporate-speak came to me. Especially under pressure.

"In my time as a Marine officer...hone leadership skills...apply to the world of finance...skills set...top MBA program... trading and investment banking...add value...reputation for quality...have the opportunity...fit in well...diversity...experiences...New York City...access to the banks...competitive advantage..."

This was what you had to do if you wanted to get into the kingdom.

"Well, Michael, that all sounds terrific. I know that you've been waiting for a response from us for quite a while, and I want to explain why. Over the past few months, we have been developing a new program called Summer Start. It's for students with exceptional leadership experience who we feel would make a great contribution to the Stern community but who might benefit from starting classes three months early. The members of the Summer Start program would join the rest of the full-time student body in the fall, and from that point on would be just like the other students. We are very excited about the idea, and this summer we are going to be running the pilot Summer Start program."

"That sounds like a very interesting opportunity..."

And a few minutes later I was in. Just like that. Through the back door. While no one was looking.

The promised land.

On the way out of the admissions office, I smiled at the receptionist, who obviously knew what had just happened, thanked her for being the greatest receptionist in the history of the world, and grabbed a fistful of the purple pens before heading out the door.

In the elevator, I thought how it was always just a handful of people who got to decide. The ones who decided which kids got to go to the gifted and talented program in fourth grade. The ones who decided who did and didn't deserve the medals for valor in combat. The ones who decided who got into the best schools. Who got the best jobs at the banks and how much the bonuses were. The ones who got to decide whether or not we would invade other countries and topple governments and bomb cities.

And I remembered the moment, almost two years before, of stepping off that bus at Camp Pendleton. The moment when I realized that things would now always be different. For better or worse. And after my discharge, I was in a new world. A new world with new rules and new people. And there in that room with Anika and the wax paper cup of chocolate Tasti D-Lite, I knew that I'd just come across the bridge once again, as I entered yet another new world. And it was strange that whether it was a jet airplane that carried you from Kuwait to California or the whim of some admissions committee in a last-minute meeting, in just a few moments or hours your life suddenly became something completely foreign and unfamiliar.

Dean Thomas Cooley stood in a corner of the room speaking with a group of Summer Start students at our welcoming reception. It was early in June, just before our classes began. I approached him and introduced myself.

"Hi, Mike," he said as he read my name tag and shook my hand. I told him about my background, then wasted no time going in for the kill.

"Dean Cooley, do you know that NYU Stern is the only top business school without a military veterans club? Everybody else has one—Harvard, Wharton, Columbia, MIT—everybody."

He watched me with a look of concern on his face, and I wondered if I'd been just a little too aggressive and that maybe my words had sounded accusatory. For a second, I had a vision that someone was going to take it all away from me. "Well, Mike, unfortunately we have changed our minds—sorry. You're just a bit too combative. Security will escort you to the door." I softened the tone of my voice considerably and explained to him where I was coming from.

"You see, Dean Cooley, students have tried three times in the past four years to get a veterans club started. But unfortunately, they've run into some roadblocks. I know that we are very strict about the number of clubs that we have here, but I think it would do the school good to be seen as military-friendly. Right now, Harvard and Wharton are where all of the military vets seem to be headed. A military veterans club would really help to add to the Stern arsenal, don't you think?"

"I think it's a great idea, Mike, and I think we should have one. Employers love to hire former military folks, and we definitely want to be seen as a military-friendly school. And it's the least we can do to pay back our service men and women for their service."

His endorsement was like a golden chip, one that I put in my pocket. There would be procedures that I would have to follow to get the club formally pushed through, but I knew that I had the firepower to clear any bureaucratic obstacles that would block my way. Because I started at the top, and the top said yes. So when someone tried to push back with some reason not to approve the club, I would pull the shiny golden Dean Cooley chip from my pocket and throw it on the table.

There were only four U.S. military veterans in the entire full-time class of 2007, which had a few hundred students. And in the years past, the numbers were similar. To me, this was a problem. One that I thought a veterans club would help solve.

———

Institutional finance and retail finance are worlds apart. Retail finance, which most people are more familiar with, is for the everyday needs of a person who earns a normal salary. Retail finance is the type that you see in your local branch office at Chase or Citibank or Bank of America. Simple things like checking accounts and home mortgages and retirement accounts.

Institutional finance—otherwise known as Wall Street—is the

part of the banking world that deals with large corporations. The bankers take privately owned companies public by creating shares of stock that trade openly on the world's listed stock exchanges. They help one $3-billion company buy another $3-billion company. They help companies manage risk by betting on the direction of interest rates or the value of the dollar or the price of oil. They create billions of dollars of stocks and bonds and derivatives and sell them in the primary market to institutions—insurance companies, pension funds, and hedge funds—that have billions of dollars to invest. Later, the banks also buy and sell these same stocks and bonds and derivatives, for profit, in the secondary market.

The magnitude of the transactions—a merger that creates a $10-billion-a-year behemoth company, or an offering of $2 billion in high-yield bonds—allows the Wall Street machine to cut off a nice slice of meat for itself. That's why bankers and traders are paid so well.

Wall Street and the clients it services deal in a global river of money unseen by most, which runs so swift and deep that its size and velocity are difficult to comprehend. Annual transactions run into the trillions of dollars.

And the top ten graduate business schools are part of a machine designed to place students at jobs in institutional finance. At finance-heavy schools like NYU Stern, the machine feeds directly into the recruiting receptacle of the Wall Street investment banks.

It takes two years to earn an MBA in a full-time program. The first year, September to May, is usually spent trying to secure a summer internship between your first and second years. The hope is that at the end of that internship in August, your employer will offer you a full-time job, with a large signing bonus, to begin a few weeks after you graduate the following May.

———

One night that summer when Meredith and I were out to dinner, I sensed that things were going to end between us. I knew that she cared for me deeply, and I felt the same way about her. But she knew that it would be many years before I settled down and started a family.

At dinner, Meredith told me about a guy she had once worked with, who was after her. From the way she told me about it, I knew that whatever it was that we were doing was going to end. It was inevitable. She was a good woman and deserved a good man who wanted the same things she did. He was a solid guy with a steady career in law and was getting to the age where he wanted to start a family. So over the weeks and months that followed, Meredith and I seemed to taper off. We saw each other less and less, until eventually we stopped altogether.

In the fall of 2005, after spending two months with the other Summer Start students studying statistics, corporate ethics, and corporate communications, we met the rest of the full-time NYU Stern Class of 2007. They were a group of highly intelligent late-twenty-somethings. Ivy Leaguers who'd spent three years working hundred-hour weeks as analysts at investment banks. People who had started their own businesses. People who had worked at nonprofits and wanted to change the world. Marketing people. Advertising people. Engineers. Someone had even worked directly for President Clinton.

All were about to lock in an orgy of stress and judgment and competition, hoping for one thing: the offer.

———

The night before our first big recruiting event, the president of the Sales and Trading Club lectured the eighty of us who were shooting for jobs as traders or salespeople at the banks. He was a second year student who already had a job waiting for him after he graduated.

"You are about to be hit by a tsunami—the fall recruiting season. Your goal is to get on as many summer internship interview lists as you can. You will spend the next three months fighting for a spot on one of these lists. Each bank will make between one and four summer offers. If you are lucky enough to get an internship, you will then spend next summer trying to turn your internship into a full-time job offer. That is why you are here. To get a job. Don't worry about your grades. In sales and trading, grades don't matter. The investment bankers, who are going into mergers and acquisitions, have to worry about their grades. We don't. So spend your time recruiting. Networking. Doing informational interviews. There is a list of one hundred questions on the Sales and Trading Club website. Answer them. Know them cold. Read the *Wall Street Journal* every day. The first corporate presentation is tomorrow night, and from then on, things are going to be insane for you guys until January."

When he paused, we squirmed anxiously in our seats, immediately eyeing each other in a new light.

"And try not to do anything stupid, or else you'll blow yourselves up at the banks. There are only twelve decent ones out there. But it will happen to some of you. You will rub someone the wrong way or say something dumb, and then they will stop inviting you to their recruiting events. When there is an invite-only event and your name isn't on the list, you are finished at that bank. And there really isn't much you can do to get back in the running there."

It was good advice, and he was telling us things that we needed to hear. And I had to laugh a bit when he used the words "blow yourself up." The first time, and certainly not the last, I heard a finance person borrow imagery from war. But I thought for a moment how different his speech was from the speech our battalion commander gave us before we crossed over the border and into Iraq at the beginning of the war. Reminding us that we would forever remember those Marines to our left and to our right, those Marines with whom we fought against an enemy who would try to kill us. How we were liberating a people from a tyrant and how the deeds that we were about to do would echo throughout eternity.

After the president of the Sales and Trading Club finished his speech, most of us were suddenly thinking the same thing: *If I am $100,000 in debt and jobless when I graduate…*

So this was the new stress. The stress of graduate school and job hunting and finance in general. The stress of being compacted within the solid walls of a process that relies on attrition to weed out as many people as possible. *You have one slip-up here, and you are finished.* I thought about the night with the cabdriver and realized that no one could ever know about what I'd done, because I'd be viewed as defective by the people in this new world. And if they thought I was defective, they wouldn't hire me. There would be a stigma. Because in the world of finance, there is little room for anything that seems to stray from the norm. So I told no one, and I kept the things that happened after I came home from the war to myself. I hoped that this transition would be a fresh start.

On the night of the first event, I gently slid the handmade gray

Sartoria Partenopea suit from its protective bag that hung on the clothes rack I'd installed on the wall next to my refrigerator. My apartment was so small that it didn't have any closets. The bathroom, refrigerator, stove, mattress, front door, and dresser were all within a few feet of each other. I could shower, shit, shave, and make a sandwich all at the same time.

I viewed that first event as a study of the battlefield terrain—the choke points, the high ground, the valleys. Who were the enemy? Where were they? How could I chop them to pieces?

I spent large sums of student-loan money assembling the correct uniform after studying the well-dressed finance people who roamed the city. And I cared for and wore this uniform—a gray or a dark blue suit, slim-fitting shirt, and silk tie—the same way a Marine cares for his dress blues. The lines of the suit must be tailored perfectly along the shoulders and the arms for it to become a part of you. Your steps and movements have a self-assuredness to them because it fits perfectly, just like a Marine's uniform.

I flashed my purple laminated NYU ID card as the guard waved me through the checkpoint. To my left, embedded in the wall, was a plaque I hadn't noticed before. A memorial to the students and alumni from NYU Stern who had died on 9/11. Her name was there.

Beth Anne Quigley.

I stopped for a few moments and gently rubbed my fingers over the raised lettering of her name.

I remembered clearly the nights just a year before, walking to work along the edge of Ground Zero. And I felt like a fraud because I had once been a warrior, but now I was about to head into a room to kiss people's asses and try to convince them that I was worthy.

Just around the corner was the hallway to the main reception room. Two large tables were set up outside the double doors. At each sat a well-dressed woman from the human resources group at J.P. Morgan. One table for the students, the other for the bankers and traders. Name tags in carefully arranged rows, rank and job title listed on each.

I scanned the tags, searching out the managing directors, or MDs, in the sales and trading positions—the decision makers with power and influence. I tried to keep a mental checklist of those I needed to meet. *I should have brought something to write on.*

We were students begging for jobs. Our mission over the next ninety minutes was to pocket as many J.P. Morgan business cards as we could.

The coveted card, the first of many filters that fall. The signal that the owner judged you worthy of responding with a perfectly composed thank-you e-mail within twenty-four hours. No card meant you were now invisible. Better luck next time, pal.

Then walking on eggshells, trying to somehow turn that thank-you e-mail into an informational interview. A thirty-minute dog-and-pony show while sitting in a folding chair next to a trader at their place of business. Canned questions with canned responses. The others on the trading desk watching you. Judging you. Deciding if you belonged there.

A gradual escalation at each of the twelve banks. Foreplay. First recruiting event: a dozen business cards, a dozen thank-you e-mails, and maybe one informational, if you were lucky. Second recruiting event a few weeks later: second set of thank-you e-mails, a few more trips to the bank for informationals. Then the one or two invite-only events as the pool of students still in the running grew smaller. The survivors. Then in December the posting of the names of those who'd been invited to interview at the banks in January. Then, after the interviews and after you had bludgeoned all your friends to death, the offer.

There would be between one and four offers from each of the banks to selected recipients among the eighty or so students who had started the process. The entire scenario is played out at each of the banks over just two months: sixty recruiting events, thirty informational interviews. Probably six hundred thank-you e-mails. Finance and marketing and accounting classes. Midterms. Finals. Sales and Trading Club meetings. The military veterans club project I was trying to get off the ground. And voice-over work for the documentary that I just didn't have time for.

The energy in the room was ugly. Nervousness. Stress. Judgment. Fear. Competition. Trying to meet as many people as possible. Trying to get them to like you in two minutes. A few hundred people confined to one space for ninety minutes, all trying to secure one of the limited number of spots. We were friends, but the friendships were new. And now we were competitors. And Wall Street certainly didn't view us as human beings. It wanted to know about our *aptitude*. To pluck those who would make them the most money. Suck us up into the mother ship and deploy us out onto the trading floors—where the energy would be much the same.

A uniformed bartender served drinks. Several servers walked the floor with trays of hors d'oeuvres. Actors and writers and musicians. Struggling. "Excuse me, sir, would you like a canapé?" The entire pecking order of the universe laid out before us in sixty feet. Managing directors, directors, vice presidents, and associates from the bank, the students, the girls at the front desk handing out the name tags, the guard in the lobby, the bartender and servers, and the people walking by the large windows that looked out onto the walkway between West Fourth and West Third Streets, who peered in at the well-dressed crowd being served fresh hors d'oeuvres. Some of them wishful school applicants who worked low-paying jobs in the city and had been rejected. Just a short time ago, I'd been one of them, watching from the dusk. Studying the well-lit room and the late-twenty-somethings with their goddamn bright ties and fake smiles and their $110 haircuts.

"So, why don't you tell me about yourself," said the MD, wearing a $4,000 suit. His tone condescending, superior, arrogant. An edginess and sense of entitlement that permeates nearly all of finance. *If this guy was a Marine officer, his own men would shoot him.*

Eight or nine of us stood in an arc around him, forming a lopsided circle. I took a deep breath. I was now in a different world. These people played by a different set of rules, all of them watching out for their own asses—and not really trying to hide it. They wouldn't run out into the machine-gun-fire-swept street to save you if you were wounded and screaming for help. Because they were probably the ones who had pushed you out there.

He asked each of us the question. And so we gave him the thirty-second elevator pitch of our lives. Trying to hit the key points that would lead to his reaching inside his jacket for the extra-heavy cardstock J.P. Morgan business card with fine raised print.

Each of us was then asked a second question: "So, tell me about where you think the yields on ten-year bonds are headed." Each of us trying to turn the conversation away from finance to something more human. Something that would make him remember us.

Dear Mr. MD: It was very nice meeting you last night. I truly enjoyed our conversation about the parallels between the worlds of bond trading and combat. Your insight gave me new perspective into how to apply the skills I honed on the battlefield to the financial markets. Thank you again for your time and I hope to have the opportunity to speak with you again soon.

They were judging our ability to make an impression on them. To talk about anything and everything in an intelligent manner. Jump through the hoops without mistakes. Ring the bell. Everyone in that circle sending the same message. *You see? You see, Mr. MD? Even among the best and the brightest, I am the best and the brightest.*

Directly across from me, an awkward student tried to join our circle. His lack of confidence a death sentence. Don't you know, my friend? You are swimming in the murky water just offshore. It is filled with us bull sharks. And we can smell your fear.

The circle did not open for him.

I made eye contact, grabbed him by the shoulder, formed a hole near where I was standing, pulled him beside me, looked the J.P. Morgan guy in the eye, shook his hand, said, "It was very nice meeting you," took the card from his outstretched arm when it suddenly appeared, and placed the awkward kid in my spot. I introduced the J.P. Morgan guy and the awkward one by name, then headed off to conquer the next circle.

Later that night, we spoke with a junior vice president who was maybe four years out of B school. He wore wire-rim glasses and had perfectly flowing, but still somehow neatly parted, sandy-blond hair. As he spoke with us, he felt it necessary to check his BlackBerry every thirty seconds, bringing the conversation with the dozen hopefuls who were hanging on his every word to a dead stop. I guess he needed to remind us of his importance and our insignificance. I wondered if he would be able to check the Black-Berry as often if I shoved it firmly up his ass.

The night was a good one. In my hands, a stack of crisp, fresh-smelling J.P. Morgan business cards. Thank-you e-mails until three a.m. Each perfectly crafted. Double-check the spelling of the name. Triple-check it, just like artillery coordinates on a map. First and last sentences always the same. Middle one or two sentences a reference to something that we had discussed. A tickler to get them to respond. Their response an open door to hint at an informational interview. But you could never be pushy. You had to cultivate it.

Then a lucky break early in the recruiting season. And I'd made my own luck, which is the best type. I got an e-mail from the dean of students notifying me of the approval of the NYU Stern Military Veterans Club. It's incredible what you can accomplish quickly if you apply pressure in the right spots. Focus your energy the way a sniper carefully chooses an aiming point. I applied the initiative and discipline and the whatever-it-takes mind-set I'd learned in the Marine Corps. I was proud to have planted the stake that would help bring more veterans to our school. The club would give veterans a voice and a way to be contacted as a group both by people who wanted to hire us and by other veterans who were trying to get accepted by the school. Formally becoming a club allowed us to better convey what we'd done in the military when we spoke to the business community. It would be a way of giving back to those who'd picked up a rifle and fought for their country—no matter what the politics behind it all was. And in some small way, it helped me to fight back against the war that had followed me home.

This is a war, I thought. I didn't know anything else. And in war you have only so much time. Only so many chances. You have a limited number of men and a limited amount of fuel and ammunition and combat power. So you must focus only on the things that truly matter in order to accomplish the mission.

The landscape upon which the battle would be fought was now clear before me. I would break the fall recruiting campaign into thirds. First make a name for myself. A solid foundation. Meet as many people involved in the recruiting process as possible. Seek out all of the military veterans who were Stern alumni at the banks. Penetrate deep. Let them know I was now the founder and president of the Military Veterans Club. Have the military contacts introduce me, personally, to the non-Stern military vets at the same banks. Get meetings with all of them. Always focus on the MDs.

During the middle third of the recruiting season, I would focus on scoring informational interviews set around the framework of the recruiting events and my expanding network. People on Wall Street talk. They know whom their competitors like. So I needed to be seen on the trading floors. Fuck classes. Use each meeting as a chance to meet others and set up more informationals. Drop the names of the others you've met at the banks so they know you know their friends. Get résumés printed on extra-heavy kid finish premium résumé paper. "Here is a fresh copy of my résumé," you say at the informationals. The heavy weight of the paper impressing them as they subconsciously equate it with you as a person. Gain momentum. Tempo. Combat power.

Then the culminating third of the attack. Play to the incestuous power of greed and fear that runs all of the financial world. Let them know that you are scarce and that others want you.

Supply and demand. They fight over you. Because if they think that someone else might steal you away, they will do whatever it takes to get you to join their team.

Don't sleep. Do three times as many informationals as everyone else. Then the interviews in January will be conversations between people who already know each other instead of one-way question-and-answer sessions.

The emotional side of my personality began to shut down. I was becoming part of the machine. I was on a conveyor belt that was slowly taking me on down the assembly line. Further away from those dark days after the war, and closer to a shiny new spot on a trading desk at a bank. But the price of it all was that during the transformation, you had to bow down to people who do not care about you. They will one day be in charge of you, and their decisions will greatly affect your life, but they have no feelings for you. So you start to become empty and cold, because there is no place for emotion on Wall Street. Just like the battlefield.

As the weeks of the recruiting season passed, the war seemed to become nothing more than a tool used to pry open the door. Kindling for conversation. A line. At times I felt ashamed of doing it, but competition was tough, so I needed to do whatever I could to differentiate myself.

And underneath the stress was still a bit of the darkness. The things I told CC, the things that haunted me in the months after the war, were still with me, in a way. But those things, once powerful and full of danger, now stood exhausted and panting. For the others who were still over there, it was different. The terrible realities of combat were a part of every new day. But for me, those things no longer existed in the present. They were part of a past darkness. And for the most part, I had made my peace with them.

That fall, Kristian completed the teaser trailer for the film, a thirty-second spot meant to generate buzz for the project, which was still at least a few years away from completion. It was shown to potential investors to get them interested.

The teaser worked nicely during informational interviews— my way of blowing the door off once I'd pried it open a bit. Sitting on the cold metal seat between two traders at two p.m. on a Wednesday afternoon at Deutsche Bank or Merrill Lynch or Lehman Brothers or Bear Stearns or Credit Suisse. The results always the same.

"So, tell me about your military service. You have a hell of a résumé." I would run through the two-minute version of the elevator pitch of my life, then finish by telling them about the film.

"Do you want to take a look at the trailer? It's on the website."

"Hell, yeah," they would say.

They would whoop when they saw the machine-gun fire and quick edits in the trailer. *Thank you, Kristian Fraga.* There's a big difference between talking about war or reading it on a résumé and watching a video of the real thing. And the guy who shot the footage was now sitting next to them. Trying to squeeze a job from the machine.

They would play it again and turn the volume up all the way on the computers, which held hundreds of millions of dollars' worth of bond positions. These flesh-eating traders loved anything that had to do with violence. Because bond trading is a form of controlled violence: two opposing parties, buyers and sellers, bludgeoning each other with clubs.

"You guys have to check this out," they would announce to the others sitting around us.

So by the third time they played the trailer, half of the god-damn trading desk would be crowded around the computer. Then the MDs would pop their heads out of their corner offices to see what was going on. And I would get an impromptu three-minute discussion with the head of the whole group as he peppered me with questions about Iraq and Afghanistan. And I would work the right words into the answers: *Initiative. Discipline. Management of chaos. Uncertainty. Management of risk. Attention to detail. Decisiveness. Knowing when to cut your losses. Effective employment of a limited number of crucial assets.* In the war, it was people and ammunition and combat power. On Wall Street, it's the banks' capital. The parallels between war and trading were true. And you could see the MDs eating it all up as their fingers slowly rubbed my résumé printed on heavy stock. Eyes twinkling as they thought about how much money I could make for them.

In October I scheduled an interview with an up-and-coming high-yield bond salesman named Lucas Detor who worked at Morgan Stanley. He was held in high regard by everyone who knew him. He'd driven tanks in the Army National Guard, worked as an agent in the Secret Service, and was now rising through the ranks very quickly. He'd made director within just a few years of graduating from Stern.

We shook hands and walked from the reception area out onto the trading floor. Lucas was a triathlete who still wore the matter-of-fact energy of a Secret Service agent. On the trading floor sat parallel rows of long tables at which the traders and salespeople sat evenly spaced on either side. Some of the traders had four large monitors in front of them—the top two stacked on top of the bottom two. The typical Wall Street bond crowd—well dressed, looking refined and intelligent, and grinding through billions of dollars of trades a day.

I carried the folding chair that was resting at the end of the trading desk and set it down next to Lucas. "Here's a fresh copy of my résumé for you."

"So you know the heavy paper trick. Nice. I like that."

I laughed and knew immediately that this was going to go well.

"So—word on the street is that you were able to get the Military Veterans Club pushed through at Stern. I know a bunch of guys who had tried that over the last few years—two or three times, I think it was—and failed. Congrats. That's good stuff."

"Thanks. The way I see it, it's all about looking at an old thing in a new way. What they missed in the prior years was that we needed to include the international veterans on the petition. Even if their service was mandatory, I still had them sign the list. I also put together a PowerPoint to help some of those guys talk more effectively about their military service, because they didn't realize the value it held in recruiting."

"Sounds good. I'm really glad you were able to get it up and running. Also, I heard about your film and checked out the trailer. Pretty amazing."

Lucas leaned over and spoke behind me to the guy who was sitting just to my right.

"Hey, Bill, this is Mike. The Marine with the movie I was telling you about."

Lucas turned back to me.

"Hold on a sec. I need to grab this call," Lucas said as the lights on his console blinked.

Bill was an MD. I could tell he felt like chatting. We spoke a bit about the film and the war and B school.

"Any hot chicks in your class?" Bill asked with a grin.

I thought for a second that it might be a trap, a test. *How unprofessional of that young candidate to have a conversation that objectified women*, I imagined someone writing on a form or something after I left. But then I took another look at him and guessed—based on his wavy hair and designer glasses and his whole vibe in general—that it wasn't.

Plus, I was a risk taker.

"Yeah, there are," I laughed. Bill perked up.

"I just got a divorce. What a fucking disaster. Never get married. It isn't worth it."

I said the first thing that came to mind.

"They say that the best time in a man's life is just after his first divorce. I think I read a quote that said that once," I said jokingly.

He laughed loudly.

"But I know a ton of ladies who would love to go out with an MD from Morgan Stanley. No kidding," I continued.

I was partly kidding, partly kissing his ass—because I could tell that was what he wanted—and partly trying to get the guy laid so he would give me a job.

"Really?"

"Yeah. I know the perfect girl for you. She's hot and she's single."

"Oh, man, you've got to hook me up with her. What color hair does she have?"

"She's a blonde. You would love her, I'm telling you. She's good to go."

He leaned behind my back and spoke to Lucas.

"Hey, Lucas, where did you find this guy? He's awesome," said Bill.

Lucas was still on the phone but heard what Bill had said and smiled at me.

"I will see her in class tomorrow and ask her, and if she's cool with it, I'll give her your e-mail."

Bill wrote something on his business card and handed it to me.

"My cell is on there. I'm having a party on Friday night at my place—it's in the Sugar Building. The address is on the back. Bring her with you."

"Sounds good."

Fuck, I hope she wants to go, I thought. *Well, Trashcan, this could be either a great move or a complete disaster.*

As soon as his phone call ended, Lucas looked at me and said, smiling, "You're too much."

I asked Lucas a few questions about selling bonds and his time in the Secret Service, and then our conversation took a turn.

"Something that might interest you is this outside project I've been working on. A buddy of mine in the National Guard said that his guys were having a rough time buying Christmas presents for their kids. The tours in Iraq and Afghanistan are killing them financially, because their pay is like half of what they would be earning at their civilian jobs. The bills keep coming in while they are overseas. It's a mess. So when I heard this, I thought that somebody needed to step in and help these families out. I just started a military charity called Reserve Aid. We just received 501(c)(3) nonprofit status last week."

"Damn. That's messed up. I had no idea. Anything I can do to help out?"

"We haven't started fund-raising yet, so any ideas that you might have, I would love to hear. We are planning to have a gala fund-raiser somewhere nice in the city to kick things off."

I thought for a second.

"How about this: I use my position as founder of the NYU Stern Military Veterans Club to round up a bunch of guys from all of the top schools who are looking for jobs. Then we go out to all of the banks and have them sponsor tables for the MBAs at the event. I don't have a job anywhere yet so I can still be objective when reaching out to the banks. It's pretty obvious that they love to hire vets from the top schools, and these military guys need jobs, so why don't we match the two needs and use it for something good?"

"That's a great idea," Lucas said, smiling.

"It's all about matching buyers and sellers, right? Well, we can have the banks write the checks out of their recruiting budgets. Come up with a résumé book of the vets who will be at the event. And it will be a good way to start to solidify the unofficial Wall Street veterans roster. Get a good list of names going at all of the different banks."

"Sounds good to me," he said.

Lucas was a good man, and I liked him from the moment I met him. He was grounded and did not have the edge of arrogance that so many in his position had. He was a family man with two—and soon to be three—daughters. He understood the importance of giving back—and went well beyond just writing a check. He rolled up his sleeves and put hundreds of hours of work into Reserve Aid. Lucas got it. In the world of Wall Street selfishness and entitlement, he was unselfish and giving. I admired him greatly and hoped that I could one day be as good a man as he.

———

That Friday, along with Leslie, the NYU Stern girl whom I'd promised to set up with Bill the trader, I took a taxi to the ultraexclusive Sugar Building in Tribeca. It was an old sugar warehouse that had been converted to gigantic multi-million-dollar apartments.

The elevator doors opened directly to Bill's apartment. It looked like he had the whole floor.

We immediately saw two MDs whom we'd spoken with at recruiting events, one from J.P. Morgan and one from Goldman Sachs. *Everyone really does know each other on Wall Street. It's its own self-sustaining habitat.* The net worth of the room was probably that of some countries.

"Hi, Peter," I said to the MD from J.P. Morgan as his eyes grew wide, probably wondering what the hell I was doing at this party.

"Hi, Mike," he said.

We spoke for a bit, and I explained that Bill had invited me. He smiled, shook his head, and put his hand on my shoulder.

"You are going to be just fine on Wall Street, my friend. Just fine."

I drank exactly one beer, made sure I was seen by everyone who looked like an MD, figured that it was time to go before I did something stupid, then headed home alone in a taxi to spend the weekend studying for Professor Silber's extremely difficult finance midterm that was just two days away.

Leslie and Bill started dating, and every time I ran into her in class, I smirked and thought about how varied the random alliances and meetings and introductions can be when you put eight million people together in a city.

———

Later that week, I arrived twenty minutes early to the Credit Suisse First Boston corporate presentation. Arriving early gave me time to get to know the human resources people from the banks. They were friendly and were good sources of information.

On the name-tag table, one stood out above the others.

MR. ROBERT C. O'BRIEN
CHIEF CREDIT OFFICER
GLOBAL HEAD OF CREDIT RISK MANAGEMENT
MEMBER—CHAIRMAN'S BOARD
AND MANAGEMENT COUNCIL

He was just a few rungs from the very top of the entire 63,000-employee, $60-billion-per-year multinational investment bank. He was like a general. *A guy like that could snap his fingers and change your whole life*, I thought.

After asking the HR folks if they needed any help, I headed inside to review the list of MDs that I had scribbled using a small golfer's pencil on the single 3 × 5 index card that I carried in my pocket. The index card was less bulky than a notebook and didn't ruin the lines of my suit. It was also easy to quickly and discreetly check between ass-kissing circles because it didn't need to be unfolded.

One of my buddies showed up a few minutes later. Our conversation easily accompanied the stress and mild form of insanity that was the fall MBA recruiting season.

"Did you hear that Hunter blew himself up at Deutsche?" he asked me with a smirk.

"No—really? How?"

"He's not totally sure, but he realized that he spelled Deutsche Bank wrong in a whole bunch of his thank-you e-mails. That might have something to do with it."

"Aw, man, that sucks. I've almost done that a bunch of times. I still don't know how to spell it. I have to hold the goddamn business card right up next to the screen every time I type it and look back and forth like three times to make sure I've got it right."

He laughed.

"Did you hear what Allison did?" I asked him.

"No."

"It was the night when we had the double firmwide presentations. Last Tuesday, I think it was. Bear Stearns and Goldman. Well, she did a cut-and-paste with her thank-you e-mails and forgot to change the name of the bank when she sent them. So she sent out like twenty thank-yous to people at Bear Stearns saying that she enjoyed learning about Goldman Sachs. I'll bet they loved that."

"Damn."

"Yeah. And now tonight we've got another double firmwide. I think they schedule two in one night just to fuck with us. I'm going to spend exactly sixty minutes at this one and then head to Morgan Stanley. You want to share a cab? I'll round up a few more people."

"Sounds good. Grab me before you leave."

As I told the story, it occurred to me how odd it was that misspelling a bank's name in a casual e-mail was considered a *disaster* in the world I now lived in—when it once had been incorrectly reading numbers on a map and blowing up the wrong people with artillery. And how once I had prided myself on not making any mistakes and delivering artillery fire with accuracy, at the correct time and onto the correct target. But now my mission seemed to be to grovel and jump through hoops and hope that some arrogant prick who never really did anything meaningful in his life would give me his business card.

A figure appeared in the doorway. A distinguished gray-haired gentleman in his late fifties or early sixties. He paused as he stood in the doorway, and his heavy energy consumed the entire room. I glanced at his name tag. Then I glanced at my watch. He was fifteen minutes early. The three of us were still the only ones there.

"Hi, I'm Bob O'Brien."

"Hi, Mr. O'Brien. Nice to meet you."

"Please, call me Bob."

"I see that we all like to get here early. Get the lay of the land," I said.

"If you're on time, you're late," Bob said.

"We used to say that in the Marine Corps."

"Marine Corps? I was Army. Vietnam."

And for the next few minutes, Bob O'Brien and I traded war stories. I felt bad for my buddy, but *oh well*, this was alone time with a titan of Wall Street, and I did what I needed to do.

It wasn't my fault that my buddy never served.

As the room began to fill up, first slowly, then in waves, it was the right time for our conversation to end. I didn't even have to ask for the card.

"Mike—let's keep in touch. Let's talk again soon, OK?"

"Sounds great, Bob. Really nice meeting you."

He handed me his card, and I slipped it into the inside pocket of my suit jacket and wondered for a second if Bob had ever been in the darkness after his war. Then I remembered that he had offered me his card without my having to ask for it, and I realized, *That was probably the most important four minutes in all of business school.*

Those doubleheader nights could wear you down. You would meet several dozen new people whom you needed to impress. You needed to always be *on*. Day after night after day after night. Class all day mixed with informationals. Subway rides. Cab rides when you were late. More meetings. Group projects and presentations and midterms. People started to break down, cracking from the stress. Those who blew themselves up at one or two of the banks early in the process started to really unravel as time rolled forward. You could sense the fear in them in the recruiting circles. Desperation. Bad energy. Loss of confidence. Wondering if they were one of the sorry sons of bitches who wouldn't get a job, as their failure with a few of the banks then spread to the others as they made their own nightmare become reality.

When I saw this, I felt conflicted. I felt pity, because some people just don't do well under stress. It isn't their fault, and there's no shame in it. They just can't handle it. I saw the same thing happen in Iraq with some of the radio operators who were monitoring some of the nets that we used. I had to fire one in particular, because he just couldn't cope with combat conditions and got details wrong and made other mistakes on the radio.

I knew that those who were having trouble handling the recruiting season wouldn't survive long in the land of the vultures and handmade suits. Being able to multitask and handle large amounts of stress is not something they can teach you in business school. If you haven't learned how to do that by then, it's probably too late. I tried to help whoever would ask me for advice, like "How do I get an informational interview?" but it was obvious that if they had to ask that question, they didn't understand the game and probably never would. Maybe if they'd been Marines, I would've helped them a little more.

In the hallway outside of the main study room at school one afternoon, I heard a girl talking on her cell phone.

"Look—I just don't have time for this. You don't understand how busy I am. It's not that I don't want to go away for the weekend with you. I just don't have time."

Then a pause as the person on the other end of the phone said something. Then her tears.

"Yes, baby, I do still love you. But—you just don't understand how busy we are. I can't do *this* right now, baby. I just can't."

We were becoming part of the machine. A machine that printed money. A machine that chopped your personal life to pieces. The teeth of its great gears grinding until it had taken everything.

I blew myself up at J.P. Morgan fairly early in the process. I arrived too early for one of their targeted events at a bar in midtown and was greeted by one of the most obnoxious and disliked people involved with the recruiting process—across all of the banks. She was a low-level VP. And she was angry. We wondered if she'd had a rough time in high school or college or something, and if she was overcompensating for it with her newfound power.

I was sitting at the front bar, reading a copy of the *Wall Street Journal*. When she arrived, through the front door, she was clearly on the warpath. And I was her target.

"What are you doing here this early?" she asked, obviously annoyed by my presence thirty minutes before the scheduled start time for the event, which was to be held in the reception room in the basement of the lounge.

"It's raining and I figured I might as well grab a cab while there were still some left."

She didn't like my answer. And I didn't care for her very much. I guess my feelings for her were obvious.

I should've just left at that point, because she alone could torpedo me as far as J.P. Morgan was concerned, and I knew that I was probably finished at that bank. But I figured I'd be a good sport about it, hang around for the next hour and a half, and eat as much of the free gourmet food they provided as I could. And soon enough, I was glad that I didn't leave. Because J.P. Morgan invited some of the math whiz kids from the undergraduate Curant Institute at NYU to join us that night. The Curant kids knew they were brilliant and that Wall Street would pay handsomely to rent their extraordinarily gifted quantitative minds. The banks needed those minds to structure all of the highly complex financial instruments that were fueling a large part of the housing boom and also the Wall Street bonus boom. And it was fun to watch the superbrilliant twenty-two-year-olds get hammered and do things that were wildly inappropriate. They were too young to really give a shit that much about anything, and their freedom from fear was beautiful. Double-fisted with drinks and ordering shots on J.P. Morgan's tab as the bank people scowled at them. One even passed out on a couch by the coat check. That made my week.

The scramble to get on the summer-intern interview lists finally came to an end in early December. The invitation to interview was e-mailed directly to each one of us, individually. Those who had not made the cut found out only when they heard others had already been invited.

I made ten of the twelve interview lists. In the end, I had a great haul. Seven offers for summer internships from seven different investment banks. The people in the career development office at NYU Stern said that they were pretty sure it was a record for Sales and Trading. I had to laugh when they told me that, because I was fairly certain that my GMAT score was somewhere in the bottom 10 percent of my class.

Go figure.

Chapter Eleven

I SAT ACROSS THE long polished-oak conference table from two of the most powerful men at Credit Suisse, waiting to begin my sales pitch. It was June 2006, eight months since I'd met Bob O'Brien that night at the corporate recruiting event. I'd finished my first year of graduate school and was in the second week of my internship as a summer associate at the bank. In addition to spending the summer trying to convince them to give me a full-time job, I was also trying to convince them to write a check for tens of thousands of dollars to Reserve Aid, the military charity that Lucas Detor founded.

I glanced out of the window for a second at the bright gray sky. It had an overexposed blown-out look that seemed strange for June but closely matched the hollow feeling you got from the fluorescent lights above the vast trading floors on the lower levels of the building where I spent twelve or so hours each day.

Both of the men sitting across from me were legends on Wall Street. Both were veterans of combat in Vietnam. Both had spent three or four decades climbing the ranks at the bank. Bob O'Brien was awarded a Purple Heart after he was wounded serving as a platoon commander. Doug Paul, the vice chairman of the Fixed Income Division, had been a Green Beret.

On the wall of the corner office where we sat—between Bob's

desk and one of the windows that looked out high over Madison Square Park and the Flatiron Building—hung the signs with the names and logos of each version of the bank as it changed hands over the years. Bob had been there for all of them, and you could sense that they had been hung on the wall proudly. On a bookshelf was a worn copy of *Barbarians at the Gate*, in which he was featured as part of the iconic RJR Nabisco leveraged buyout in 1988.

"Gentlemen. Imagine for a moment that you are a young husband and father of three from Texas or Ohio or West Virginia. You've been hit by an IED. Your legs are gone because they have been blown off by the shrapnel. And when the gas tank on the Humvee exploded, you were severely burned over 60 percent of your body. Your wife has to take care of you and the kids. But the VA is so backlogged with disability benefits cases that you won't see a dime for at least fourteen months. There are no rich grandparents to step in and help out. And the Army Reserve or National Guard or whoever has cut you off because you've been deactivated and they stopped paying you once you were discharged from the hospital."

I paused.

"Families are at risk of losing their houses or being evicted from their apartments. Lights are being turned off. This is a real problem that is only going to get worse as both of these wars continue. These guys don't have money to buy their kids diapers. It's a disaster.

"Their problems are unique. Reservists tend to slip through the bureaucratic cracks because they live a double life of civilian and warrior—and that leads to major complications after multiple deployments. Especially when they are wounded.

"Lucas Detor, an MD in high-yield at Morgan Stanley, started the charity. I am now on the founding board of directors, and we are swinging for the fences with this first event four months from now. We could really use your help."

There was a pause in the room, and I watched and waited for their response. I felt like I'd aimed my bullet well, and I hoped that it had hit its mark.

"We like this idea a lot, Mike, and we want to help. How certain are you that you will get good attendance from the first-years at the other schools? I ask this only because I need to know if we can use money from the recruiting budget," Bob asked.

"If Credit Suisse sponsors the event, the first-year MBAs who are looking for jobs will show up. I have already spoken with the presidents of the Columbia and Wharton military veterans clubs—the closest schools geographically—and they have both pledged a minimum of seven first-year MBAs each. The four of us from NYU are a lock. So the risk of no-shows is, in my mind, minimal. For the schools further out, this is an opportunity for them to get down to the city for informational interviews. The guys from MIT are chomping at the bit and already have at least ten people who want to come. That number can easily be stretched with guys from other schools, because demand is strong for the seats, given that we have a top-tier sponsor."

Bob and Doug looked at each other and each raised their eyebrows. I sat perfectly still in my pressed flat-front khakis and my custom-fitted blue-and-white-striped banker's shirt.

"What are the sponsorship levels?"

"Lead sponsor is $50,000. Cosponsor is $30,000, and with that you get three tables."

They looked at each other again. Then Bob spoke.

"Put Credit Suisse down for a $30,000 cosponsorship. If you can't find another cosponsor, come back to me and let me know. Also, put me down personally for one table."

"Me too," added Doug.

"Thank you, gentlemen. This is going to help a lot of people."

Almost in an instant—$50,000. For a charity that hadn't yet raised a dime. It didn't seem real. Just like it didn't seem real to me that no one told you what it was going to be like to come home from a war. What wasn't in the brochure you read when you put on the uniform was that after you fought bravely and did your time, things would fall apart, your life would end up in pieces, and you would be hanging and twisting out on the line, emotionally, physically, or financially.

So we were at least going to do whatever we could to spray some water on what I saw as a raging fire. At least we could divert some of that massive money river that flows through finance and use it for something good.

"Wow, Trashcan. You are going to make a hell of a sales guy," Lucas said when I told him the news of the fifty grand. Within a week, Morgan Stanley signed on as the other anchor cosponsor.

———

Two months later, I accepted a full-time position that would begin the following summer, after my graduation, in Credit Suisse's leveraged-finance group. I was to be a desk research analyst, working directly on the trading desk, profiling the financial health of companies that were in danger of missing payments on the debt they had sold to investors—a great way, a prestigious and relevant way in the eyes of others, to start a career in high finance. And I was doing it at one of the best trading desks on Wall Street. This group of just a few dozen traders and salespeople were responsible for bringing in *billions* of dollars of revenue to the bank.

I was lucky. Of the twelve summer associates—one or two

each from the various business schools that had made up our intern class at the bank that summer—only four of us received full-time offers. I had climbed a mountain and planted my flag squarely on top of it. I was proud of accomplishing my goal. And happy that the signing bonus would erase my school debt and that there would still be some left over.

But something felt off.

The internship took up all my time and energy. There was nothing left for anything else. I hadn't seen my parents all summer. My dad was scheduled to have double hip-replacement surgery in a few weeks. It felt like I'd abandoned him during the months of pain that led up to the decision to have the surgery. I had fallen behind on my work for the documentary. Kristian was asking me to start doing preliminary voiceover work, and I didn't have enough time to give him. I had not seen or spoken with Meredith in months, but I'd heard that she was now on the verge of getting engaged. And my buddies who were still serving in Iraq and Afghanistan felt like distant actors in a play that no one was watching.

I watched a rerun of a show on the Discovery Channel. It was an entire episode on the guys from First Battalion, Fourth Marines, my old unit. Mike Borneo and his boys had fired some of the first shots of the battle of An Najaf in Iraq, which became one of the toughest fights of the entire war. The combat got especially heavy in the Wadi Al-Salam Cemetery on the outskirts of the city, one of the largest cemeteries in the world. It stretches for miles and has hundreds of thousands of tombs, many that are taller than a man. This city of the dead was a treacherous maze in which the enemy, who knew the terrain, could hide and shoot from just a few feet away. Dave Lewis, one of the lieutenants I had served with in One Four, had taken shrapnel to the face. But

I hadn't seen or spoken with any of the guys from that unit since I'd flown out to California almost two years before.

So a threshold had been crossed. I now belonged to a different world. A world that revolved around bonus season and earnings before interest, taxes, depreciation, and amortization. I didn't even notice it while it was happening. But with each step I took further into that world, each meeting I attended or e-mail I carefully crafted or managing director I tried to win over, I bowed down just a little more. My master, which was once the war, was now a bank. And I'd sold myself wholly to it.

There'd been something else nagging me all summer, and I'd been trying to ignore it. The daily grind of the sales and trading life was—*transactional.* Repetitious. Do a trade. Do a trade. Do another trade. Hit your revenue goals for the month. Or don't hit them. Stress. And those goddamn fluorescent lights. The judgments and opinions and doublespeak. Now that I had lived it for twelve weeks, I saw the reality of day-to-day life on the trading floor, and I suspected that maybe it didn't particularly appeal to me. Especially for the next twenty years of my life. But where else could you make that kind of money?

Nowhere.

It was October 8, 2006. I opened my eyes as I awoke from a deep and satisfying sleep. The type that seems possible only in the fall when you crack the windows a bit and let the cool air swirl throughout the room. And there was an electricity to those days as the weather started to change. Now a second-year student who would graduate that spring, I was all set for a great day in my budding career: an investment banking class, a meeting with a senior Credit Suisse executive, a Reserve Aid board of directors meeting, and my first recruiting event as a representative of the bank for the first-year MBAs who were looking for internships.

Charlie Murphy, a senior MD in the Credit Suisse mergers and acquisitions group, was to guest-lecture my investment banking class later that morning. I had not yet met him but had traded e-mails with him to arrange a face-to-face after class. He said he had heard great things about me and was looking forward to it.

The Reserve Aid board of directors meeting in the Citigroup building in midtown was to be the final session before our inaugural gala dinner, which was now just a week away. The event was completely sold out, and we had generated almost $350,000 in ticket sales. We asked the New York Athletic Club to squeeze in a few more tables than normal because demand was so high. The pressure was on to make the event run smoothly, but it was good pressure, because it felt like things were under control.

After the board meeting, I would rush back downtown to a conference hall at NYU Stern for the large on-campus Credit Suisse corporate recruiting presentation for the first-year MBAs. The same presentation that I had sweated through as a job seeker the year before.

Though still a student, I was now a representative of the bank whose mission it was to help locate the one or two most talented students in the pack and sell them on Credit Suisse. The first-years had listened to me speak on panels about recruiting a few weeks before, and many had asked to meet with me one-on-one to get some straightforward and focused recruiting advice. Credit Suisse was proud that I had chosen them of the seven offers, and I was proud that they felt me worthy of working in their leveraged-finance group.

I had become known as the recruiting star from the prior year. The prize pony. And I was now a company man.

I went for a run through the West Village and up and back on the path that ran along the Hudson River. It was a beautiful fall day in New York City. My mind drifted to the mental checklist of last-minute items for the gala. Call the florist to confirm the table headpiece order. Get final confirmation on body count from the heads of the other veterans clubs at Columbia, MIT, Wharton, and all the rest. Ensure that the printed programs were still on schedule. Make sure the color guard had the correct time and address. Make sure the guys from Sirk Productions would be ready with the patriotic video we had put together. The list stretched on.

As I climbed the stairs to my apartment, I heard my cell phone ringing. I burst through the door and grabbed it off the tiny countertop.

It was 10:18 a.m. I glanced at the caller ID.

My heart stopped.

"Mike, this is Major Gelerter. I am afraid I have some very bad news." His voice had the tone of a caring father talking to his son. Major Gelerter had taken over command of our artillery battery after Major Russo had rotated to another assignment. He was a good and fair leader, and I'd enjoyed working for him. I hadn't spoken to him in years, and I was afraid of what he was about to tell me.

"What is it, sir?" I asked.

"Unfortunately Rob Secher was killed in Iraq yesterday."

I said nothing for a few moments.

"How did it happen, sir?"

"He was shot by a sniper while on patrol in the town of Hit. From what I understand, it was a head wound and he went quickly."

"Fuck, sir. No. Not Cubby. Not Cubby, sir."

The tears were already starting to fill my eyes. Walls collapsing and things snapping and breaking. Sliding. Falling.

"I know. I know. We all loved him. He was a damn good Marine and an even better friend."

No words came to my mind. Only disbelief and sorrow. There was a silence for a few moments.

"I will be escorting Rob from Dover Air Force Base back to Memphis. The funeral is set for Friday."

"I will be there, sir. I will fucking be there."

"I know you will, Mike."

"Is there anybody you want me to call, sir? I can take some of the load from you. I am sure you have a lot of preparations to make."

"Thanks, Mike. Can you call Joe Holecko? I don't have his contact info."

"No problem, sir. I will take care of it."

"Alright. See you in a few days."

"Bye, sir."

I collapsed on the bed and sobbed.

Cubby.

After a few minutes, I regained a bit of control. Wiped the tears from my eyes and splashed some cold water on my face from the sink in the bathroom. I looked at myself in the mirror. *Carry on* with the mission of the day. Swallow down what happened. Just like the war.

But I wasn't sure if I could this time. Because one of my best friends whom I loved as my own brother had just been killed fighting in a war and all of these things back home that I was so concerned about were so goddamn insignificant and idiotic and based on the opinions of others whom I tolerated only because they could make me rich.

In class I sat in the back row. Anie Borja, a trusted NYU friend who'd worked for Bill Clinton, sat next to me. I told her what happened as the class was starting. I listened as Charlie Murphy spoke about investment banking. She looked over at me about halfway through the lecture. I sat still, head forward, as tears fell silently from my eyes.

"Are you OK?" she asked in a concerned whisper.

"Not really."

"Why don't you leave?"

"I have to meet with Charlie Murphy, and I don't want to cancel. It's our first meeting."

On her face, caring. And disbelief.

During the second half of the lecture, deep breaths. Hit the sadness with a hammer. Push it down.

I didn't think Charlie could sense what had happened, and because it was the first time I'd met him, I didn't want to tell him.

I hopped on the subway and headed to the Citibank tower in my banker's suit. The meeting was in a conference room on the forty-third floor. Up where the helicopters flew. You could see the whole city. Blinking lights. The span of the cityscape. I sat at the conference table with Lucas and the three other members of the board. One was the youngest person ever named partner at the law firm Kirkland & Ellis. The other two were high-yield bond traders, one at J.P. Morgan and the other at the multi-billion-dollar hedge fund Old Lane Capital.

"Fellas, I lost one of my best buddies today, in Iraq. Captain Robert M. Secher. I don't think it has really hit me yet. But I was wondering if it would be OK if I said a few words about him at the event. Maybe even cut together a minute or so of video with him in it. I want people to know how good he was."

"No problem, Trashcan," Lucas said without hesitation. "Do

what you need to do. And sorry for your loss. I'm sure he was a great man."

As the Credit Suisse presentation started later that night, I pulled Norm Parton, the COO of the leveraged-finance group, aside by the name-tag table. His energy was friendly and it was easy to trust him. He looked young for his age except for the one patch of gray on his otherwise full head of brown hair. I told him what happened. He gave me a hug and said in an earnest way, "Sorry for your loss, my friend," and he told me that he could imagine how "something like that could take the wind out of your sails." One of the girls from HR heard the conversation.

I went through the motions that night. Did my duty, but I was starting to sway. I was bleeding, but I couldn't let them see my wounds. Or so I thought. At the end of the night, as I was heading home, the girl from HR stopped me at the elevator.

"Mike, it's OK if you are like... really upset. It's OK," she said with a soft smile. I thanked her and stepped into the elevator.

That night I lay in bed staring at the ceiling. I couldn't cry. So I opened the last e-mail I got from Cubby. I must have read it a hundred times that night.

```
Date: Wed, 28 Jun 2006 09:30:05 -0500
From: Rob Secher
Subject: Re: address
To: Mike Scotti


Dude,
I can't find that letter, my shit is in
such a state of mess right now. I'm sick
and tired of this stupid ass war and the
stupid ass Iraqi army which we are here
```

babysitting. I'm also sick of the fact that it is obvious that trying to create this army is failing since the "plan" is constantly changing and changes even before the current changes can take place. I'm sick of field grade officers, it honestly seems like the only people you can trust are company grades and SNCOs and NCOs. Everyone else is drinking the Kool-Aid.

There is so much bullshit that goes on and to watch the indifference and lack of capabilities of the Iraqi army is disheartening and frustrating. This army is the polar opposite of our military. These are the losers of society. These are the people who would be nobodies and beggars and thieves and probably insurgents. This army is a pathetic collection of souls and I would never trust them with the security of a nation. On that note, the only way to deal with them is to accept that they suck and then just be nice to them, there is nothing else we can do.

Our presence only worsens the matter since it is really the chicken or the egg scenario. We're here because of the insurgency and the insurgency is here because of us. The Iraqi army is just along for the ride. Those fuckers do jack and shit while Americans are out fighting the war and dying for THEIR country. American servicemen fighting for a people (the Iraqis) who just don't give a shit.

This place in general is just a bad situation and it gets nowhere. The insurgency in our little AO has not changed its tempo in over a year! All that talk about "death throes of the insurgency," it's all bull-shit that's being fed to the US on TV. From what I have seen in my little piece of the pie around Hit, this war is going nowhere.

But oh well, I'm a MOTIVATED Marine! (said as only Stefan can say it). Aren't you happy to know that the suck hasn't changed one bit. Doesn't it make you happy you got out while the gettin' was good!

Jim will be home in August and I'll still be here until next February . . . fucking miserable! So tell me what you're up to. Any new chicks? Are you going to Russo's wedding? I have his e-mail if you need it. Take care and enjoy life, don't hold back!

Your Friend,
Rob (Cubby)

I remember my first night on duty at the barracks when I was an awkward young lieutenant confused about what to do and I called you at home at midnight on a workday and got your name wrong when I asked for Lieutenant See-cher instead of Se-shair but you were cool enough to laugh about it and I could feel your smile through the phone and you were always doing that—smiling—even though you were the toughest of us all and we called you Cubby and you were always too nice to the ladies in the bars and they always went home with the douchebags instead and I watched the video of you that day we were all in the truck on Highway 10 coming back from San Diego and I asked you what type of chicks you liked and you said "The ones with big boobs" and we all laughed. But no matter how many times I rewound the tape it could never bring you back then I thought about the goddamn bullet that smashed your face and your skull and wondered and hoped that you didn't feel it Cubby oh please God I hope you didn't feel it. Then Jim called the day after we all found out and he in California and me in New York on the phone crying not believing and he said that we have both seen guys bleed out on the side of the road but this time it was Cubby. No it wasn't but yes it was. And why was it him and not us he was the nice guy always smiling and we were the assholes. And then we hung up and I cried and I wondered if you had the chance to sneak a sip from that bottle of Jack Daniel's I had sent to you before they got you Cubby I can't believe they fucking got you. Then I thought about how the sniper had you in his sights and carefully controlled his breathing and gently squeezed the trigger and he did that terrible thing to you and that he was a warrior just like we were so I didn't hate him really but I wished I could tie him to a chair and slit his throat and let the blood run down all over his clothes.

We flew in from all over the country. The big reunion wasn't supposed to be for this. *Jesus, is this really happening?*

I met Joe Holecko in the lobby of the hotel. He and I had stayed in touch since we both got back from the war. Over the years, we partied in Brazil, New York City, San Diego, and Mexico. He was one of my best friends.

He would be involuntarily recalled out of the IRR two months later to do another tour in Iraq. I would miss the cutoff for the recall by one week because my eight-year contractual commitment to the Marine Corps would have only fifty-one weeks left on it, and they were calling up only Marines with at least fifty-two weeks left. We would take a trip to Aruba and lose money in the casinos and go on booze cruises and be too drunk when we talked to the women on the boats. Just in case that was the last time we would ever be able to do things like that together.

"I'm warning you, man, Memphis is an evil, evil town," Joe said in a very serious tone. He was speaking from experience.

My cell phone rang. It was our buddy Jim calling from one of the rooms, asking where we were.

The man behind the front desk grew stuffy and annoyed that I was on my cell phone so close to his workspace. I sensed his disapproval. And his passive-aggressive energy set me off.

"Listen, you fucking son of a bitch. I am here for Captain Secher's funeral, and if you have a problem with me talking to one of my buddies on this cell phone, then just go ahead and say something." I squeezed my phone so tightly that the screen cracked and I thought about picking up the lamp that was on the table next to the house phone and beating him with it until his skull cracked open and they would have to squeegee his blood off the floor.

And I didn't give a fuck if he called security because I would've beaten them to death too.

"I'm sorry—I'm sorry—we're just..." Joe said to the clerk as he ushered me outside.

And though I'd gained my footing in the time I was living in the world of bankers and business schools and *always acting in an appropriate manner*, the war would always be a part of me. And when you were back among the things from the old world, it could *just like that* come back upon you. And the anger I felt against the man behind the desk was the same anger I felt at whoever had stolen the food from the rifle squad. There would always be the old world of the war, and the new world. And when they touched under circumstances such as the unexpected death of a close friend and the passive-aggressive mannerisms of some unhappy hotel clerk, the results could be pure madness.

In the church, Major Russo—now Lieutenant Colonel Russo—was one of the people who gave Rob's eulogy. It was the first time I had seen him shaken and nearly at a loss for words. But those he found were simple and pure and good and made all the more real by his emotion. I didn't even try to hide my tears this time. *Fuck it. Let them fall.*

———

At the cemetery, Marines in dress blues carried Rob's flag-draped coffin from the hearse to a small covered structure at the edge of the graveyard where he was to be buried. His family sat in a row of seats in front. Hundreds of us stood in a semicircle around the structure.

Somebody whom I did not know said some words, but I did not listen. I just stared into the back of the person who was standing in front of me.

The guns fired the volley that marked the death of another young man. Bite down hard. Empty, hollow, gray. Descending.

Two Marines ceremoniously folded the flag. Joe Russo solemnly knelt down on one knee as he presented it to Rob's mother, who was sitting in the row of chairs nearest to the coffin. I did not watch as he did that. Instead I stared at the coffin and tried to remember Cubby. The smiling warrior with the glasses and the freckles and the sandy-red hair.

After the ceremony, Joe Russo approached.

"Scotti, you're invited to come to the actual burial. It's not just for guys in uniform, you know. You earned it, Scotti."

"That's alright, sir. I feel weird going without being in uniform. You know—being a civilian—but...thank you, sir. I appreciate that."

And after I said it, I wished that I hadn't said it. But it was too late.

I said it because I was ashamed of getting out while guys like Cubby stayed in and ended up paying the price. I said it because I was ashamed that my life had become largely based upon the pursuit of wealth. And I said it because I just didn't want to see them lower him into the ground.

"To Cubby."

"To Cubby."

The twelve of us who had flown in for the funeral all raised our glasses later that night. The pitchers of beer sprawled out in front of us at the local Hooters. The perfect place to honor our fallen. A warrior who was braver than all of us. After a few hours and a few rounds of drinks and more than a few stories, most of the group headed back to the hotel.

But not Joe Holecko and me.

"Dude, let's head to Beale Street," I said to Joe.

"OK."

So that was that. Things took a left turn on us. Barhopping along Beale Street, each round of drinks added to it. Bleakness. Permanence. Cubby was gone. Somewhere along the fuzzy line, all the bars on Beale Street closed on us. They tried to shut it off. But we were not ready to accept it.

Delay it. Make him last a little while longer.

"Tunica," Joe said. "The casinos just across the state line. They never stop serving."

"Alright. I probably shouldn't drive. But fuck it. Let's go anyway," I said.

The chemical smell of the rental car. The long straight road that stretched into the night. The haze. The silence.

Then the lights of the casino. Third base at the blackjack table. Hit me. Hit me again. Busted. Fuck it. Bet $100. Bet $500. Down two grand, just like that. "Waitress, another beer please." Hit me. Hit me again. ATM card locked. Cash advance against the credit card. Down another three grand. *Good. Take it all.* Max out the other credit card. Call the bank. Make it last. Don't stop. Off the rails. *Please—take it. Everything I have left. I don't care anymore. I don't care about signing bonuses or networking or generally accepted accounting principles. About half-Windsor tie knots, proper Excel formatting, or the London interbank offered rate.*

Then a tap-tap-tap on my shoulder.

"Sir, are you friends with that gentleman over there?"

"Yes."

"I'm sorry, sir, but he is going to have to leave."

I didn't bother to ask why. I just accepted it.

Back on the road to Memphis in the early morning light.

"What time is your flight, dude?"

"I think it's like nine twenty a.m."

"Mine's at like nine thirty. We're probably going to miss them."

Too drunk to be driving. Trying not to swerve. Early morning commuters dressed in business casual as I speed by them at ninety miles per hour. A fleeting thought that maybe I should just jerk the wheel and hit one of these eighteen-wheelers head-on. But no, I had Joe with me, and besides, I was not that man anymore. I couldn't be that man anymore. I had to not be that man anymore. I would mourn Cubby, but I would not let myself die there on the road.

"Dude, I forgot to write my paper for my ethics class. I guess I'll have to do it on the plane and turn it in late. It's about this company Refco that I used to work for. They had like $400 million in bad loans that they hid when they sold the company, and like $500 million in fake fucking bonds."

Talking helped me focus on the road as I tried not to swerve. Joe was passed out next to me, but I talked to him anyway.

"I still can't fucking believe that Cubby is gone, man. I still can't believe it. I don't think I'll ever be the same. We're still young, but I'll never smile again."

I looked over. Joe was still unconscious.

Four days later, the night before the Reserve Aid inaugural fundraising dinner, Marc Perez and I spent seven hours at the editing machine at Sirk Productions' offices, putting together a tribute video for Cubby. It was tough to watch him in the footage. I grew teary when he spoke. I spoke to the screen as though he could hear me. "C'mon, Cubby, where is that shot of you smiling on the deck of the ship as we pulled out of Sydney Harbour just across from the Opera House on the way back home from Afghanistan?" Watching the footage made me miss him even more, but I was grateful that I had taken it. I was grateful that I'd captured the good times that we would never share again.

Everybody showed up for Reserve Aid. The room filled to legal capacity. I told the bankers and hedge fund managers and traders what a great man Rob was. We slowed down some of the footage of Cubby smiling into the camera on the deck of the troopship on the way back from Operation Enduring Freedom. The caption read: CAPTAIN ROBERT M. SECHER. UNITED STATES MARINE CORPS. KILLED IN ACTION. AL ANBAR PROVINCE, IRAQ. OCTOBER 6, 2006. From the podium, I saw the tears in the audience as I fought back my own. I doubted that anyone who was there would ever forget him.

The head of the leveraged-finance division pulled me aside at one point.

"Mike, you have done with this charity in six months what it usually takes three or four years to do. Congratulations."

"Thanks. I appreciate that. So does this mean I can count Credit Suisse in for $50,000 next year?"

He laughed.

For the first time in years, since leaving the Corps, I felt that I was a part of something that was bigger than myself. That I used my energy for something good. Something that was true. Something that brought light to the lives of others who were in their own dark time. For the first time in my life, I realized—though it sounded like the most tired of clichés—that it is, in fact, true: by helping others, we help ourselves.

During the ceremony, Reserve Aid's executive director asked all vets from operations Iraqi Freedom and Enduring Freedom to stand. As I looked around the room, all the guys standing were around the same age as me. And many of them, with the same look in their eyes.

Chapter Twelve

"This morning on the way to work, I hoped an anvil would fall on my head," my buddy Kevin announced at eight a.m. on a fall Monday morning as we sat in front of our screens. I always laughed when he said things like that. Kevin worked at the computer terminal on the trading desk behind me, our backs to each other. We would lean back and turn our heads to the side whenever we wanted to talk. Kevin was tall, in his midthirties, a proud new dad with a wife and young baby at home.

"I know exactly how you feel, man. Exactly," I replied in a low voice, so they wouldn't hear us.

"Time check—how many hours left until the weekend?" he asked.

"Approximately 105. And a half."

"An eternity."

"Yes—but look at it this way... there are only 248 hours until our next paycheck. And 864 hours until Thanksgiving. And, most importantly, only 629 minutes until we get to go home today."

Kevin gave me the evil eye.

"I feel like I'm chained to this fucking desk, man. Human beings were not meant to do this. Or at least not guys like me," I said to him.

It was October 2007. It had been five months since I'd graduated from Stern and a year since Rob was killed. I spent the summer after graduation in the Credit Suisse associate training program, along with the others who had been hired from various MBA programs.

Kevin and I worked in the private side of finance, We had access to sensitive information. Security was tight. We worked behind electronically locked access doors where you had to swipe your ID card to get through the carefully constructed information wall that separated us from the other parts of the bank. Those doors were in addition to card swipes in the lobby and just outside the elevators on our floor. Logging our every move.

They called our room the Bubble. There were no windows to the outside. Just a constant bath of fluorescent light and recycled air that blew from the vent above our heads.

"I'm calling maintenance. This vent blows directly on my face. Aren't you guys cold?" one of our coworkers would ask. We would laugh, because every week it was the same. She would tape manila folders over the vents to try to stop the flow. Then one night each week they would miraculously disappear.

On my first day on the desk, a few weeks before, I'd discovered that my workstation was directly between the only other associate-level employee in the group, which was filled with managing directors, and the wall. And it appeared that she knew only a bit more than I did and probably viewed me as a threat to her advancement. This would almost ensure that I wouldn't learn anything about my job. On most of the other desks I saw, the newbies always sat next to the most senior person on the desk, so that they could be mentored and would learn to avoid stupid mistakes.

So when I started, I spoke with my boss.

"I understand clearly what my job is. But so I can see how to actually do the analysis…can you and I just run through one company analysis together, from start to finish? If you walk me through it just once, I will get up to speed very quickly. I will take detailed notes and will practice on as many other companies as you want to give me. Just show me exactly how you want the research and analysis done—one time, correctly—and I promise I will not let you down."

"Well, I want to see exactly where you are with everything, so why don't you just take a look at Claire's Stores for me and let me know what you think."

I looked at him and said OK. On the inside, though, I was frustrated and angry at the complete and utter lack of leadership. The job was not rocket science, but since I'd never been trained specifically for this, I just wanted him to show me how to do it one time. A simple request. A logical request, because he was the one who was supposed to be training me.

But maybe he knew what was about to happen to him and just didn't care anymore. Over drinks one night when things got a bit loose, I heard some of the traders talking about him behind his back. This kind of gossip and backstabbing was somewhat typical of the world in which I now lived.

"He's sleeping. Don't wake him up," one of them said. So I knew then that my boss was a marked man.

One day, after searching for forty-five minutes for a certain legal clause in some paperwork, I leaned over and asked the other associate—Stephanie—a question. She was in her late thirties and always seemed to know everything that was happening in our group. Her eyes scanned over the top of her monitor and out across the trading floor in search of new bits of information.

"Stephanie, why don't they standardize these credit agreements? They could have a checklist format that lists the most popular terms and then just check off the ones that apply to this deal instead of burying them in pages of legalese. Then they could just have a small separate section for terms that are nonroutine. Seriously—this is ridiculous. The content of each of these is like 85 percent similar, but because they're all in different formats, we spend our time digging for the 15 percent that's unique to this deal."

"Because then the lawyers wouldn't have jobs. And neither would we." She spoke as though quoting a rule that was supposed to be left unspoken.

"Am I talking to the customer in the context of them being a buyer or a seller?" people would ask while covering up the receiver on the phone as they were about to discuss the companies they covered. It was then that I knew my job consisted largely of bullshit. Both sides of the mouth.

Individually, most of the people in the group where I worked weren't bad. But the culture made things almost unbearable. Twelve to fourteen hours a day spent staring at Excel files. Sedentary for months. People protecting their own jobs and clients and personal territory. A barely perceptible undercurrent of mistrust. The silent rage. A hum of bad energy that swirled through the recycled air. Through the phones and the Bloomberg terminals and the quick, secret glances.

And the hedge funds all had their own internal analysts anyway. Which made me realize that my work didn't really mean anything at all. It was boring. It was soulless.

So it became a march of meaningless days strung out end to end. How long until that single day during bonus season when the whale hunting was good? When it became worth it for a few moments and the bank paid you for the year of your life you'd spent sitting there.

Just a few months before, in July 2007, things had begun to collapse in the financial world. Two hedge funds at Bear Stearns failed. Then Standard and Poor's started downgrading a lot of bonds that were backed by mortgages. A disaster for the owners of the trillions of dollars of mortgage-backed securities throughout the world. One of our instructors in the new-hire training program that summer had told us ominously in his English accent, "I think we are on the edge of something here."

A few weeks later, my boss received a call to report to the office of the head of the group. *Poof!* After ten years on the desk, he was gone. "He got shot," people would say. That's what they called it. When you got laid off, you'd been shot. *If only they knew what seeing someone shot is really like,* I thought. And for a second I remembered what it was like to pull over to the side of the road and see dead children who had been blown out of vehicles. What it was like to look out over a field of corpses. People who, just a short while before, had been fathers and husbands. Or into the face of a man who'd been shot in the eye. Or to see the docs frantically working on a wounded human being, cutting away his clothing as you could see the color of life draining from the surface of his skin. To feel the sting of the voices over the radio as they asked for helicopters to come pick up the dead and wounded. The nausea you felt after you realized you knew some of the people they were talking about.

I watched the arguments that would break out on the trading floor. The traders ruled the roost and largely decided how much everybody got paid each year. The salespeople always found themselves caught in the middle—between the traders, whom they worked for, and the customers, who were the salespeople's meal ticket.

"Are you out of your mind? What the hell is wrong with you?

Tell them to forget it and to not come to us with any more low-ball bids like that, or we are never trading with them again," one of the traders yelled at one of the older salespeople. His tone that of a tyrannical master whipping a slave.

The room was silent as we watched the two very senior people go at it. I snickered and wondered what I would have done if he had talked to me that way. No matter how long you have been there or how old you got or how much money you made, there would always be someone above you to shit all over you on a daily basis.

Then there was the nightly entertaining of clients. On some nights, I would accompany the salespeople on $1,000 sushi and sake dinners with hedge fund traders. Powerful players in the debt markets who could give their business to any trading desk among the dozen banks. As a result, there was a lot of ass kissing that went on. So for the salespeople, it was arrive at seven a.m., work the phones until six p.m., then head out to entertain clients until eleven p.m. or later, two or three nights a week. Then head home, catch some sleep, then back to the office at seven a.m. the next day. And this would be their lives. For decades.

Managing directors who ran desks could make $3 to $5 million in a good year. Conversations about pay were subject to an informal rule: inside the building versus outside the building. Early in my time there, one of the traders explained to me that inside the building, $500,000 *wasn't really that much money* but that people outside the building just didn't understand that. But when I would read the monthly status updates for families that Reserve Aid was assisting, I would think of those $1,000 dinners and what the trader had said to me. These were families who didn't have enough money to pay the electric bill. Young Marines in west Texas who had been wounded in the war but had no way of getting to rehab at the VA medical center eighty miles away. Or the single mother who'd served in the Alabama National Guard in Iraq but was now living out of her car with her young daughter, frantic because she was behind on payments and they were trying to take her car away. Reading these stories but then eating $1,000 dinners made me feel like an asshole.

After seeing what the salespeople went through each day—the bad energy and stress and constant probing—I no longer wanted to be one. Unfortunately, becoming a salesperson was the entire reason I was there. I mentioned my concern to a trusted confidant who'd also served in the military and worked as a salesperson at another bank and made several hundred thousand dollars per year. "What? You mean you don't want to kiss people's asses all day for a living?" he responded as he downed his single-malt Scotch and looked vacantly out the window of the bar.

As the months rolled on into early 2008 and the financial meltdown continued, one of the biggest problems on the desk was the growing fear of the massive layoffs that everybody knew were just around the corner. It was crushing morale. A RIF, they called it—reduction in force. A nice sanitized description. Collateral damage. Everyone showed up for work at seven a.m. each day wondering if this day would be the last. And if it was, you were in trouble because no one else was hiring, as all of the other banks were doing exactly the same thing.

You would catch people staring vacantly at their screens as they worried if they were one of the thousands who would be put up against the wall and shot. *Do you have any last words?*

Their thoughts were written on their faces. The weight of their lifestyle was pulling them down. Things that weren't easy to turn off: Mortgage payments. Private schools. And the status of their fortunes, tied to the price of the stock that they couldn't legally sell for another three years.

The looming layoffs seemed to be all that anybody talked about. Normally at this time of the year, people would be speculating on the amount of their bonuses. But at this point they just wanted to hold on for dear life.

To try to lighten the mood, I turned to a bit of gallows humor, just as we did in the Marine Corps when we knew things were about to get rough. It would be just for my little corner of the trading desk. On a small piece of paper, I drew a tombstone with the letters RIF on it with a question mark next to the word *date*. Next to the tombstone was a poorly drawn grim reaper holding a large scythe.

Stephanie didn't think it was funny.

One day, just a week or so after I drew the picture, Stephanie's computer started acting strangely. Her e-mail account was working really slowly. She put her head in her hands.

"Oh God—it's a sign. I'm going to get shot," she said.

"Don't be paranoid. Just call IT and have them take a look at it. I'm sure it's nothing," I reassured her.

"Where are all of the desk heads?" she asked.

We looked around. The senior MDs were nowhere in sight. The hairs on the back of my neck stood up. Like when the bugs stopped chirping in the fields around our defensive positions near Al Kut. Or when the people all suddenly disappeared from the streets of Baghdad.

Not good.

Her phone rang. Someone said something on the other end.

"OK," she said, turning pale. She gathered her things quickly and without saying a word, stood, turned, and walked out the door.

"Shit, dude, Stephanie just got shot," I said, stating the obvious to Kevin and to Brian McNamara, who sat on the other side of Stephanie.

Word spread quickly as hundreds of other calls just like that one hit the bank in a massive wave. Carnage everywhere. A massacre. Some divisions that sold products that were at the center of the financial meltdown, like the collateralized debt obligation (CDO) desk, were completely wiped out. The heads of the desk were making the calls in the basement meeting rooms, flanked by HR people. They would summon the target to the basement. In front of them, folders detailing the conditions of the termination, the amount of severance, legal documents to sign, and a kit for job-placement assistance. Then once you signed the documents, they would ask for your company ID. Then they'd ask you for your company credit card, which they would cut in half in front of you with a pair of scissors.

When things like that happen, the difference between the resilience in morale of people who are fighting for a cause and those who are working for a large paycheck becomes apparent. Those who are united for a cause—for a mission—become stronger and more powerful. They dig deep inside themselves, and they persevere.

But those whose motivations are less heroic become frozen with fear. Unit effectiveness drops. Productivity drops. And the wrath continues and feeds on the fear, whether it's a war being fought by mercenaries who don't believe in it or traders and salespeople who say things like "I'd sell my kids for a twenty-percent return" and are only half joking.

With Stephanie gone, there was more space in our small corner. I brought in some weights, two dumbbells and a curling bar that I kept stashed underneath the desk just in front of my feet. I might as well get a few sets in during the day. The others at the desk looked at me like I was a lunatic.

One Friday, we had an event at the Water Club, an exclusive floating restaurant and ballroom on the East River. One of the senior executives in the group mentioned that he was heading out to his house in the Hamptons for the weekend. About twenty minutes later, a seaplane went barreling past us as it took off directly from the river.

"There he goes," someone said and pointed out the large window at the plane banking to the right.

"He's like a character from a novel," I joked. Those who had been around the bank for a while were types who drank vodka martinis and had houses that had names. They were definitely interesting, but *These just aren't my people*, I thought. Something about having that much money now seemed somehow off to me. Especially when I thought about the young soldiers and Marines returning from war with broken bodies and a financial situation that was a mess.

"You know what's missing from Wall Street, brother?" I said to Kevin one day. "Trust. Leadership. Unselfishness. On the Street, fear, jealousy, greed, and suspicion are the only things that matter. People look at new hires as people who are just sucking up the bonus pool. They're all pissed off that they're not getting promoted more quickly or not being paid enough. People here have this 'I'm watching my own ass' mind-set. And they're always looking for the next move. You can spend two or three years at one bank and then jump ship to another bank and double your salary *overnight*. When somebody is out for a few hours to go to a doctor's appointment, everyone asks them the same thing: 'So, did you get the job?' With a system like that, how the hell are you supposed to rely on each other and create a real team? There is no unit cohesion here. All this talk about teamwork is bullshit. Wall Street is nothing more than a bunch of independent operators who happen to work together."

"Well, what do you expect, man? This is Wall Street, not the Marines."

"I know, man. You're right. But could you imagine a desk that was run like a Marine Corps battalion? With Marine Corps leadership and where the people actually cared about one another? It would probably make fucking trillions."

Then my thoughts drifted off to the Marine Corps leadership training we'd received as enlisted recruits and as officer candidates—when our young minds had learned the importance of values like honor, courage, and commitment. I never realized how valuable those things were—and how important they were to me personally—until I started spending my life in a place that was completely lacking in all of them.

Here, even basic leadership skills were absent. Simple things like setting an example. Developing a sense of responsibility among your subordinates. Knowing your people and looking out for their welfare. These are the things that build great organizations, that make people want to work harder for the cause and not think twice about it.

Instead I was counting down the seconds until I could get out of there each day. A complete waste of our time, my talent, and their money. I would sit at the desk and shake my head when I thought about the irony of it all. The energy and the time I'd spent to get there and the uncertainty of those years after I'd come back from the war, when I'd looked to get to this place—and this very job—to save me.

I could understand the mistake now. I'd assigned a value, a level of importance, to something that was just an illusion. Wall

Street was not a magical kingdom of wealth and power and prestige. It was a place where people did one thing: they moved money around. They stared at screens and made spreadsheets and talked with clients on the phone. It was bullshit and it would never be something I'd enjoy, no matter how much they paid me.

I'd tried to swap one existence, being a United States Marine, with another, being a Wall Street analyst. But I couldn't do it. The underlying beliefs and motivations and sense of what is honorable were completely different. And in my eyes, only one held the truth.

I thought of a night so many years ago, sitting in a dirt fighting hole with two young machine gunners on the edge of our defensive perimeter in southern Afghanistan just after 9/11, our toes numb and our stomachs empty and our hearts full, waiting for an enemy attack. Someone approached in the darkness behind us. We gave the verbal challenge and received the correct password from an unfamiliar voice. The figure appeared.

"Hi, I'm General Mattis."

We couldn't believe who was standing next to us. It was unheard-of for someone of that rank to be this far forward. The commander of Task Force 58 and all the Marines in Afghanistan at the time. It was three o'clock in the morning, painfully cold, and we were deep in enemy territory. But the good general was doing the best thing that a leader could do. *Walking the lines. Meeting the men.* And he was doing it alone. So that he could talk to us as men, not with our bosses around to stifle the conversation.

"How are you doing, Marines?"

"We're doing great, sir. Every clime and place," the nineteen-year-old next to me said with a smile on his face. A reference to "The Marines' Hymn."

"Good to go, Marines. Do you need anything?"

"No, sir. We're all set," I said.

"A little trick I've learned over the years that's especially good for machine gunners: if you think you hear something out there, take off your helmets for a second and cup your hands by your ears and listen. These Kevlar helmets can fuck with your hearing."

"Roger that, sir," we all said in unison.

"Have a good night, Marines."

"You too, sir."

And he continued through the darkness, alone, to the next fighting hole.

"What a fucking great guy," one of the Marines said.

"Yeah. I would die for that motherfucker."

"Why can't all officers be like that?" asked one of the machine gunners.

As I sat at the trading desk, I remembered the day that the entire artillery battery, Bravo One Eleven, pitched in to buy a World War II–era M1 Garand rifle for Major Russo as a gift for his change-of-command ceremony. He was getting ready to turn the battery over to a new commanding officer. The lieutenants had all pitched in to buy it for him, and Cubby and I had found one for sale in the classified ads. The enlisted Marines in the battery got wind of the plan, and within a few hours, we had three times the money needed to buy the rifle. The Marines loved that man so much that they were falling over themselves to pitch in—from their meager $20,000-per-year salaries—to show their admiration, respect, and thankfulness for such a brilliant and un-selfish leader. I was certain that a higher level of leadership was not possible. He was the best.

Now I awoke each weekday morning after a broken night of sleep. Tired and groggy. Full of dread. The sleep broken not because of bad memories from the war any longer but because I would stare at the ceiling and think about the fact that I was miserable doing the thing that I had struggled hard to achieve. That in a few hours I would be sitting at the desk waiting for another day to end. Then I would be back there in bed again with nothing to look forward to except another day of the same.

What happened? It wasn't supposed to be like this. People would kill to have my job. Why was I so *ungrateful*? I'd planned my strategy before I started working there. Be the first one on the desk in the morning. Be the last to leave. Ask my teammates if they need help. Do whatever it takes to make a name for myself. Stay positive. Work any hours they want me to work. My first day, I'd planned to give a speech during the morning meeting: "Hello everyone. I am very happy to be here and know that it is a privilege and not a right. I am here to learn so that I can become a productive member of this team as quickly as possible."

I never made the speech.

Instead, I swiped my ID in the turnstiles in the massive marble lobby each morning. And as I did, I checked my soul, my pride, and my conscience at the door.

One afternoon on the trading desk, while entering formulas into an Excel spreadsheet and wishing I was somewhere else, I thought about the commencement address at my graduation from NYU Stern. Aswath Damodaran, the world-renowned corporate finance professor whom the students voted professor of the year for the sixth time, gave the address at Madison Square Garden.

Many said that Aswath Damodaran was the best applied corporate finance professor in the world. I agreed. But he was also something much more than that. He was a visionary who understood the human element of finance and the motivations of his young students and the consequences that the endless pursuit of personal wealth has on the lives of financiers as the years tick by. He posted videos of his lectures freely on the Internet in the belief that knowledge should be available to everyone and not just people with 700 GMAT scores and access to a hundred grand in tuition money.

"Remember one thing," Damodaran said. "There is no greater power than the power to walk away. Don't make it just about the money. Do something that makes you happy. Something that you enjoy. So don't live just for the weekends. And if you are headed off to be an investment banker—you won't even get those."

His words hit me hard because I knew that he was speaking one of those undeniable truths that guide the lives of those who have found their correct path. The path that shines with happiness and fulfillment. The path that allows you to live directly in the moment without yearning or scheming or politics.

I took his words about the power to walk away to heart and I decided that I would live, for the short to medium term at least, a variable-cost life. I didn't want to own anything that would weigh me down. No mortgage payments or expensive watches. And no more pissing away money on the weekends on expensive dinners to soothe the misery of the job that was sucking the life from me. The savings would give me the power to bolt if I needed to. The flexibility to move fast, which was the concept the entire Marine

Corps war-fighting strategy was built upon. Keep things light and mobile so you can move them around the earth with speed: the non-heavy-asset expeditionary mind-set. Freedom.

I used the signing bonus to knock down the debt I had run up during school, and then I saved every cent possible.

The managing directors' offices on the north side of the building had windows that looked across East Twenty-Fifth Street. One day, after a meeting with some traders whose offices were on that side of the building, I walked past one of the windows. I stopped for a moment, looked up, and saw the balcony of my brother's apartment jutting out into the Manhattan skyline directly across the street from the bank. It was the same balcony from which I had watched the bankers on the floors above us work late into the night in December 2002. The night I got the call that we were deploying to the Middle East along the border of Iraq. The night that I knew our lives would soon depend on our training and the decisions that we would make in those moments when everything was on the line.

I walked back toward my trading desk, past that elevator bank and the people sitting at their screens, down the overlit hallway, through the security doors, and into the Bubble. So all around me, this money. But it wasn't enough. Something pressing against me and stopping me each day from buying all the way in. Maybe the war had changed me. I *needed* my life to have meaning, but I knew that the life I was living had none.

The last sentence from the last message I ever got from Cubby kept ringing through my head. *Take care and enjoy life, don't hold back!* Words written by a man who stared death in the face every time he went out on patrol. Words written while he was still in the middle of the war and the danger of a violent end was always close. When the real truth about life becomes most apparent.

One Thursday afternoon, I sat in Penn Station waiting for the train to take me out to the shore for the rehearsal dinner for a high school buddy's wedding. I sat at the bar in front of a window that looked out onto the terminal. The faces of the commuters were like those at a funeral. Everybody seemed so miserable. Overweight men in their forties clutching brown paper bags that held a few tallboys that they would down on yet another train ride home. Back to the wife and kids out in New Jersey. Monday mornings back in the office responding to the question How was your weekend? by saying things like "Went by too fast, just way too fast."

In my own hand, a bottle of Coors Light. The cold-activated label with blue mountains on it, turning white from the heat of my fingers. "When the mountains turn blue, it's as cold as the Rockies," I said out loud.

I'd been suspecting it for a while, but now I was beginning to admit that I had just spent a large chunk of my late twenties and early thirties climbing the wrong mountain.

I had been through too much—too much war, too much recovery—to be miserable six days a week. Monday through Friday at work and Sundays knowing I had to go to work the next day.

I went to dinner with my brother Dan. He could tell that something was bugging me.

"What's up, little brother?" he asked.

"Well, I haven't even been at my job for a year, and I'm already tired of a life that consists mainly of staring at a screen all day. Revenues and expenses and inventory adjustments and Excel spreadsheets. People would kill to have this job, and I feel like sort of an asshole for thinking this way, especially because people are getting laid off and I should be thankful that I have a job, but it feels like there should be more to life than this."

He smiled and I saw the recognition of my problem register in his mind.

"You have to do what makes you happy, little brother. That's what matters. You will wake up one day and be forty. And you will ask yourself where all the time went. All those years. I worked from twenty-five to forty-one as an attorney. And I never really enjoyed it. I just wasn't happy with what I was doing with my life. And now I can never get those years back. Don't go after the money. Jobs like finance and law are the ones that pay the most but are also the ones that people like you and me enjoy the least. Your time and your happiness are more important than the money. It takes a while for people to figure that out, and some of them never do, but it's the truth."

Dan had walked away from an extremely lucrative and secure career as a securities lawyer. He woke up one day with his pockets full but his soul empty. And he had the courage to say that he'd had enough. So he took a risk. He started his own company, Daniel B. Scotti Design & Development, that built luxury homes in the Hamptons. Applying the creative talent that had been begging to leap from inside of him for sixteen years. I'd never seen him so happy, so fulfilled. He was doing what he loved.

And then there was my brother Dave, the actor, who always had the balls to not give in to the pressure. The only one of us three brothers who lived his own life, a true life, from the beginning. His life: a calling. One driven by his love for the art of method acting and by his natural talent for it.

No office cubicle job for him. No sanitized existence with stale recycled air. Only his calling. His craft. A poet when the poets were the ones with their backs against the wall. When there was no money and he had to work jobs that were beneath him because those were the only ones that would give him time to audition.

I admired both my brothers, and I still learned from them, just as I did when I was little.

"You know, I heard somebody speaking with the vice chairman the other day, and your name came up. He said that you should be earmarked for management," one of the more senior salespeople on the desk said to me after a morning meeting.

"Really?"

"Yeah, and then he said, 'The only thing is, how are you going to control a guy like that?'"

"No shit." I laughed. But on the inside, the alarm was sounding. Why not build me up and support me, then give me a mission and turn me loose?

I wanted no part of it—spending the next twenty years being controlled and playing politics and being scared of how I was viewed by others.

It was then I made the decision to pull the Eject lever.

"Dude, I can't quit for another four months, or else I have to give back my signing bonus. And I already spent it paying back loans, but you can bet your ass that as soon as my contract is up, I am out of here," I said quietly to Kevin the next day.

"Great, you'll be free, and I'll still be stuck in this place," he said with a grin.

"How many hours left until the weekend?"

That Sunday was the first in nearly a year when I woke up without a feeling of dread for the upcoming week. Just because I *could* be on Wall Street didn't mean I *had to* be.

I'd decided against killing myself quickly in the dark time after the war, and now I'd decided against killing myself slowly over decades of being bound by big paychecks to a job that I didn't like. *Get out while you can.*

One Monday morning in June 2008, almost a year after I'd started working there, I headed out of the Bubble, across the trading floor, and into Norm Parton's office. He and I had become friends since that day at the corporate presentation at NYU when I'd told him about Cubby's death. Norm's son, who was interested in film, had interned at Sirk Productions. And Norm was a champion for Reserve Aid among the traders at the bank, helping to ensure that they donated each year. Over the months, there was a second round of layoffs, and the rumor was that there was a third just around the corner.

"Norm, you and I are friends, and I feel comfortable coming to you with this. My one-year contract is up in a few weeks, and I am probably going to leave once it's up. I don't know if there is another RIF coming or if my name is on the list if there is one, but you can shoot me if you want. I would rather you shoot me and save some guy with a family and mortgage from getting whacked, a guy who wants to be here, than survive this RIF just to move on a few weeks later."

Norm had a look of sadness and concern in his eyes.

"I understand, Mike. And I'm glad you came to me. I'm sorry to see you go, but I know that you will be successful in whatever you do. You know you could have come to me if you felt like things weren't going well with your on-boarding process."

"I know I could have, Norm. And I really appreciate it."

It would be a few more weeks before the day came. The rumors of the RIF continued to build. I brought my weights home in preparation for the day I'd get the call from the basement and become one of the walking dead. When it did, I wouldn't have a chance to come back upstairs to gather everything. It was down to the basement, then directly out the door, once they had your employee ID card.

The morning of June 30, the sense of the impending massacre was in the air. People paced anxiously about. At my computer, I ate a breakfast of oatmeal and scrambled eggs from the commissary.

I watched as the heads of the desk disappeared.

"Alright, fellas, let's snap a picture for posterity," I said with a smile as the three people who worked closest to me gathered around for the shot.

The phone rang. It was the head of distressed sales.

"So *you* are the reaper?" I asked as I picked up the line.

A few minutes later, after my execution in the bank's bowels, I walked slowly through the polished marble lobby toward the exit. As I passed through the heavy brass and glass revolving door for the last time, I snapped another picture—a reminder to myself of the sense of freedom and happiness I felt to have cast off the golden handcuffs, in case I ever felt tempted in the future to return to the green pastures of Wall Street. I slowly walked along Park Avenue as the sun shined brightly in the blue summer sky.

I thought how great it was that my emotions would no longer be tied to the health of the financial markets. That I would no longer have to live in fear of the opinions of others or be beholden to the golden master. Now my time would be my own. The price of it all was uncertainty and a lack of financial security.

But I'd rather take my chances. Jump off the roof and learn to fly on the way down.

Maybe I'll take a walk in Central Park, I thought.

So I turned north. As I walked, a great weight was lifted and I felt that I saw things clearly—things I *knew* to be true—for the first time in years. I thought maybe not everybody has a price—because I'd just walked away from those who would've paid handsomely for me.

And as the residue of the bank seemed to be washed away by the warm summer sun, I thought of the wars I'd fought and the friends I'd lost and what really mattered in my life. Of how I was part of a new generation of veterans who would probably deal with many of the same issues together and how that was something bigger than just me. And, as I'd learned, as veterans coming home from the war, maybe we needed each other even more now than when we were fighting in it. And we needed to let each other know that *it's OK if you're not OK*. That war does things to everybody and there's no shame in it. And that once you realize this, you can begin to do what you need to do to become well again.

I knew that I loved my country and what it stood for: freedom and the right to pursue my own happiness. I knew that I would never again trust a politician who had never served in combat. I knew that I loved the Marine Corps and the purity of heart that it fostered and the fact that guys like Joe Russo and Rob Secher were a part of it. And I knew that when you allowed yourself to become vulnerable, you became strong. And I knew that I could dwell and focus on the past and the ugly, or I could choose to focus on the future and all of its unknown beauty.

So I walked slowly north along Fifth Avenue, watching the tourists and the street vendors on the corners. Slowly north toward Central Park. Past the building where we held the Reserve

Aid dinner each year. Down the stone steps. Through the trees and fields of green where couples nuzzled gently on soft cotton blankets. The air warm and the sky lazy and happy and blue. Tall buildings standing guard along the perimeter. At the duck pond, a young boy sat on a bench with his father, holding the remote control for his toy battleship bobbing slowly in the water.

And I remembered a young man seven years before standing on the bow of a warship in a time of war. Looking out into the nothingness as the ship cut through the dark water en route to Afghanistan. Our mission clear and true. Young men going off to fight a war. For the country. For their Corps. For each other.

Out there on the ocean, the light was perfect. Perfect. And I wished I could breathe it in—for always. Breathe it in and it slips into your bloodstream and makes your heart beat strong and loud.

And that day, as I walked slowly along the edge of the pond, with the ducks swimming and the children laughing and the toy battleship bobbing, the light was perfect. As I stood and watched for a moment, I knew I didn't have all the answers. So I just took a deep breath as the sun shimmered on the water. And my heart beat strong and loud.

Just like it was supposed to.

Epilogue

In March 2010, the documentary film *Severe Clear* was released in theaters on a limited basis in several U.S. cities.[3] It was later released on Blu-ray in the United States and under the title *This Is War* in the United Kingdom, Israel, Australia, and France. The film tells my story and the story of those who fought with me in Iraq. The film's title is a reference to a term that pilots use unofficially to describe a rare weather condition in which the skies are so clear that visibility seems almost infinite. The sky on the morning of September 11, 2001, was severe clear.[4]

At a screening of the film in Austin, Texas, I was surprised to find Jeremy Davis, along with his family, waiting in the ticket line. He was with me that day in Iraq when we came upon the taxicab.

Jeremy sat next to me during the screening. I watched him and the others around me as our story unfolded. He winced at the gunfire. In the scene with the little girl's brain, he sat perfectly

---

[3] Stephen Holden, "A Marine Searches for Meaning in the Sand and 'Steel Rain' of Iraq," *New York Times*, Mar. 11, 2010, http://movies.nytimes.com/2010/03/12/movies/12severe.html.

[4] Debra Burlingame, "'Severe Clear' on 9/11," *Forbes*, Sept. 11, 2008, http://www.forbes.com/2008/09/10/terrorism-anniversary-pentagon-oped-cx_db_0911burlingame.html.

still, eyes wide. The nightmare from our past that was once again alive on the fifty-two-foot screen in front of us.

During the closing monologue—my final voiceover in the film—the tears fell from Jeremy's eyes. And then they fell from mine. When the lights came on, the audience applauded loudly; Jeremy stood and clapped loud and hard, with everything he had. This was his story as much as mine. For years it had been lying asleep inside of him, but now it was awake. And now the world could see what it's like for men and women who fight in war.

"You told our story, LT [lieutenant]. You told our story." We looked at each other and hugged. "I love you, brother," we said. Because I'd seen the film so many times, I didn't anticipate how powerful it could be for those seeing it the first time. Many people in the audience looked like they had been through combat. Eyes uneasy. Exhausted. Kristian had clearly hit the mark.

Later that night, we sat at dinner with Jeremy, my family, and the guys from Sirk Productions. Jeremy sat next to me. About halfway through the dinner, he leaned over and said, in a low tone, "I buried her brain. That little girl—I buried her brain. You buried her little pink slippers and I buried her brain by the side of the road that day. Remember? Eric Sibert was with us." His eyes grew distant.

"Yeah, man, I remember. That was fucking terrible."

"It seems like that was another life."

"It *was* another life. And now you and I are sitting here in this restaurant eating these good steaks and drinking this wine. And all of that shit is in the past forever. It feels good, doesn't it? To know that we never have to go through that again."

"Yeah, LT. It feels good."

"I'm glad you're here to experience all of this with me, brother."

"Me too," he said.

"And I'm glad you're still breathing, brother."

It felt good to have Jeremy close by. The calming effect of a buddy who charged through the gates of hell with you. Who saw all of the same faces of the dead. The faces that followed us home.

In Dallas, the rain fell thick and angry outside. I wondered about tornadoes. I stood just inside the front entrance of the theater, watching the crowd roll in, wet from the rain. You could pick the vets out easily. They were the right age, but more important, they had the look. They were there seeking something. Lions coming to the watering hole to drink. A few of them wild-eyed and unshaven, looking lost, eyes darting from left to right. Others were well put-together, looking curious but otherwise completely at ease. And others were much older, wearing the weight of the decades along with the patches on their jackets. These were the guys. All of them. My guys. Our guys.

I noticed three guys in their midtwenties sitting together in one of the rows near the front of the theater. The three of them approached me after the Q&A. The tallest of the three, who had shoulder-length hair, stood quietly next to his two buddies as one of them spoke to me.

"Sir, we were in One Four in Iraq with you. We remember you."

"No shit, fellas?"

"Yeah, you were in Weapons Company and we were in the rifle companies. You didn't know us, but we knew you."

"That's awesome. I really appreciate you guys coming out to support the film. I wish I would've known. I would've gotten you some free tickets."

"No worries, sir. We just wanted to say that the movie was fucking awesome. We really loved it. And we feel like you told our story."

"Thanks, man. This film is for all of us. And this film helped me get through some pretty dark shit after I first got back from the war."

When I said that, the tall one suddenly looked off into the distance for a second.

"Look me up on Facebook, guys. If you want copies of the DVD or to just bullshit about anything, let me know. Even if it's just to blow off steam. Sometimes shit can sneak up on us, and it's really fucking hard to ask for help. Take care of yourselves, fellas. And Semper Fi."

———

Later that night, I received a message on Facebook:

> Hi—My name's Ryan. Me and my 2 buddies met
> you tonight in Dallas at the Studio Movie
> Grill. I just want to say for years I've
> wished I could hook my head up to a machine
> and show people what I went through the
> first time overseas and you have done that
> for me. You showed everyone what it was
> like for me back in 2003 when I was 19
> years old and fresh out of high school.
> Into the Marines as a machine gunner and
> sent overseas right after boot camp and SOI
> [School of Infantry] to fight and kill.
> Then having to deal with it all after you
> got back. You touched home when you told

the story of the little girl. I had something like that happen to me but it was a
bus loaded with mothers, daughters, sons
and 2 dirt bag Iraqi soldiers coming at us
shooting. The only thing for me and my sister gunner to do was light it up. But no
one can understand the toll it takes on
someone when they realize what just went
down and the weight on your shoulders of
the lives you just took. I fought back
tears on the drive home. I can't thank you
enough for making this movie.

Semper Fi
Corporal Ryan C Pounds

When I asked Ryan if it would be OK to share his story, this
was his response:

I'm OK with you telling my story. Yours
helped me talk about mine and has lifted
some of the heavy burden I've been humping
around for some time now. Maybe my story
will help others talk about theirs. I've
had too many friends turn to drinking to
help them deal with it and I'm sad to say
it kills me to watch them tear their lives
apart. You know Marines, like you said, are
not ones to go get help. It's hard, but
watching them only helped me to speak up so
I didn't go down the same path. There's not

```
much in the world for us grunts once we're
back and for some of them it's hard to make
that change back to the real world. And I
appreciate the DVD. For once I can show
people the true story—not no Hollywood
bullshit!

Thank u again
Ryan
```

About a week after I received Ryan's message, I received another from Daniel Lange, whom I'd served closely with in the war but hadn't spoken to in seven years. He was the Marine who was screaming over the radio during the friendly-fire barrage in Baghdad. In the subject field of the message was one word: Everything. When I saw the subject, I knew what it was about before I even opened it.

```
Hey man, I hope you remember me. I just
wanted to say this movie could not have
come at a better time for me. I am starting
my counseling sessions at the VA on the 4th
of August for all the shit that went down
over there. I just ordered the movie and
had it overnighted so I will watch it as
soon as possible.

Daniel Lange
Apocalypse FO
```

And from his wife:

THE BLUE CASCADE

I know that you don't know me at all. I am Daniel's wife and wanted to say thank you for making this movie. I truly understand now what all happened with my husband. For some reason, as his wife, I had this crazy thought that he went and did some things, ate good food and was never in harm's way. I never truly understood and would actually compare what we did at home to what he did when he was gone. I want to thank you for setting me straight and opening my eyes to what you all actually went through.

I also want to thank you for what you did for my husband. He now has a way of telling others what he went through. He also has a way to show all of us why he is the way he is. I knew he had changed a lot since that time, but never really wanted to know why, ya know? I watched it twice and both times I cried thinking about how close he was to danger.

I would like to also tell you how proud I am of both of you as well as all the other men and women that put their lives in danger in order for us all to live free and safe. All that you all have done for me and my whole family. You don't know us, but you fought for us. I want to thank you.

Crystal Lange

In the summer of 2007, the National Suicide Prevention Lifeline, a national network of more than 130 independently operating crisis call centers linked to a series of toll-free lines, was established.[5]

Callers were initially asked if they were veterans of military service. In 2008, nearly thirty thousand veterans contacted the hotline. The following year, over sixty thousand veterans called. And in 2010, over eighty thousand veterans reached out to the suicide prevention hotline.[6]

On January 11, 2010, Secretary of Veterans Affairs Eric K. Shinseki, in a speech at the Suicide Prevention Conference in Washington, D.C., acknowledged that "of the more than 30 thousand suicides in this country each year, fully 20 percent of them are Veteran suicides. That means, on average, eighteen Veterans commit suicide *each day* [emphasis added]. Five of those 18 are under VA care at the time they take their lives."[7]

On May 10, 2010, the Ninth U.S. Circuit Court of Appeals noted in a ruling that it takes the Department of Veterans Affairs an average of *four years* to fully provide the mental health benefits owed veterans and that it often takes *weeks* for a sui-

---

[5] John Draper, "Suicide Prevention on Bridges: The National Suicide Prevention Lifeline Position," National Suicide Prevention Lifeline, June 16, 2008.

[6] Bernard A. Lubell, "War's Other Casualty: Suicidal Thoughts Plague Returned Veterans," *Medill Reports*, Feb. 17, 2011, http://news.medill .northwestern.edu/chicago/news.aspx?id=178771.

[7] "Remarks by Secretary Eric K. Shinseki," Department of Defense—Veterans Affairs Suicide Prevention Conference, Washington, D.C., Jan. 11, 2010, http://www.va.gov/opa/speeches/2010/10_0111hold.asp.

cidal vet to get a first appointment. The court stated that the "unchecked incompetence" in handling the flood of post-traumatic-stress-disorder and other mental health claims was unconstitutional.[8]

One of the first things that I realized after speaking with hundreds of veterans and their families across the United States at various screenings was there are a lot of people who are suffering out there because of the war. And not only the people who fought in the war, but also the people who love them.

One thing that the veterans and their families seemed to appreciate was that someone had told the story of what it was like to fight, in a way that was easily accessible. Like the mothers who had a look of understanding in their eyes as they thanked Kristian and me for letting them know what it was like in war. For letting them know why their child came back a different person. The film served to help bridge some of that gap of isolation that forms between loved ones who lack the shared experience of something as profound as war. And it was also clear that many of those with whom I spoke might benefit from speaking more about their thoughts and emotions. But I wondered if things like shame or isolation or fear prevented them from doing so.

The toll that these wars have taken on the mental health of a large portion (20 percent[9]) of a generation of warriors is becoming an ongoing tragedy. In my mind, the emotional aftermath

---

[8] Paul Elias, "Court Blasts VA Mental Health Care System," Associated Press, May 10, 2011, repr. *Marine Corps Times*, http://www.marinecorpstimes .com/news/2011/05/ap-court-blasts-veterans-administration-mental -health-care-system-051011.

[9] United States Department of Veterans Affairs—National Center for PTSD, "How Common Is PTSD?" July 5, 2007, http://www.ptsd.va.gov/public /pages/how-common-is-ptsd.asp.

of combat should not be some private epidemic secretly unfolding behind closed doors across the country. It must be brought into the national conversation to be dealt with head-on, and quickly.

If we want to help, we will have to erase the social stigma that seems to accompany any mention of depression or PTSD. As individuals, and eventually as a society, we will have to acknowledge the true nature of what war does to the human spirit. To start things off, we can send a simple message to those who have served:

It's OK if you're not OK.

Summary of Action

1st Lieutenant Michael T. Scotti
for Navy and Marine Corps Achievement Medal with Combat "V"

1st Lieutenant Scotti has distinguished himself in combat as an artillery liaison officer (ALNO) while attached to 1st Battalion, 4th Marines, 1st Regimental Combat Team, 1st Marine Division from 25 March to 7 April 2003. Lieutenant Scotti performed his duties as ALNO in a highly professional and meticulous manner while under enemy fire during six engagements. While operating under confusing and extremely fluid situations, Lieutenant Scotti was able to receive multiple artillery calls for fire, process them and submit them for approval from the FSC [fire support coordinator]. At all times his professionalism and meticulous attention to detail ensured that information passed from the forward observers was disseminated to the battalion staff and contributed to the overall situational awareness of battalion operations. His tireless perseverance ensured that even under conditions of minimal sleep over 48 hours of sustained combat operations he operated efficiently and accurately in coordinating artillery fires for the battalion. Without Lieutenant Scotti's intense devotion to duty and perseverance under fire, the battalion would not have received the critical artillery support that it needed to destroy enemy positions in the attack and repel their assaults during defensive operations. His actions over this time period deserve to be recognized because of their flawless execution, their critical nature to battalion combat operations, and their execution while often under intense and close enemy fire.

1st Lieutenant Scotti proved instrumental in planning and coordinating artillery support following the battalion's first engagement south of Al Garraf on 25 March 2003. Based on guidance from the Battalion Commander he ordered illumination fires [flares] in the city of Al Garraf as a psychological warning for possible Saddam Fedayeen hidden in the city. The battalion was able to pass through the city unscathed because of the contribution of artillery fires coordinated by Lieutenant Scotti. As a testament to the effectiveness of this tactic the next unit to pass through was ambushed and suffered casualties as a result.

The same day he continued his commendable performance by coordinating the artillery fires in support of a battalion defensive engagement south of the city of Ash Shatrah. During a heavy enemy probing attack, Lieutenant Scotti used enemy SALUTE [size, activity, location, unit, time, and equipment] reports to call devastating fires for effect on key enemy avenues of approach from the enemy-held city towards the battalion's defensive perimeter. The effects of the artillery fires cut key enemy reinforcement routes and prevented them from moving heavy machine gun vehicles into effective range of the battalion. These fires also supported the disengagement of the battalion's forward CAAT [combined anti-armor team] platoon that had come under enemy RPG and heavy-machine-gun fire. Lieutenant Scotti continued to coordinate artillery fires that neutralized enemy positions engaging the battalion's flank positions. All of Lieutenant Scotti's actions were done under direct enemy fire and were subject to at least 2 observed medium anti-tank weapons that impacted near the AAVC7 [amphibious assault vehicle, or amtrac, model 7] he was working out of.

The following day, 26 March 2003, Lieutenant Scotti continued his stellar performance under fire as he coordinated artillery missions supporting a battalion attack to secure the key main supply route through Ash Shatrah and cover the movement of RCT-1 [regimental combat team number one], in its entirety, through the heavily defended city. While working from the battalion jump CP [command post] in an AAVC7 positioned as part of a mechanized rifle company strong point position, Lieutenant Scotti coordinated 5 artillery missions extremely close to friendly positions within an extremely confusing urban environment. Three missions supported engaged rifle companies and resulted in the destruction of key enemy strong point positions. Two missions were directed at enemy mortar positions that were adjusting on to the battalion commander's jump CP, silencing them and eliminating the growing danger of the mortar rounds impacting closer and closer to the critical vehicle. These actions were accomplished while directly on the forward edge of the battle area with 2 RPGs fired directly at the jump CP AAVC7 and numerous bursts of small arms fire actually impacting the vehicle.

Lieutenant Scotti continued his outstanding contributions to the battalion's success throughout the remainder of the campaign enduring enemy fire and planning artillery fires to support the battalion's operations. These included an attack to fix the 5th Brigade of the Republican Guard's Baghdad Division in Al Kut on 3 April 2003 and supporting the battalion's river crossing of the Diyala River on 7 April 2003.

Because of Lieutenant Scotti's commendable skills as an artillery liaison officer, the battalion received the critical artillery support it needed in a timely and safe fashion under challenging combat conditions. He constantly kept his forward observers informed of the changing artillery situation as firing batteries repositioned on the battlefield and maneuver units continued their attacks. Lieutenant Scotti's support proved instrumental to the success of the battalion's fire support coordination center and he ensured that all his information was accurate and timely to ensure the safety and responsiveness of the artillery supporting fires. Because of his attention to detail and meticulous communication skills the battalion was able to prosecute 16 fire-for-effect missions with complete safety and maximum effect on the enemy undoubtedly saving the lives of Marines in contact with the enemy. His devotion to duty and commendable actions while under fire deserve recognition and were in keeping with the highest tradition of the Marine Corps and United States Naval Service.